NOBODY EVER SEES YOU EAT TUNA FISH

NOBODY EVER SEES YOU EAT TUNA FISH

DAVID BRENNER

ARBOR HOUSE / NEW YORK

Design by Richard Oriolo

Manufactured in the United States of America

10 9 8 7 6 5 4 3 2 1

Library of Congress Cataloging in Publication Data

Brenner, David, 1945–
Nobody ever sees you eat tuna fish.

1. Brenner, David, 1945–   . 2. Comedians—United
States—Biography. I. Title.
PN2287.B685A36   1986   792.7′028′0924 [B]   86-1055
ISBN: 0-87795-730-4

ALSO BY DAVID BRENNER

Soft Pretzels with Mustard
Revenge Is the Best Exercise

NOBODY
EVER SEES
YOU EAT
TUNA FISH

DAVID BRENNER

ARBOR HOUSE / NEW YORK

Design by Richard Oriolo

Manufactured in the United States of America

10 9 8 7 6 5 4 3 2 1

Library of Congress Cataloging in Publication Data

Brenner, David, 1945–
Nobody ever sees you eat tuna fish.

1. Brenner, David, 1945–   . 2. Comedians—United
States—Biography. I. Title.
PN2287.B685A36   1986   792.7′028′0924 [B]   86-1055
ISBN: 0-87795-730-4

To the great love of my life,
VICTORIA

CONTENTS

CONTENTS

ACKNOWLEDGMENTS

Whenever a book is written, there are people to thank. It is rarely a solitary effort. So, here it goes in no particular order and, hopefully, without forgetting anyone.

I thank Arbor House Publishing for starting all this book-writing business; the fine job done by their editor, Fred Chase; Aspen, Colorado, for providing me with an environment so conducive to thinking and for writing; Chuck and Barbara Besanty for making all the arrangements in Aspen; my secretary, Susan Bennett, for making believe she enjoyed typing and collating my manuscripts; the Xerox Company for making copying so easy; Federal Express for making sending copies so fast and convenient; Drs. Milton Reder, I and II, for keeping my back in good enough condition to take the brunt of the hours of typing; Olivetti for still manufacturing a manual portable typewriter for those of us who drum our fingers on the keys too much to use electrics; George Schultz, owner of Pips and my pal, for reading the first draft and offering suggestions; Dave Shalek for making the strong cappucinos that kept me awake during the late hours of rewriting; all the known and unknown professional and amateur photographers who took the pictures seen in this book; the kids from the streets of Philly who painted my life with the hot colors; all the "nice" people about whom I wrote; my personal manager, Steve Reidman, for all his suggestions and comments and for doing his job perfectly so I had a free mind for writing; Artie Moskowitz, my William Morris agent, for helping me to earn enough money so I won't have to try to live off the royalties from this book; my sister, Bib, for her comments and suggestions; my big brother, Moby Dick, not only for his support but also for his creative writing genius so well felt in the following pages; all you marvelously loyal fans for making so much of my life so wonderfully exciting and fulfilling; my attorneys Robert Cinque, Ric Silver, and Leora Herrmann for extracting me from the legal pressure cooker so I could once again be creative; my accountant, Bill Zysblat, for giving me financial peace of mind; my mother and father, who throughout my life have taught me so much, loved me so much, inspired me so much, and filled me with all the dreams and then gave me some of the stuff I needed to turn them into realities; and, last, but not least, my four-year-old son, Cole Jay, who has unknowingly taught me so much about myself and about life.

To all of you—thank you.

Dying is easy. Comedy is hard.

—Edmund Gwenn, actor;
spoken on his deathbed

Tough times don't last, but tough people do.

—Robert Schuller, evangelist

"If you could be anyone in the world, who would you be?"
"You're looking at him, pal."

—David Brenner, comedian

NOBODY EVER SEES YOU EAT TUNA FISH

INTRODUCTION BY MEL BRENNER

When my kid brother first became a celebrity, I asked him, "When you have it all, what's left to worry about?" David answered, "Losing it."

This conversation took place in a hotel in Milwaukee in 1977. David earlier that evening had finished a show in concert, a tour de force in which he had delivered two solid hours of stand-up comedy on an empty stage to a packed theater. It was when I'd watched that performance that I knew he was more than a comedian; he was a humorist.

Late into the night in the hotel suite, we were having a private brothers' talk. About old hard times and new good ones, the meaning of it all. A celebration. For all of us. "In a close family," David said, "only one person has to be rich." He was quoting a Brenner tradition that went way back. On that philosophical note, we turned in, snug in our good fortune. But something wasn't right.

In our beds in the dark room, we watched a bright light from a nearby building flash on and off. Twenty-four hours a day it announced the time and temperature, we learned later, but all we could see now was that relentless glare. Despite our posh room, the windows were greasy, so that the flashing light made the room look dismal. And a familiar scene came to us at the same hilarious moment—the old gangster pictures, Edward G. Robinson or Humphrey Bogart, fallen from fame and power, sweating it out in a dilapidated hotel room, a café light outside blinking on and off. The reminder was clear. We laughed ourselves to sleep, with maybe a hidden tear or two.

Nobody these days sees you eat tuna, David. Except your family. And it's all right with us.

INTRODUCTION BY BIB BRENNER

Tuna was the beginning of our family's individuality. Undoubtedly, you've heard David talk about our mother's cooking skills. Everything he says is true. She has to be the only person I know who makes lumpy boiled water. Unfortunately for my brothers and me, my parents liked fish. I say unfortunately because in those days when you brought a fish home, it was the whole fish: head, fins, scales, and bones. It was the bones that made us dislike fish. They were constantly getting caught in our throats. As a result, my mother would make tuna for us whenever my parents had fish for dinner. Now, my parents always wanted us to be individuals. To carry out this teaching, Mom would make our tuna the way each of us liked it. David ate his straight out of the can. Mel preferred a little salad dressing in his. I, on the other hand, liked celery, eggs, and salad dressing on mine.

So, David, don't think of tuna as a poor man's food. Think of it as something that helped develop our individuality.

FOREWORD

I've been very lucky, so far. The canvas of my life is covered with vibrantly rich and explosively bright colors. There have been some very difficult times, of course, but never any boring ones. Somehow, from my early days in the streets of Philadelphia's poor neighborhoods to these days on the prestigious Upper East Side of Manhattan, my life has been a great adventure. I have also always been surrounded by wonderful friends and a loving family. What had been pictures of unattainable dreams and fantasies that I had seen so often only in my imaginative mind, I have seen with my very eyes. Yes, I have been extremely lucky, indeed.

I now share with you some of my thoughts and experiences. You have been very good to me. You have helped to make a lot of my life possible. This book is one small way of thanking you.

On these pages, I want to make you laugh. You know that already, because I am a comedian. I also want to make you think and to feel. I believe that all of us are a part of one another. I offer you these parts of me.

I

SPECIAL PLACES

THE STREET CORNER

Next to my parents, the most influential aspect of my life was the street corner. It is a big-city phenomenon. An American institution. It is where friends gather, primarily, because there are so few places to go. You stand on the corner of an intersection, usually in front of some kind of a store. For us it was Moe's Candy Shop, 60th and Osage streets in West Philadelphia. Sometimes you leave the pavement to hang out inside, where you buy a double thick milk shake, a hoagie, a cheese-steak sandwich, a candy bar, or an ice cream. Sometimes the hangout owner will let you run up a tab. Moe never did, but he was still a good guy. You sit in a booth and talk about sports, school, parents, gang fights, and, of course, the most popular subject of all—getting laid.

Other than your home, the street corner is your whole world. It is where your values are discovered and set and, sometimes, where your whole future is determined. It is your safe spot, the one place in the whole big universe where you feel like you belong, where you know you are not just another piece of faceless flesh. You mean something to somebody, to the neighborhood guys and girls. You are an important somebody to the gang on the street corner. It is where you laugh and sometimes even where you cry. It is where you talk about all the fun things and about the deep-down-inside-of-your-gut things. It is where you brag about your achievements and ask questions about your failures. It is where your friends look into your soul and see what you are all about. It is a place where I lived for twenty-one years of my life. It was almost as vital to me as the blood that ran through my veins. I owe a lot to the street corner. I would not be where I am, what I am, who I am, were it not for that little area sixteen feet by ten feet, once the most important and valuable piece of real estate in the entire world. That's why I named my corporation Street Corner Enterprises.

THE BARGAIN HOUSES

When you're poor, you either get hand-me-downs or store-bought rejects, seconds, thirds, fifths, tenths, one hundredths, according to the severity of the flaw or flaws. Growing up, I had gotten such items as a reindeer sweater on the front of which only appeared reindeer legs with a head at one end and a reindeer ass at the other end; a genuine leather belt that had no holes for the buckle, so they had to be punched in with a red-hot ice pick; an Arrow dress shirt with only one sleeve, which was in the back. My mother once bought herself a pair of nylon pantyhose with a crotch that hung so low she could carry home groceries in it.

In my neighborhood of West Philadelphia, there were two reject stores—the New York Bargain House and the American Bargain House. They were right next door to each other, and the owners were bitter enemies. They were having price wars between themselves constantly, posting their sale prices in the window.

In one window would appear the handwritten sign "For sale. Irish linen sheets, regular and king size, with such minor refractions that not even the hawkeye of Mrs. Reba Gerber could find them. Ask her. The ridiculous low price of $6.50."

Everyone would then traditionally await the reply from the other bargain house, and in about two hours it would appear in the window: "Mrs. Gerber needs glasses. His rejects can be seen by Ray Charles. My sheets are as close to firsts as Romeo is to Juliet and only $5.95."

An hour later. Next door: "Romeo killed Juliet and you will kill yourself if you listen to those lies. His sheets look more like horse blankets. Just to prove I'm right—$5.00 each."

"Better you should give the $5.00 to the Neo-Nazi Party. Two of the best sheets in the neighborhood and the world for $9.00."

"No one calls me a Nazi and gets away with it. I'll take a loss to prove my Americanism. Two sheets with matching pillowcases for $7.95."

In addition to the sign war, the two owners would often appear outside their stores, screaming and cursing at each other and oftentimes coming close to actual blows. Finally one of the owners would stop competing in the price war, claiming that the other one was crazy and so was anyone who bought from him. That was the starter's gun going off. Everyone in the neighborhood would rush into the winning bargain store and buy out the entire stock of sheets and pillowcases.

This war went on forever. The only things that changed were the items on sale. Their feud was one of the most intense and lasting in the neighborhood. These two men hated each other with a vengeance, and everyone living there profited from it by getting all kinds of wonderful bargains.

One day one of the owners passed away. A few days later, the other owner had a going-out-of-business sale. Shortly thereafter, both stores were sold and turned into new businesses. The surviving owner had moved out of the neighborhood, never to be seen again.

When the new occupants of the stores checked out their newly purchased properties more closely, they discovered a secret passageway between the two, as well as a connecting door between the two apartments above the stores where the previous owners had lived. Why would two bitter enemies, rivals, fight-to-the-death competitors have connecting doors between their businesses and homes? Further research revealed the answer. These two archenemies, these two men who threatened to kill each other with their bare hands, as witnessed thousands of times in front of their respective businesses, these two men of bitter hate were brothers.

The swearing, cursing, threats, and other personal abuses were all playacting. All the price wars were fake. Whoever outlasted the other would just take all the other's stock and sell it with his. For more than thirty years these two brothers had conned an entire neighborhood, a neighborhood made up mostly of cons. Their merchandise may have been seconds, but their brains were first-run.

THE SHOEMAKER

I guess I am what people call a star, a celebrity, and, for some, maybe even a hero of sorts. Well, let me tell you about my star, my celebrity, my hero.

When I was a kid, I had two pairs of shoes: one for every day and one for special occasions such as weddings or funerals. They were both hand-me-downs from my older brother, who was much older, so their toes had to be stuffed with toilet paper to prevent my feet from slipping out of them with every step that I took. Now, when the everyday pair wore out, and they wore out quite often because of the rough way I played in the streets and alleys of my neighborhood, I had to make a choice. Either I stayed home from school for two or three days, missing all the lessons, while my mother took my shoes to the shoemaker and we waited for them to be finished; or if I went to the shoemaker first thing in the morning, say six-thirty, I could wait while he fixed my shoes and not miss any school. I chose the latter, not because I liked school—I hated it—but because I didn't want to risk missing so much work that I'd get left back and spend even more time in that damn place.

In the shoemaker's store, I'd sit in a red leather booth and watch the old Italian shoemaker work on my shameful shoes. He would take these beat-up, scuffy shoes, which had a heel worn right down to the nails and a sole that was flapping in the wind, with holes in the top and sides, and shoelaces that were broken and knotted so many times you could hardly recognize what they were, and he would perform magic. First, he'd rip off the old heels and put on new ones, carve out two soles from a large piece of leather, pick some nails out of his mouth, and hammer the soles onto the shoes. Then, he'd take a sharp knife and trim them to the shoe. He would sew up the holes, cut off the old laces and string in new ones, polish and buff them, and hand me a pair of shoes that looked brand new. A miracle.

When I was a little kid, the shoemaker was a hero to me. He still is. You see, it is our society that has determined that I have more value. Oh, sure it is true that the shoemaker cannot do what I can do. He cannot make crowds of people laugh, but I can't take a beat-up pair of shoes and make them almost new. So, the next time you see a shoemaker, please think about it.

THE ROLLER COASTER

My childhood pal Stan "the Dancer" Levinson recently reminded me about the following story.

I still believe that the most thrilling amusement park ride is the roller coaster. One of the best ones, outside of the Cyclone in Coney Island, was the one in Willow Grove Park in Philly.

One night, one of many summer nights spent there, we went to Willow Grove Park and got on the roller coaster. As we were speeding and shaking around the curves and feeling our stomachs do flip-flops as the cars lifted off the tracks on their downhill run, the six of us poured catsup all over our heads, faces, and shirts. When the ride came to a stop, in front of the hundreds waiting in line to go on, we staggered off.

"What a helluva ride!"

People took one fleeting glance at our dripping bloody heads and faces, screamed, and ran off. So, what Stan the Dancer actually reminded me of was that as kids we were a bunch of real sickos—but, man, did we have fun.

LONG SUMMERS

Remember, as a child, when you got out of school for the summer vacation how long it lasted? Forever. We would play for months and months, year after year, and it was only the first week of July. Dozens of street games, hundreds of hours of play, thousands of new and beloved old experiences, millions of hours of fun and laughter. The summer seemed endless, filled with great adventures. Nothing in the whole wide world could beat summer. A few months that lasted more than forever.

Now summers are over practically before they even begin. You no sooner hear that it is the first official day of summer than you are listening to the announcement of the first day of autumn.

What happened to those long summers? I don't understand.

THE MOVIES

When I was growing up, there was no greater pleasure, no greater experience, no greater way of spending time than going to a Saturday matinee at a neighborhood theater. What in this whole wide world could beat five cartoons, two cliff-hanging chapters, and a cowboy, gangster, or war double feature? Nothing.

We used to get in the movie line two hours before the box office would open. Every once in a while we'd rub our fingers over the outside of our pockets to be doubly and triply certain we had the ticket money. As soon as we got back the torn stub of the movie ticket, we would charge into the theater. A couple of guys would save seats in the row closest to the screen, while the rest of us dove under the seats to look for boxes of candy discarded the night before by grown-ups. There would usually be a few pieces of uneaten candies in a box, a few jujubes, Good & Plenty, Goldenberg's Peanut Chews, M&M's. I used to think adults' fingers were just too fat to dig down into the boxes to get out the last of the candies, but then I couldn't figure out why they didn't just open the other end of the box. Grown-ups are dumb but not that dumb. Whatever the reason, we were thankful because we didn't have enough money to buy our own.

As soon as we all got into our seats, the spitballs, paper wads, paper clips, would start flying through the air. Peashooters came out of concealed places inside of shirts and slingshots from inside pants legs. War would break out on several fronts, accompanied by lots of screaming and running up and down the aisles. There would be a gang wrestling match in front of the first row and a couple of scattered fistfights. Then the magic moment would arrive and complete silence would envelop the theater and truces were immediately called. The lights would start to dim, the music would start to fade. The moment the theater was completely dark, the air would explode with thunderous applause, whoops, whistles, and then another burst of silence, a reverent respect for the opening of the curtain. And then there it would be—the giant white screen. I'll never forget the sound of the giant curtain sliding open. Then the picture would start and so would the yelling, screams, whistles, jumping, running, and fighting.

Those kids rich and lucky enough to have store-bought guns would bring them to the theater. The rest of us would have our homemade rubber-band pistols or clothespin guns shoved in the waistbands of our baggy, hand-me-down pants. Whenever the bad guys would appear on the screen, everyone would whip out their guns, aim at the screen, and make mouth sounds of guns being fired and bullets ricocheting. More mouth-created bullets were ejected in one movie in one afternoon than on any real-life battlefield. The light from the projector would pick up the hundreds of split peas fired from peashooters and wads of silver paper fired from rubber bands. It was the prototype of a light show.

Then that wonderful world of dark excitement would end. The movies would be over. Everyone would charge out to the streets, blinded by the strong rays of the summer afternoon sun. The movies would be over but not the fun. No sooner would we be heading up the street toward our houses than someone would yell the magic words "Let's play the movies."

Everyone would then pick his favorite character from whatever film we were going to reenact. Everyone would get a role. If there were more kids than roles, we'd make up additional parts. Once again the fake bullets would be flying. Sometimes our movie would last longer than the real one. Sometimes it lasted even longer than a real battle.

What fun. What wonderful, wonderful fun. I loved it. God, I wish I could sit in a theater today with my clothespin guns in each hand, firing my fake bullets at the bad guys on the screen, and later on join my friends to play the movies. As an English poet wrote long ago: "I long for the days that are no more."

I know that if there had been Saturday afternoon matinees when Keats was a boy, he would have added a line about the movies to the poem.

THE POOLROOM

I was a late-in-life child. My father was past the age when he would play kid's games, as he had with my much older brother and sister. In spite of our age difference, my father and I always had a special rapport. I could tell just by the tone of his hello, the way he'd nod, or by a certain look in his eyes whether he wanted me to hang around him. Sometimes he would say the words I always liked to hear:

"I'm going up to Sixtieth Street for a few minutes, Kingy. Want to come?"

"I'm going to go have a drink. Want to sit at the bar with me?"

"There's a great shoot 'em up cowboy movie playing at the Spruce. A hundred shots a minute. Want to go?"

"I'm going to smoke a cigar on the porch. Want to sit out there?"

"I'm going to take a spin in the car. Want to go? You can shift gears."

Then there was my all-time, super most favorite: "I'm going to shoot some pool. If you promise not to tell your mother, you can hang out with me."

No activity with my father topped going to the poolroom, where he would meet all his cronies, as he used to call his friends. He was very popular. No one was funnier than my father. Everyone loved to be in his company. When we walked into the poolroom, all the men would stop shooting to say hello to my dad. They'd all shake my hand, too. My dad would crack them up with his never-ending collection of dirty jokes and original one-liners. He always had a quip or ad-lib about everything and everyone. No one could come close to competing with him. When Lou Brenner walked in, so did uproarious laughter and lots of fun. He was a pretty good pool shooter, too.

My father would lift me up and deposit me on the high judge's seat, so I could see all the table action in the room. I'd watch my father shoot pool, listen to him curse when he'd miss a shot or his opponent would make one, laugh along with the others at his jokes, watch him blow his cigar smoke into the overhanging table lights or spit tobacco juice into a brass spittoon. I'd watch as the tough-looking, brightly painted women—or, as my father called them, broads, bimbos, or hot tomatoes—would come in to joke around and tease the men.

I had a special ranking in the poolroom, partly because I was the only kid there, but mainly because I was Lou's kid. Everyone always treated me special because they loved my father. I did, too, and I loved being there with him.

I, too, am much older than my son. In a few years, I'm going to take him to the poolroom as my father took me, because, as my father said to me when he was born, especially knowing the environment of his mother, the posh Greenwich, Connecticut, "Kingy, you're the only one who can teach Cole Jay about the streets." I hope that I can instill in my son the riches one finds between the street corner and the eight-ball table. It would be a great moment in my life if people were to walk up to Cole Jay, as he sat in a poolroom judge's chair, and joke with him because he was David's kid.

We can only try to pass on our treasures to our children. We can only hope that they will want them and will learn how to use them properly. It worked for Lou's kid Kingy; now I hope it will work for Kingy's kid, Cole Jay.

TOYS AND GAMES

When I was growing up, I had no store-bought toys. Poor kids never do. It's nothing to get upset about. It's simply the way of poor life. So, we made our own toys. They were great. For example:

Skato (skate-oh): Take a wooden orange crate and stand it up on its end so it now looks like a double-shelf end table. Take a two by four that's about three feet long and nail the upright box onto one end of it, the open shelves facing the long end. Nail a six-inch piece of broom handle on the near end of the top of the box. Steal your sister's or someone else's sister's skate, take it apart, and nail the front two wheels to the bottom front of the two by four and the back two wheels to the back. Now place your left foot on the middle of the two by four, gripping the two broom handles, and move your other foot along the street the same as you would on a scooter or a skateboard. You're flying on a skato.

Gutter raft: Save popsicle sticks from the few times you are lucky enough to have the money to buy one and from the ones you find in the street. Weave them together like a basket until you have a raft. Wait until you hear some kid scream, "The vegetable man's horse is pissing on Osage Avenue!" Grab your raft and run as fast as you can to Osage and place your raft in the gutter with all the others. Run alongside it as the horse's piss rushes the rafts to the sewer at the corner. You are yellow-water rafting.

Weapons: Put two wooden clothespins together. Now you have a gun. Take your mother's curtain rod down and put it through your belt. Now you have a sword. Take a garbage-can lid. Now you have a shield. Take some clothesline and wrap black plumber's tape around one end and on the tip of the other end. Now you have a whip. Put some large chunks of coal in your pockets. Now you have hand grenades. Roll your T-shirt sleeves up past your shoulders. Now you're ready to take on anyone.

Slide: Take a very large cardboard box from the loading dock of a supermarket. Open it up at the seams, flatten it out, lay it down on the front steps of a house. Stand at the top and slide down.

Rubber-band guns: Take a block of wood six by three inches. Nail half of a clothespin to one end, to make the handle of a revolver. Knock a large nail in the bottom, to make the trigger. Cut bands of rubber from an inner tube, then stretch them from the front of the gun to the back, under the clothespin. By holding the trigger nail with the finger and pressing the bottom of the clothespin, the rubber band will be released and will fly through the air toward its target—usually the back of someone's head. Use longer wood and bigger inner-tube bands to create a rubber-band rifle. Maybe a telephone pole and a slice of a rubber raft could be turned into a cannon. I don't know. I never tried.

Baseballs: Take a small rock, as close to round in shape as possible, and wrap it tightly in black plumber's tape, until it is the size of a baseball. This will perform like a real, store-bought baseball, until it is hit with a bat about a dozen times, at which time it'll start to flatten out until it resembles a small flying saucer. Even in this condition it is still able to be caught on the fly and can be reshaped for the next batter. Please note: Footballs and soccer balls require larger rocks and much more tape; basketballs are impossible.

Flying Heroes: To play such greats as Superman, Captain Marvel, Captain America, and Wonder Woman, simply tie a pillowcase around your neck, letting it droop down your back. Now extend your arms and start to run down the street as quickly as you can, until the pillowcase rises like a cape. You're flying. As you get older and your neck becomes thicker, a bath towel will have to replace the pillowcase.

Beeries: This was sometimes called deadman's box. You take the tops of beer or soda bottles and remove the cork disk from inside. Smooth the top by rubbing it on the cement pavement. Then, with the inside facing up, you move it along the pavement by releasing your middle finger off your thumb as you do when you give someone a "beazle" (snapping the finger off the top of someone's head). The object is to move your bottle top, or beerie, from one chalk-drawn numbered square on the pavement to another until you have put it inside all the ten numbered squares. Then you shoot it into the square with the skeleton head and crossbones drawn in it. This is the deadman's box. You are now a potent killer and you go after everyone else's beerie. When you hit their beerie out of the master square, they are dead. The remaining beerie wins.

Iron tag: One person is "it." The object of the game is simple: The "it" person must tag someone when that person is not holding onto iron, such as the schoolyard fence, a manhole cover (not the best iron because the "it" person just waits until a car is coming down the street and then the manhole-cover holder usually runs like hell), cellar grating, sewer cover, awning pole, etc. Once you are tagged, you become one of the "it" person's assistants, also capable of killing. A slick runner and shifty mover could make the game last over the weekend, becoming the best "last" there ever was.

Scaling: By pressing the bottoms of your canvas high-top sneakers against the opposite brick walls of an alley, you can inch your way up like a human fly. The objective is to either go all the way up to the roof of one of the buildings, where you could recover all the roofed balls, or to just hang about ten feet above the alley walkway until some other kids walk through and then drop on top of them. This is one of the least favorite games among parents.

Dead baby in the air: You simply throw a ball into the air yelling out someone's assigned number, such as "Dead baby number seven." The kid assigned that number would stop running and return to catch the ball. Once he succeeded in getting it, he would yell, "Freeze." He was then allowed to take seven flying giant steps and then try to hit someone with the ball. If he missed, he was "it" again. If he hit you, you were "it." Running inside of houses or into cars was not allowed.

Ball games: There were way too many games involving bouncing balls (stolen from the five-and-ten) to describe, but, because ball playing was such an important and wonderful part of my life, I'd like to simply put my favorites into an honorary mention list:

Stickball	Halfball
Wallball	Hoseball (*played with cut-up*
Stepball	*pieces of rubber garden hose*)
Boxball	Wireball
Atlantic City baseball	Chinkball

Capture the flag: You choose up sides with as many players as there are kids. One team keeps their shirts on, the Shirts, and the other side removes their shirts, the Skins. You go into a darkened building, such as a church recreation room, school gym, or empty warehouse, so dark that no one can see. You hang a flag (someone's T-shirt or a rag) on the wall at one end and another flag on the opposite wall. Then both teams line up against their own wall in the total darkness. A couple of guys are goalies and the rest are players. Someone whistles and it begins. The objective is to capture the other team's flag. There are no rules. You can do anything to anyone from the enemy team to stop him or when you capture him, including beating the hell out of him. This rule, and the possibility of being a skin, kept the girls from playing—damn it.

Three feet off the ice: One kid is "it." He stands on one side of the street. All the other kids are lined up along the opposite sidewalk. He selects one kid by name and gives him permission to make a certain number of some kind of moves into the street toward his side. There were many particular kinds of moves, including scissors (spreading your legs wide open like a scissor and spinning out), frog leaps (crouching and leaping like a frog), giant steps (running and leaping steps as in step, step, jump), and baby steps (one step after another with the heel of one shoe pressed against the toe of the other). For example, the "it" kid would say the following: "Dee-Dee, you can take three scissors and four baby steps off the ice. Beb, you can take one giant step, one frog leap, and twelve baby steps off the ice. Stan the Dancer can take forty-two baby steps and Morty the Bird can take five giant steps, which is the same as five baby steps." (The Bird was and still is the shortest guy in our gang.)

Sometimes the order simply was in feet, such as "Big Micky can take six feet off the ice," at which time Big Micky would run as fast as he could across the pavement and leap six steps across the street.

After everyone was in the street, the object was to suddenly dash the rest of the way across the street and reach the sidewalk without getting tagged. Once tagged you helped the "it" kid, until there was only one or two left. If anyone made it across, he would have to face everyone else in the next round.

Red rover: This was similar to three feet off the ice, except the kids trying to get across the street would be divided into the colors red and green. Then the "it" kid would announce that either color would try to come over to his side of the street by announcing "Red rover, red rover—green can come over." All the greens would charge across like crazy trying not to get tagged. Then the reds would come over with the "it" kid and any reds that were tagged trying to get them. This was repeated until the numbers dwindled, sometimes until everyone was now trying to tag one kid.

Statues: One kid would take another kid's arm and spin him around and around and around, finally letting him fly through the air, spinning down the street until someone yelled "Freeze," at which point he stopped and froze in the position of a statue. After all the human statues were in place, the "it" kid tried to guess what the statues were representing: baseball players, Mrs. McConnell taking a dump, Superman, a meteor, etc.

Bottle of pee: All the kids would urinate into a glass milk bottle. Then we would tie a long string around the bottle neck, balance the bottle on the railing of a porch of the street crab—the one who chased you away from playing in front of their house or kept any balls that landed on their property. The other end of the string was then tied around the front-door doorknob. We would then ring the doorbell, run like hell, and hide so we could secretly watch. When the grouch opened the door to see who rang, the milk bottle would fly through the air, landing and smashing in the vestibule or living room of the house.

Hide-and-Seek: I saved this one for last because next to stickball, this was my favorite game. We played it for hours. Kids found places in which to hide one could never imagine anyone getting into, let alone hiding in: garbage cans, sewers (holding on of course), atop store awnings, inside thrown-away mattresses, manholes, inside automobile hoods. One of my favorite places was inside a church. Most of the kids figured I'd only hide in a synagogue. I don't have to explain the rules of this game because it's universal and ageless. My son loves to play it and we do, except I always know where he is hiding and I am very limited in places to hide because I am too big—physically, that is, not mentally. So, in a sense, the game has lost something, some of the thrill of the unknown. It's a game strictly for kids, but I play it with Cole Jay anyway. Come on, how many words are better to hear than someone tagging the home base and yelling, "One, two, three O'Leary. Freedom for all!" Also, when you become an adult, it is so rare that you find a home base and even rarer to find freedom for all.

I absolutely loved all my homemade toys and street games. There were so many I just couldn't take the time and space to

write about them all. I had no money, but I had many friends
and a lot of fun playing in the streets. One day you stop playing
with toys and there are no more games in the streets. It's the
day boys discover girls. And let me tell you—they're more than
worth it. However, every once in a while I'd like to get some
black plumber's tape, a broom handle . . .

A SHRUNKEN HEAD

When I was a kid, the last store on the Atlantic City boardwalk,
heading for the Inlet, was Lee's Curio Shop. He sold everything
you could imagine and beyond what you could imagine, including an ashtray with a donkey sitting on it that when you turned
over exposed the donkey's ass, magic ink you could spill on a
friend and watch it disappear in minutes, a picture of Jesus
Christ whose eyes followed you as you walked from side to side
and closed and opened as you walked away and toward, a model
of the Taj Mahal built completely out of seashells, a horse built
entirely from toothpicks, and a mystery box containing God
knows what.

My favorite item was displayed in the window among the
hundreds of other oddities—a real shrunken head. The eyes and
lips were sewn shut. It had a long mustache and long black
silken hair. It was twenty-five dollars, an enormous amount of
money for a seven-year-old. I wanted it so badly. All I could
think about was how impressed all my friends would be and
how I could use it as a bargaining tool in the neighborhood
stores:

"I'd like a couple slices of American cheese, Mr. Saylor."

"It'll be twenty-five cents. You got a quarter?"

"No, but I'll show you a real shrunken head."

I'd get the cheese, and hoagies, and steak sandwiches, a scarf,
a baseball, the answers to the math test, a week of history homework. I could talk myself out of fights. I could date the best-
looking girls in the school. The possibilities were endless. All I
had to do was buy that shrunken head; but there was no way I
could save up that much money.

When I was in my early teens and working steadily after
school, I could have easily bought the shrunken head, but by

that time its value to me had diminished greatly. However, whenever I would go down to the shore, I would walk to Lee's Curio Shop and look in the window at the shrunken head. It was always there because I guess no one was enough of a putz to buy it.

Lee's Curio Shop eventually closed and was torn down. I wonder what he did with that shrunken head?

THE STEAM BATH

In Yiddish it is called the *schvitz*, which literally means "sweat," and figuratively, "the steam bath," a place where men used to go after work, usually on Fridays, to sit and talk business, play gin rummy, complain about their wives and children, whisper about their gentile secretary lovers and other main topics of conversation.

It was a diehard fact that one was not a man, in the true and accepted sense of the word, until one attended the *schvitz*. A true man was christened, if you pardon the expression, in the steam baths.

In Philly, the main *schvitz* was the Camac, so named because it was located on Camac Street in Center City. At age twelve, Dee-Dee, Beb, and I decided that it was the proper time to become men, so we took the bus downtown and paid our visitation fee at the Camac.

We undressed, placed our street clothes in the rented wall lockers, wrapped around us the terrycloth bath towels they supplied, and entered the steam room.

We sat on the wooden slabs, trying to adjust our eyes to the thick steam so we could see the mysterious man's world about which we had heard so often. Finally we were able to focus. Sitting on wooden slabs all around us were approximately twenty-five to thirty of the much heard about and revered "men." They looked more like a school of white whales that had been washed up on a beach. The world's largest collection of massive, swollen stomachs hanging directly above the tiniest penises. Their tits were bigger than most women's. They had jowls like old bulldogs. Most of them had bald heads that shone like New England lighthouses. The only sounds emanating from these strange creatures were the sounds of heavy wheezing, coughing, clearing of throats, and the passing of gas. The only movements from them were spitting on the floor, picking their noses, scratching their asses, and fondling their testicles.

We got up and left. If this was what it meant to become a man, I wanted to remain a young boy forever.

II

THE STING OF YOUTH

THE FIVE-DOLLAR BILL

As soon as Beb and I came out of the Sugar Bowl Luncheonette at 60th and Ludlow streets, I saw the purse lying on the pavement. We were across the street from our elementary school—William Cullen Bryant. I scooped it up and we went down an alley. Inside the purse was a five-dollar bill. No identification, nothing! Now, at age eight, I hadn't seen too many five-dollar bills. This was the find of the century!

"Beb, you hold onto the bag. I'm going to run across to the schoolyard and get the guys. Then we'll all go to Moe's and get us some hoagies and double thick milk shakes. Wow, what a day!"

A few minutes later, I was running back with the eight or nine guys I had rounded up, each of whom was freaking out that we had a whole five dollars to blow. I saw Beb standing across the street talking to two cops seated in a patrol car. I ran faster.

"Beb, what the hell you doin'?"

"Is this the kid who found the purse?"

"Yeah, I am. Where is it?"

"Right here, son."

"Okay, you seen it; there's no ID in it, so give it back to me. I found it."

"The woman who lost it may come to claim it."

"Then just give me the five-spot."

"That's hers, too."

"Jesus, don't I get anything for finding it?"

"If the woman wants to give you something, she will."

"Suppose she don't show?"

"Then it's yours."

"How long we gotta wait?"

"Thirty days."

"Thirty days? You gotta be shitting me."

"That's the law. You come to the station in thirty days, and if no one claimed the bag, it's yours."

"Where's that? Fifty-fifth and Pine?"

"Right. See you, boys."

The police car drove off, and I turned to Beb and punched him in the arm as hard as I could.

"Owww! What's that for?"

"For being a schmuck! Why the hell did you give the cops the money?"

"I was standing by the curb waiting for you to come back when they pulled up and looked at me funny-like. I got scared and told them about finding the purse."

"Jesus! What's today's date?"

"May fourth. Why?"

"Because on June fourth you and me are going to the police station, and you'd better pray that lady didn't claim her purse or I'm going to give you a five-dollar ass kicking!"

First thing in the morning, on June 4, Beb and I walked into the police station at 55th and Pine streets. We told the desk sergeant about the purse. He looked through some book and told us that no purse had been handed in. Beb and I had gotten ripped off by the cops!

That night at dinner I told my family what happened. First thing the next day, my father, Beb, and I were at the police station again. The same desk sergeant told my father that we needed the names of the officers if we wanted to file a complaint. My father said that they could look up who was in car number 384 during that shift on May 4. The sergeant tried conning us some more by saying that they didn't keep such records, and that unless we could positively identify the two officers, nothing could be done. As my father was pursuing the argument, I saw the two cops walk in!

"There they are! Get 'em!"

A very strange thing to be yelling about cops, especially while inside a police station, but I kept on pointing my finger at them and kept on repeating, "Get 'em!"

I remembered one cop because he looked like a prison warden named Captain Muncie played by the actor Hume Cronyn in a Burt Lancaster movie.

The sergeant had no choice but to call over the two officers. We all discussed the issue. Of course, the cops denied the entire story. The sergeant said that nothing could be done. My father was livid.

"It's tough enough trying to teach kids to be honest in this kind of neighborhood," my father yelled. "How the hell do you expect these two boys to have any respect for the law now?"

Somehow we did, and I still do, but from that moment, through my teen years and early twenties, right up to the day he was transferred, retired, or died, whenever I saw "Captain Muncie," I would ask him real loud where my five dollars were, and if there were strangers around, I would quickly tell them the story of how he stole the money from me. Once, when he took out a five-dollar bill, I grabbed his arm and told him that if he ever did that, I would rip it up, mix it into a bowl of broken glass, and make him eat it. It was way too late.

Did I get my five dollars' worth? Not really. Did "Captain Muncie" get his money's worth? I'd like to think so.

WHITE WOLVERINE SALVE

The magazine ad read that one could make a lot of extra money and possibly win valuable prizes by simply using one's spare time to sell White Wolverine Salve door to door. I was ten years old. I was already smart enough to doubt the claims, and even if they were true, the last thing I wanted to do was walk from door to door in my neighborhood selling a salve that was supposed to cure everything from mosquito bites to vampire-bat bites, with poison ivy and constipation somewhere in the middle. It would be a stupid thing to do, so I immediately filled in the coupon with the name and address of my best friend, Dee-Dee. This was in retaliation for him throwing my books under a truck, making me late for my science class.

A few weeks later, several large cartons of White Wolverine Salve showed up at his doorstep. Dee-Dee shipped them back at his own expense. I confessed that I did it and all the guys on the street corner had a great laugh and teased Dee-Dee about it. Dee-Dee didn't laugh.

A few weeks after that I received a Book of the Month Club membership, three best sellers, and a bill. I shipped them back. A couple of weeks later, Dee-Dee got a shipment of oversized men's shoes to sell door to door. Then I received my first encyclopedia and a bill. Dee-Dee got his twenty-four magazines and a bill. My mother asked me why I signed up for a baby diaper service. Dee-Dee's mother asked him why he had French tickler condoms shipped to the house. My mother then insisted that I carry all the newly arrived brass pots and pans back to the post office. Dee-Dee soon made his trip to the post office to return the shipment of plastic window curtains. The next week I shipped back the ant farm. A few weeks later, Dee-Dee carefully returned the male and female hamsters. Shortly thereafter, I received my ninety-five-dollar COD hand engraving of Niagara Falls. It wasn't as much trouble to send back as Dee-Dee's unpainted put-it-together-yourself bedroom suite. I stored the three dozen collapsible floor lamps in my cellar. Dee-Dee lined the walls of his halls with the dozen easy-to-sell retread truck tires. I put the metal detector next to the six vacuum cleaners. Dee-Dee hid the six-foot by six-foot paint by number canvas of circus clowns under his bed. I slipped the semitruck tire jack into the trunk of my father's car. Dee-Dee hid the dozen vibrators under his underwear in his bureau.

Dee-Dee's mother telephoned my mother. The two-year mail-order war was too much for both of them. We held a summit meeting. A truce was negotiated. Dee-Dee and I shook hands, promising never to do it again.

What really bothered me was that I had already filled out the form for the 2,000 pounds of lawn fertilizer—and Dee-Dee didn't have a lawn.

FISH EYES

You wouldn't think someone would ever tell a story about fish eyes, especially not on a stage or on TV in front of millions of people. Someone would have to be nuts to even come up with something about such a strange subject and even nuttier to tell anyone about it. Well, this nut has done it and it happens to be one of the public's favorite routines, and it often gets requested when I'm performing. But I enjoy the Fish Eyes routine much more than anyone who has ever heard it because it is a true story, and every time I retell it I relive the wonderful moment with the true-life scenes flashing before my mind's eye. Fish eyes in the mind's eye. Now that's some weird wording. Why not? It was some weird event. But I've got to tell you that there was more to the true story than I've ever told, so for those of you who are already fans of the Fish Eyes routine, you are about to hear more about it, and for those of you who have no idea what I'm talking about, I shall relate the entire story, bridged and unabridged.

Ladies and Gentlemen and Children of all ages (drum roll, please), I am proud to bring to you, from its very beginning to its very ending, the very true and hopefully very funny story of little David Brenner and his fish eyes.

Let's have a brief background of the Louis and Estelle Brenner offsprings. The oldest, Mel "Moby Dick"; the middle, Blanche "Bib"; and the itsy bitsy little baby, David "Kingy." Very close and very much in love with one another in spite of great differences in age and life-style. Whatever sibling rivalry existed was expressed lovingly in the wildest, weirdest, most bizarre practical jokes and most disturbingly creative attacks. The oldest was the most devious. For example:

My brother offered me a delicious new drink and I discovered—pure carrot juice. He pretended to join me in drinking some. I didn't pretend, taking the biggest gulp of all time of the most rancid-tasting liquid of all time, almost causing me to

33

throw up on the spot. The oldest rolled on the floor bursting with laughter as I charged upstairs to brush my teeth and gargle. The youngest strikes back. Every night I poured just a few drops of the awful carrot juice into my brother's milk. Every night he complained that his milk tasted rather peculiar, but continued to drink it until all the juice was consumed. As the last glass was finished I announced what I had been doing. His turn to brush and gargle.

The oldest also had the sickest sense of humor. His idea of fun was to sneak up on me while I was reading or sleeping and place a dirty sock of his on my shoulder or over my face. Now remember that this is a man tormenting a boy, a full-grown man with a Ph.D. degree, a college professor, a brilliant intellect, a sick son of a bitch. I'd be watching TV and all of a sudden I'm smothered with a dirty gym sock, or I'd be doing my homework and suddenly would smell something rotten, only to see the sock my brother was dangling in front of my forehead. I was never safe in my own house, not even when I went to sleep in the bedroom I shared with my big, demented brother. When he would return home after a date, he would sneak up to the bed and lay a dirty sock over my sleeping face. Sometimes, he would pile as many as a half-dozen socks on my face. Of course, I struck back as best I could. For these sock wars, we wouldn't put our dirty socks in the clothing hamper to be washed. My mother was always complaining about the missing socks. So as not to aggravate mother and in order to better aggravate each other, we both began wearing the same socks for a week or so while throwing clean socks into the hamper. My mother was happy and we developed more deadly sock bombs.

My best attack ended the war forever. While my brother was out on a date, I rigged a series of clothesline pulleys across the ceiling of my bedroom, through which I put a string, on the end of which was a rancid sock. When lowered, this foul article of clothing would come to rest directly above my brother's pillow. A second dreadful sock was rigged so that it could be pulled across his pillow. I then tied the string to my hand and forced myself to stay awake until my brother returned from his date.

In the middle of the night he came home. I faked deep breathing as I heard him climb into our bed. I waited until I heard the familiar sound of his sleeping breathing, then I ever so slowly pulled the string that released the sock so that it hung a few inches above his nose. As he sniffed, twisted and turned onto his side, I pulled the string that brought the other sock slowly sliding up onto and across his pillow, coming to rest directly at his nose. He sniffed, coughed, and opened his watering eyes, and stared at the moldy cloth object perched at the tip of his nose. I then released the pulley string so that the first sock came pummeling from the ceiling. A direct hit—right over his face. My brother gagged and shot up. I rolled around the bed in hysterics. Moby Dick, on the merits of originality and ingenuity, conceded victory and called a truce. So ended the War of the Socks.

Warfare with sister Bib was of an entirely different nature. She had a proof-perfect aim. She could hit just about any target, from any distance, with just about any weapon, her favorite being a rubber band with a semistraightened paper clip or a V-shaped wad made from tightly rolled paper. Then, too, she could throw anything, from a sofa pillow to a stale end of a rye bread, with the same deadly skill. I would tease her, she'd pick up something, I'd run as quickly as I could, she'd haul off and throw, I'd get smacked with it. I never learned my lesson. What I should have done was tease her from behind a protective shield or from another city.

Now for the fish eye incident. One day I challenged a friend of mine to a game of stickball. I guess that's strictly an eastern big-city game, so I'd better explain. The way stickball is played is as follows:

1. You steal your mother's broom, place it on the curb, stomp on it to break off the straw, and rub off the splinters on the pavement. This is your bat.
2. You then steal a high-bouncer pink Spalding ball from the five-and-ten and cut it in half with your switchblade knife, being careful not to let any of the smelly fish juice that's inside get on your hands. Let the ball dry in the sun for ten minutes or so.
3. You can play shortways, which is where the pitcher throws from the middle of the street and the batter hits

the ball toward the building behind the pitcher. A single is anything that gets past the pitcher; a double is anything that hits above the first-story window but below the second-story one; a triple is above the second-story window; and a home run is on the roof.

4. If you are playing longways, the black Chevy is a single, the telephone pole a double, Mr. Connelly's porch a triple, and the sewer a home run.

5. One strike or two tips or two fouls (the porches longways, and the ends of the building shortways) are an out. There are nine innings, same as in baseball. Home runs over the roof or into the sewer must be retrieved by the batter.

The fellow I challenged to a game was the best, or second best, according to me, stickball player in the neighborhood. We were to play longways on my street. Kids from all over the neighborhood came to see the playoff.

We flipped a coin and he won. I would bat first. I got myself positioned at home plate, a small pothole in the street. The first pitch was a big mistake on his part. It was low and on the outside, just where I liked it. I knew it was going to be a home run as soon as the bat left my shoulder, and it would've been, if I didn't get hit in the back of the head with a small red brick.

I collapsed to the street. I didn't know what or who had hit me. I saw who as soon as I rolled over onto my back. There she was, my sister, running across the roofs.

The game was called off. I got to my feet dizzily and staggered toward my house. A huge lump was already coming out on the back of my head. It looked like a person was following me. When I got into the house I didn't say anything to my mother, because there was an unwritten rule in the streets that one never squeals. It was a sacred law.

I weaved into the kitchen, where my mother was preparing fish for dinner. The lump on my head reflected a large shadow on the wall.

Now, preparing fish for dinner was different in those days. Nowadays you go to a supermarket and there's a fish counter and inside are all the fish already prepared for you. You reach in, you take a white thing wrapped in cellophane paper marked "Fish." It could be anything—a gym sock, anything. When I was a kid, it was a lot different, especially if you were poor. Your mother either went to the local fish market or she bought the fish off a pushcart. No matter where you bought it, you had to prepare the fish yourself. It wasn't cleaned. You bought the whole fish, with the head and the tail, a little hat, eyeglasses, sneakers, the works. Then the fishman would wrap it up in a newspaper. I still feel a little squeamish when I open a newspaper, because as a kid, sometimes you'd open a paper and under the headlines there'd be this open-mouthed carp staring at you.

Next, your mother had to prepare the fish herself. She had to cut off the head and the tail and put in her own mercury. It was entirely different then and it was difficult.

While my mother was preparing the fish for dinner, I was standing there wobbling, thinking of how I could get revenge on my sister. I glanced down on the drainboard of the sink and saw a pair of fish eyes staring at me. I scooped them up and put them in my pocket. I got some Krazy Glue and glued them to my forehead, and then climbed into the dirty clothing hamper in the hallway with a flashlight in my mouth, the light flashing inward. I waited until my sister opened the hamper to throw in some of her delicacies, then I turned on the flashlight. When my sister saw my red cheeks and the four eyes, she fainted, but, as she fell, she slammed the lid of the hamper against the end of my flashlight, lodging it in my throat. Immediately, I climbed out of the hamper and started running down the hall. My mother saw me, thought I had jammed a pipe in my throat and my eyes were coming out of my head. She collapsed on the spot. I charged downstairs. My father glanced up. Nothing ever bothered my father. He just looked at me and said, "How ya doin', four-eyes?"

This is where I stop the stage and TV rendition of the story, but this is not where the real-life story ends. I shall continue.

My father followed me into the kitchen, where I was removing the fish eyes from my forehead, after having successfully extracted the flashlight from my throat. Lou took a long puff on his cigar and slowly blew the smoke up to the kitchen ceiling. He removed the cigar from his mouth and looked at me. Then in his soft Godfather-type whisper, he spoke: "Kingy, I want you to take those fish eyes into the backyard and throw them into the garbage can or else I'm going to see that you eat them for dinner."

I didn't need more convincing. I ran out into the backyard, opened the garbage can lid and . . . well, I looked into the eyes of the eyes. It was as if we had become friends. I just couldn't throw my newfound friends into the garbage just like that. They were pleading with me to save them, silently promising that they could offer me more fun. I opened the lid and rattled the can noisily, as though I were throwing away the eyes, which was really dumb because there was no way two eyes could make that much noise. You could throw away an entire cow more quietly.

I then carefully put the fish eyes into my pocket and went into the house. I apologized to my sister and mother for the incident. Then I casually walked into the dining room and as silently as possible slid open the top drawer of the dresser where the glue was kept. I took the glue and ducked out into the back alley. I then reglued the fish eyes to my forehead and walked up to 60th Street, the bustling shopping area for the neighborhood.

I would walk up to a store whose front window was painted halfway up in order to use the space for advertising and then I would tap on the window lightly but loudly enough to be heard while simultaneously raising my head so that the fish eyes would appear first and then my own wide-open eyes. Women shoppers would scream. I did it to about six stores. The rumor was flying that a monster was loose on 60th Street. The neighborhood was terrorized. I was very happy.

I returned to my house and placed the two fish eyes in the center drawer of my bedroom dresser, a hand-me-down from my brother, who had as a child put a big ball of roofing tar in the center drawer. I think he was trying to corner the black-tar market.

Well, you know the attention span and memory span of young children. It isn't very long. The world is all new and all exciting and there is so much to enjoy and remember that one forgets so much, such as a pair of fish eyes casually placed in a drawer.

The summer rolled along. July came and with it a horrific

heat spell. The second floor of our house began to stink. Then the first floor. The whole house reeked of a strange and horrible odor. Although we really could not afford to call an exterminator, we were forced to, because we would gag upon entering the house, and my father's search for the dead animal had failed. We had no choice—Morris the Exterminator Man.

He arrived in his exterminator truck, which had a huge water bug on the roof almost as big as the truck itself. The water bug was on its back with its legs up in the air and Morris's slogan was painted across the side paneling: "Nobody Gets Away Alive From Morris the Bug Killer."

Morris came into the house and sniffed around. He went up the stairs to the second floor. I could hear him open the door to my bedroom and enter. I think I even remember hearing him sniffing around in there. I know I do remember hearing him scream and seeing him charge down the stairs.

"What is it, Morris? Have you found it?"

"Yes, it's a dead animal."

"What kind of animal?"

"I don't really know, Mrs. Brenner. I've never seen anything like it in my life. It's in the center drawer of David's dresser. It's this real small, soft, black animal and from the look of its eyes, I'd say it's been dead at least two years."

My father, mother, sister, and brother snapped their heads in my direction. I leaped to my feet and ran out of the house. There was no way I was going to have fish eyes and tar for dinner.

That's the truth, the whole truth, nothing but the truth about the pair of fish eyes as it all happened during one of those glorious summers so long ago in the days of my wild, woolly, disturbed—and fun-filled—youth. Would I do it all over again if I could? You're damn right I would.

LUNGER

Lunger. Just the sound of the word is sickening. I understand that its origin is from tuberculosis victims who would cough up and spit out a ball of phlegm from deep down inside their lungs.

Mrs. Schroat was my art teacher and ninth-grade homeroom

teacher. She didn't like me and I didn't like her. She made a habit of suspending me from class or school. I made it a habit to give her just cause for such actions. My mother spent as much time in Mrs. Schroat's company as I.

As we were nearing the end of the semester, I was on my best behavior because of my fear that Mrs. Schroat would flunk me in art class and make me attend summer school.

In homeroom I shared a double desk with my pal Beb. To occupy our minds and keep us at our best behavior, Mrs. Schroat would spend the homeroom period reading from and acting out a classic.

One morning while acting out a very dramatic recitation by Fagin from *Oliver Twist*, she screamed out his lines and something flew out of her mouth and landed smack in the middle of Beb's desk top. It was a huge lunger. Beb leaped to his feet, pointing at his desk.

"You shot a lunger on my desk, Mrs. Schroat."

The entire class got hysterical. I was doubled up in gleeful pain. Mrs. Schroat was red as a beet.

"That's enough. Barry, you and David are suspended. Report to the vice principal immediately."

"Why me, Mrs. Schroat?" I said. "What did I do? Your lunger landed on Beb's desk, not mine. Look, my desk is clean as a whistle. No lungers. See I'm rubbing my hand on it."

"David, you have just increased your suspension to three days. One more word and it's a week."

"A week? You shoot a lunger and I get a week? Good thing you didn't vomit on his desk or I'd probably never go to school the rest of my life."

Bedlam broke out. My classmates were howling. Fuel for my humorous furnace.

"Matter of fact, I'm glad you didn't take a shit on his desk or I'd probably get the electric chair."

She leaped out of her seat and came toward us. It was the closest I had ever come to getting hit by a teacher. Beb and I both took off for the door.

On the way home, after our suspensions, I grabbed Beb in a headlock, and rubbed my knuckles along his head. This was called nuggies. Beb was forever nudging me or getting me in trouble and I was forever giving him nuggies. To this day, he swears that the reason he went bald in his late teens was because of my nuggies.

Oh, by the way, I didn't flunk art class and didn't have to go to summer school. However, when I graduated, Mrs. Schroat sent my mother a letter in which she wrote that for the rest of her life, whenever she sees the capital letter *B*, standing for Brenner, she will shudder. Personally, I hope she's been shuddering and lungering her artsy ass off.

KING DONG

Most kids love class trips. I hated them, starting with the stupid permission note from your mother, to carrying the brown bag with the tuna fish window stain on it, to holding some pudgy kid's hand in the don't-get-lost buddy system (as though you're going to drown in the marble floor of the museum), to getting constantly reprimanded for talking or laughing or having a good time.

One class trip turned out to be an exception. We were going to the zoo—again. Come on, once you've looked into the gaping mouth of a hippo, you've seen all there is to see about a hippo. There's no need to check it out every few years.

We were waiting in line to enter the monkey house. My pal Dee-Dee was in front of me, holding his "buddy" Ruth's hand. She was a very quiet, well-mannered, bright girl from the right side of the tracks. Sort of a quasi teacher's pet, but very nice, nevertheless.

Bored as I usually was on such outings, I was looking around restlessly. Across the dirt road alongside us was a very large gorilla in a cage. I noticed that he was staring directly at Ruth. I nudged Dee-Dee, who looked and started giggling, which started me giggling, which got the teacher angry. According to the teacher's manual, she called out for us to stop giggling. According to the human nature manual, this only makes one giggle more so.

I glanced again at the gorilla, who was now doing more than

looking. He was stroking his large erection. I went. So did Dee-Dee. We were both out of control. The teacher was livid.

"Okay, you two, share the joke with the rest of us so we can all have a good laugh."

"But . . . but . . . but . . ."

"No, 'buts,' David Brenner. I demand that you tell us immediately what is so funny."

An opportunity like that may come only once in a million school years, maybe even a trillion.

"The gorilla is jerking off to Ruth."

The roar of laughter probably startled every animal in the zoo. The only ones not laughing were Ruth, the teacher, and the gorilla.

Yes, of course, I was suspended from school—again. But, man, it was worth it.

BIG MICKY'S BIG DUMP

When I was a teenager, if you came home in the wee hours of the night, say four or five, one or both of your parents would get on you for staying out all night and doing who knows what, but if you came home eight or nine in the morning, your parents would think you slept at a friend's house, so, when we were about to break the parents' time barrier, we would just stay up all night and wouldn't get it for staying up all night. I know it's nuts—but this is the way it was.

One summer night we had driven down to Atlantic City for a good time. After we had it, the six of us piled into my 1941 Buick convertible and headed back to Philly. Even though I was always heavy-footed on the gas pedal, we didn't get there until five in the morning, too late to go home. We had to drive around for a couple of hours.

I was roaring down the Industrial Highway, which leads to the airport, when Big Micky, who stood six feet five inches, said he had to go to the bathroom but not where he could do it standing up. There are no businesses along this highway, so no public bathrooms. I told Big Micky that I would cut off at the next light and head into town. We could be there in twenty minutes or so. His cramps got worse. It was time for emergency action, quick thinking.

"Look, Micky, I'll pull over and you can go. There are Kleenexes back there."

"Are you crazy, Brenner? I can't do that. What about all the traffic?"

"All the traffic's coming toward us heading for the city. No one's behind us. See. Look at all the trucks and cars over there, bumper to bumper."

"No way. My luck a parade'll pull up behind us and then . . . Oh, God, the cramps are killing me."

"Micky, if *you* have an accident in my car, *I'll* have an accident in my car."

"Ohhhhhh. Pull over, Brenner. I'll do it." I pulled off the road. Micky grabbed the box of Kleenex and got out of the car. I turned to Beb by the other front door.

"Beb," I whispered, "look in the side-view mirror and let me know just when Big Micky is getting started."

"Okay, Dave. He's got his pants down around his ankles, now he's squatting. Okay, he's started."

I floored the accelerator and the car screeched ahead. As I turned to get back on the road, I looked in the rear mirror. Micky was squatting on the shoulder of the road, a look of disbelief on his face, his bright-red face. The oncoming traffic came to a dead stop. Truckers were blowing their horns, people were getting out of their cars, lots of them were cheering and applauding Big Micky. We were hysterical.

"Oh, Dave, that's the best one you ever pulled off. Man did you see his face?"

"Man, did you see his ass?"

"Half the city has."

"Now when they say this highway is a real dump, they'll mean it."

"Dave, we'd better go back for him."

"Are you insane, Dee-Dee? If I pick up Big Micky, that's exactly what he'll do to me and then throw me in front of a moving truck. No way, man. I'll drop you at your car and you can go pick him up."

"Then he'll kill me."

"What'll we do, Dave?"

"I don't know about you guys, but I know exactly what I'm going to do."

I still don't know how Big Micky found out what hotel I was staying in in New York. I thought the knock on the door was room service. Big Micky's big left fist crashed into my little right ear, sending me spinning back onto the bed. He leaped on top of me, his fists flying. I covered up. He was cursing like crazy. I guess you could say he was angry.

"Micky, stop hitting me for one sec. I've got to tell you something."

"Okay, say what you got to say, then I'm going to finish beating the hell out of you."

"There's not too much hell left in me now, but here's what I want to say. If you stop punching me, I'll treat you to the best dinner in Manhattan and then I'll take you over to the West Side Highway so you can take a good dump. You'll like it much better than the Industrial."

In spite of himself, Micky cracked up. We both got hysterical recalling the event in Philly.

Yes, we had the great dinner. No, Big Micky used the bathroom in my hotel room. Of course we remain good friends to this day. After all, we went through a lot of shit together.

MRS. CROOKED MOUTH

The kids in the neighborhood called her Mrs. Crooked Mouth because her mouth was twisted over on one side of her face. They could've also called her Mrs. Mean Mouth because whatever came out of that opening between her chin and nose was almost always mean.

Every Saturday afternoon she did her shopping in the supermarket where I worked as a combination stock boy and bag packer. No matter how big a shopping bag I gave her, she would always scream for a bigger bag, constantly getting me in trouble with my boss. If I did give her a bag big enough for all her purchases and then some, she would still scream. "What're ya tryin' to do, give me a hernia? Put it in two bags."

One busy Saturday afternoon, Mrs. Crooked Mouth showed up in the checkout line for the second time. She had forgotten to buy a can of tuna fish. She put the can on the counter and watched the cashier ring it up. I picked up the can of tuna fish and threw it loudly into our largest shopping bag and yelled, "Is the bag big enough for you, Mrs. Crooked Mouth?"

Everyone in line within earshot laughed. Mrs. Crooked Mouth reddened and stormed out.

The following Friday night, as I was hand-trucking cartons of stock deliveries into the store to be put into the storeroom or on the shelves, I saw Mrs. Crooked Mouth standing by the double doors. It was the first time I had ever seen her on a Friday night. I started moving closer to the doors with my heavy load of cartons of Sunshine prune-juice bottles. I noticed the doors were closed. I rested my hand truck upright and went to open the doors. I couldn't find the little rubber doorstops we had always used to keep the doors open.

"I'll hold the doors open for you," said Mrs. Crooked Mouth. She was smiling—I think. Anyway, I was shocked to hear her volunteer to help me.

"Thank you, Mrs. . . . Thank you."

"My pleasure."

I placed my foot against the bottom of the hand truck, pulling the heavy boxes toward me. I headed for the doors, pushing faster and faster, in order to get the truck over the little speed bump in the doorway.

I saw them coming toward me, but it was too late to do anything about it. Just as the wheels of my truck got to the bump, Mrs. Crooked Mouth let the two swinging doors go. I smashed into them and went flying into the store, cartons crashing to the floor, sticky prune juice splashing on customers, gushing and oozing all over the floor. Customers screamed. My boss screamed, too. "You're fired. Get a mop and clean up this mess and then get the hell out of here."

"Wait a minute, boss. You really think I'm going to mop up this crap if I'm getting fired? What am I, a putz? I quit. Mop it up yourself."

I stormed out of the store, looking for Mrs. Crooked Mouth. She was nowhere to be seen. But next to the door, leaning against a brick wall, was a large shopping bag, and I didn't have to look inside to know what was there—you guessed it: a single can of tuna fish.

THE MAN WHO ATE HIS FINGER

I guess every neighborhood in every city and every town, large and small, has that character who entertains the children by doing something weird. Our local street jester would slide the tip of his index finger along his middle finger, separating it from the rest of his index finger, and then would put it in his mouth and chew on it, the stump of his finger in view, bloodless. Then he would put the stump into his mouth and miraculously re-unite it with the missing fingertip, leaving not a trace of any separation. Of course, it was done simply by substituting the thumb of the other hand for the tip of the finger, covering the separation with the index finger of the other hand, so it only ap-peared to be sliding along and off the finger. Then the tongue is stuffed in the cheek to make it look like the fingertip is being chewed. It's strange how as you get older the people who did such tricks for you as a child, who you thought were so funny, suddenly seem like such idiots. What's even stranger is how much fun I get out of doing the eating-the-finger trick for my son. He loves it—for now, anyway.

THE EGYPTOLOGIST

At age fourteen, I was six feet two inches tall and weighed 126 pounds. Thin is not the word for it. Strangers used to come up to me and tell me that they admired the way I had survived the concentration camps.

Even back then I believed that when something is wrong and until you can correct it, the best thing to do about it is to have some laughs with or about it. So, when my "crowd" was invited to a house party, I would sometimes dress in a black three-piece suit, put on ghoulish-style makeup, and part my greased slicked-back hair in the middle. When we arrived at the party, I would stand in the corner of the room staring into space. It was only a matter of time before one of the girls would ask one of my friends, "Who is that creep in the corner?"

"Oh, he is one of the world's best Egyptologists, and certainly the youngest. Matter of fact, he just returned yesterday from Egypt, where he was studying life after death."

This piqued enough curiosity that the girls wanted to meet me. Each would be escorted to me and introduced. I would say a very slow hello, take my hand out of the pocket, where I had been holding onto a plastic bag filled with dry ice, and offer my hand to shake. When the girl grasped my ice-cold hand in the warm living room, the reaction was always the same. She would scream her head off and run away. I would then put my hand back in my pocket, hold onto the bag of dry ice, and wait for my next victim.

You would never think that being dead at such a young age could be so much fun, would you?

BUGGED IN BED

Whenever we would go out of town, my friends and I would rent only one hotel room regardless of how many of us there were, because we had very little money.

The most innocent-looking guy would rent the room. One by one, spreading the movement over a period of time, we'd all enter the room. We would then flip coins to see who would sleep where, starting with the beds, of course, and working down through armchairs, floor, bathtub, to the bathroom floor.

One weekend night three carloads of us, about eighteen guys, packed into the one room in the Times Square Hotel in Manhattan. Big Micky and I won the flip for the only bed. My sleeping partner was six five and weighed about 250 pounds. After a wild night of fun in Coney Island, we returned to our hotel room. The minute Big Micky's body hit the sheets, I was crammed into a space about four inches wide. Now I was always thin, but not that thin. I knew I had to get Micky out of the bed or I wouldn't get a moment's sleep, not only because of my limited share of bed space but also because of my fear of Big

47

Micky rolling on top of me and flattening me out like a cartoon character who just got run over by a steamroller.

I slapped my leg real loud, cursing under my breath. A couple of minutes later, I slapped my arm and cursed a little louder. Micky stirred. A couple of minutes later, I slapped my neck, chest, arm, leg, and forehead, cursing very loudly this time.

Micky sat up. "What the hell you doing, David?"

"What do you mean, Micky? Doing what?" I slapped my leg and cursed.

"That."

"What?" I slapped my leg and cursed again.

"That."

"This?" I asked, slapping my rib cage.

"Yes, that."

"Oh, don't let them bother you. I had them all the time when I lived in South Philly. You get used to them. Good night."

I turned over on one side, slapping my rear end and cursing as I did it.

Micky spun me over on my back. "Who are 'them'?"

"Bedbugs, but they . . ."

Before I could finish my sentence, Big Micky was out of the bed. No one else accepted my invitation to join me in the bed. Not only did Big Micky sleep on the floor, he slept in his suit, tie, and shoes.

What was amazing to me was how the moment Big Micky got out of the bed, so did the bedbugs. Absolutely amazing. Well, good night. Zzzzzzzzzzzzzzzzzzzzzzzzzzz.

THERE THEY ARE, MOM!

This is one of my mother's favorite stories. If you ignore the violence and concentrate on the irony, it may become one of yours.

I was standing in my bare feet in my living room on Sansom Street, looking out the front screen door, as I waited for my mom to call me in for dinner. I was thirteen years old.

At first I thought the four boys were having a footrace up the street and that the smallest and youngest one was winning by a few yards.

"We'll get you, Jew boy!"

It was no race. It was more of the ugly anti-Semitism I had been seeing and hearing since I remember seeing and hearing.

I was barefoot and my sneakers were upstairs, so I couldn't go after them. I did the only thing I could think of doing—I ran out onto my porch and yelled for them to leave the kid alone. I doubt they even heard me. I watched as the Jewish kid cut around the corner with the three older boys only a few feet behind him. Frustrated, I told my mother what happened. We both hoped the kid got away.

A couple of months later I was sitting by the living-room window reading the newspaper. I glanced outside and saw those three boys ambling down the block. I threw my newspaper on the floor and leaped to my feet. This time I was wearing my canvas high-top sneakers. This time they would pay for their stupid hatred.

I yelled to my mother, who was in the kitchen, "There they are, Mom!" I charged out onto the porch and screamed at the three boys. "You, pricks. Here's a Jew boy your own size."

They just stared at me. I jumped down all the front steps and started running toward them. As I got closer, they turned and bolted down the street. Near the corner, they turned into the alley. I was gaining on them. As I ran into the alley, I saw the last of them duck under a large bush that grew out of a back-yard and covered the alley. I knew this alley. This was my block. I knew every inch of it. The alley they cut down was a dead end. Behind the bush was the brick wall of the garage on Chestnut Street. I walked slowly up to the bush.

"You guys might as well come out. I know there's no way out of there."

After a couple of minutes, the first one stuck his head out of the bush. I grabbed him by the hair and pulled him the rest of the way out. It took only a few punches and kicks to lay him out. The second and third ones came out one after another. My fury gave me the strength to knock out the first one to appear with only a couple of punches. As I was beating my fist into the last of them, holding him by the collar with my left hand, as he was slumped on his knees at my feet, I looked into his bloodied face. He was not one of the three guys I had seen chasing the Jewish boy. I let go of his shirt. He fell to the ground. I turned over the two others. I had beaten up the wrong guys.

When I told my mother what I had done, she couldn't stop laughing. Even to this day, she sees the humor in it and laughs as heartily as she did the first time. I guess that in some strange way it was funny—except to those three fellas I left lying in that alley. Let's hope they read this now and find the humor in it. I hope so for many reasons, including not wanting to be walking down some street someday and see three men running toward me with their clenched fists waving in the air and simultaneously screaming out the word *revenge*. After all, I sure would hate to beat them up again.

FLASH FIGHT

Dusk. A hot summer night. A group of about six sixteen-year-olds hanging around the corner of Don's Hoagie Shop at 60th and Pine streets in West Philly. I was watching some of my friends pitching quarters against the wall of the shop. I glanced up to see two guys walking toward us. One was broad-shouldered and had the bopping gait of a street tough. The other was small and wiry and was drinking beer from a bottle. I didn't recognize them. I went back to watching the quarters spin through the air, landing to the whoops or curses of the tosser.

The little one with the beer bottle bumped right into me, knocking me off balance. Then he had the nerve to blame me. "Watch where you're goin'."

I could smell whiskey on his breath, as well as beer.

"I should watch where I'm going? In case you didn't notice, you were the one moving and I was the one standing still. So, it's me who's telling you, peabrain, to watch where the fuck you're going."

Everyone had stopped pitching coins and watched. The little guy drew closer to me. I clenched my fist, ready, at his slightest move, to bring it down on the bridge of his nose and flatten his face like an Eskimo.

"Do you know who I am?" he asked through sour breath.

"No. Who are you?"

"I'm Flash."

"Oh, yeah? Then why don't you flash up my ass and tell me when the next load of shit is coming?"

My friends burst out laughing. The little guy made no move. I wanted him to. Suddenly he was pushed out of the way and I was facing the broad-shouldered one. I recognized him. His name was Pepe and he had been sent to jail for manslaughter, having beaten someone to death with his fists.

"I'll take his place," Pepe hissed at me. He began to remove the leather gloves from the epaulets of his black leather jacket, a uniform he refused to discard even in the summer heat. He started slipping them over his square hands slowly, sneering at me. I felt two hands grab my arms from behind and I was soon flying through the air. It was my friend Paul, the strongest and also one of the gentlest fellas in our crowd. He was the only guy in the neighborhood who could straight arm lift two phone books on the straw end of a broom from the pavement to his eye level. He got that strong carrying cow carcasses in a meat-packing plant all his childhood. I watched as he took his shoes off quickly and tossed them into the street.

"And I'll take Brenner's place. Let's go."

The next few moments were a stare-down contest between the gloved Pepe and the shoeless Paul. Finally, Pepe broke the silence. "I'm gonna go get the Greeks."

"Get the whole fuckin' United Nations," I called out.

All of us laughed as the temporarily defeated Pepe and his sidekick took off down 60th Street. We knew he was heading for my end of the neighborhood, from Sansom Street to Market, where there was a large pocket of Greeks. We divided up, running through our turf, spreading the word about what had happened and gathering the guys in our gang for a rumble. Within a half hour there were about forty of us standing on Don's corner ready for the big street fight.

As we were waiting for the Greeks, I had to satisfy my curiosity. "Paul, how come you threw your shoes into the street?"

"Dave, I've never seen you scared, but you were this time. I could tell. Why were you?"

"I don't know. Maybe his rep."

"No, that wasn't it. You stood up to Pepe fine until he did something. Until he started putting on his tight leather gloves. Think about it. Right, aren't I?"

"You're right, Paul. Until he did that, I was ready to go at it with him. Even planning how to knee him in the balls."

"Yeah, but the reason the gloves shook you up was because it was as if he did this all the time, a pro, getting into uniform for another fight. I figured I'd have to do the same thing to him, but I didn't know what. Then the idea of the shoes came to me. Did you see his face when I threw them on the trolley tracks? He kind of shit. He didn't know what the hell I was going to do with my feet, karate or what. I didn't know what the hell I was going to do with them either, but it worked. I'll keep them on for the Greeks, though."

We laughed and waited, smoking, pacing, cursing real loud, talking about how we were going to kick Greek ass, building our confidence. Then we saw them. A few blocks up 60th. Like a small herd of cattle, about thirty-five heads.

As they drew closer, I recognized a few of them as neighbors of mine, kids I had grown up with, but, when it comes to a street fight, your only neighbors and friends are the guys fighting on your side—everyone else is the enemy.

When they stood directly in front of us, I was the first to speak. "Yo, Sonny, what are you going to do? I beat your ass once already this year and I'm going to do it again tonight. You belong to me."

"No, I belong to you, punk," called out Pepe.

"I want him," chimed in Flash from inside the crowd.

"He's mine," growled one of the biggest guys I had ever seen. He wasn't Greek—he was Greece. His massive body made his extra large T-shirt skin tight. Two Christmas hams hung out from the sleeves. Only the tattoos and hands at their ends were indications that they were arms.

Everyone wanted me. It was going to be one hell of a night for me. Nothing better than to be the most popular target in a street fight. I had been there a few times, because it was my wisecracks that got us into trouble many times, but it was also my gift of gab and sense of humor that prevented a lot of battles as well.

It was that time: the final moments before fists would fly through the air. I could feel my muscles tighten. I was planning how to duck away from the ape and get past Pepe to Sonny or Flash. Suddenly a baby-blue Lincoln Continental convertible came screeching to a stop at the curb. It belonged to one of the three older brothers of one of the guys in our gang. The whole family was tough. He flew out of the driver's seat, the hate exploding from the gangster-looking face.

The other front door opened slowly and just as slowly out stepped this very good-looking Irish guy, handsome enough to have been a leading man in Hollywood, and a friend of the older brother. He reached back into the car and took his three-year-old son out of the arms of his wife and held him above him, looking into the little boy's face. "Now, I want you to watch your Daddy kick ass."

As he was returning his son into the arms of the mother, my friend's brother opened the trunk of his car, reached inside, pulled out a World War II forty-five automatic, cocked it to put a round in the barrel, and slipped it into his belt. He joined the front line, shoulder to shoulder with his kid brother.

The Irishman slowly walked in front of all of us. He stood between the two warring armies and directly in front of the T-shirted ape who had challenged me. He looked into the enemy faces slowly. Then he spoke very softly. "Who is the toughest Greek?"

"I am," declared the ape. It figured.

I don't think anyone saw the punch. It was lightning fast. All we saw was the ape collapsing to the ground unconscious. Irish looked into the faces again and again spoke very softly. "Who is the second toughest Greek?"

No one answered. Even Pepe took a step back into the crowd, hoping he wasn't to be the next victim of this deadly street fighter.

The silence was split wide open by the screech of the police sirens. Red cars were coming down all four streets of the intersection, lights flashing. Either a neighbor had called the police or a worried mother of one of the boys. It didn't matter who called. We were in trouble.

There was a standard plan for such an emergency. Don, who had been a former member of the toughest street gang in the history of Philadelphia, the Green Street Counts, had prewrapped hoagie sandwiches ready. Whenever any of us was in trouble with the cops, we would run into Don's and he would whip one of the sandwiches onto the counter and back up the alibi that the kid was having lunch whenever whatever happened. It was a great back-up system, but it wasn't set up for eighty guys. Neither was the small luncheonette.

The overspill unable to make it down an alley or over the porches or behind bushes or around the police cars was rounded up by the police and put into paddy wagons.

A group of cops pressed into the already overcrowded hoagie shop. The sergeant was in front. What he saw was astounding. Greeks and Jews gnawing away at hoagies, arms around each other, best of friends. Of course, we all claimed to be having dinner, knowing nothing about any rumble. Don was our witness.

I looked out of the front window at the police rounding up kids for the wagons. In the thick of it all, I spotted my friend Beb. He was standing in the middle of the street, looking intensely for a trolley car. When it came, he got on like nothing was happening around him, as though the streets were empty. I laughed because of his cool play, but more so because I knew Beb didn't have carfare. He never had any money. I knew what he was doing—what we all did when we were broke and had to get somewhere. Beb was fumbling through his pockets, searching for the change he knew he had, unless it dropped out of his pocket or was stolen, searching and searching until the trolley came to a stop a few blocks from his house, and then he would allow himself to be thrown off.

The police left Don's. We cheered. Usually we gave Don back the hoagies so he could rewrap them and sell them, but this time, I guess because we were all so relieved not to have been arrested, and more so because each of us secretly didn't want to fight in the first place, we ate all the hoagies, and truly did become friends that night.

The ones who were arrested were detained at the police station until their parents were notified, then they were released. The usual. As far as the rest of us, there was never again any incident among the Greeks, Jews, Irish, Italians, Portuguese, Albanians, or anyone else who was involved in the night of the Flash Fight. There were a lot of other fights, though. There always will be, as long as there are hot summer nights in a slum.

WHAT A URINAL

It was my first day as a messenger for the rotogravure section of the *Philadelphia Inquirer*'s Sunday newspaper. By midmorning I had to go to the bathroom. Going through large double doors, I entered a very big room lined with wall lockers. In the center of the room was a large urinal. It looked like a round horse trough. In the middle was a thick pipe with small holes around its top.

I was in the middle of urinating when the doors swung open and about twenty pressmen, covered with blotches of ink, noisily entered. They stopped talking as soon as they saw me. I thought it was because I was the new kid. I smiled and continued my business. They slowly moved around to their lockers. Some of them sat on the benches and stared at me.

When I finished, I pressed my foot down on the rubber ring I had seen at the base of the urinal. As I suspected, water came shooting out of the holes at the top of the pipe where . . . Wait a minute, what the hell were those glass soap dispensers doing on a urinal? The answer was all too embarrassingly obvious. I had just peed in the workers' wash sink.

It was too late to apologize, and not being able to think of an intelligent explanation, I simply continued as though I had done nothing wrong. I turned the soap dispenser over my hands, keeping my feet pressed on the ring, and washed my hands. I took a paper towel on my way out. No one said anything. As I got to the door, I spun around and faced all the workers who were still staring silently at me. "You guys are lucky I didn't have to take a shit."

I walked out. As I headed down the hall back to my office, I could hear the continuous roar of laughter. From that day on, I was the hit of the pressmen. I made a lot of good friends from that one mistake.

A GOOD SON

We were a group of teenagers sitting around the kitchen table of my friend's apartment playing nickle-dime poker and having some laughs. I left the game to go down the hall to the bathroom. As I passed my friend's parents' bedroom, I heard them call out from inside the darkened room. "Donny, come kiss me and your daddy good night."

I didn't feel like explaining that I wasn't Donny, then returning to the kitchen and getting him, then going back to the bathroom, etc., so I walked into the bedroom, leaned down, and kissed each of them on the cheek. As I was leaving, the mother called out to me, fondly, "You're a very good son."

As I headed for the bathroom, I thought, Yes, I am.

III

A POOR BOY'S DREAMS

SAND CASTLES

I spent a lot of my childhood in pre-casino Atlantic City, New Jersey. It was a splendiferous place for children. What better fun is there than racing a big ocean wave to the shore or diving under it or riding it in like a submarine torpedo, or sitting on top of a friend's shoulders and having a horse fight, or teasing girls by pinching their legs in the water and telling them that it was crabs, or making believe you and your friends are marines storming a foreign beachhead, or finding rare seashells that could be worth thousands of dollars, or studying how seagulls fish for their dinners, or how sand crabs burrow into the sand never to return, or shooting a skimmer stone across the water for a five- or six-skimmer record, or staying in the ocean until your lips turn blue and your fingers are as wrinkled as a one-hundred-year-old's, or eating an ice-cold popsicle, or diving below the water and hooking up with a friend who can also keep his eyes open underwater, or sitting on your big brother's shoulders as he wades out to the deep part, or swimming out to a sandbar and standing only ankle-deep way out there, or tossing horseshoes and quoits, watching lifeguards practice rowing to an imaginary drowning victim, watching a sailboat glide along the sunlit water, peering into the distance at a tanker passing by on the way to some exciting foreign country, standing near the water's edge and watching your feet become buried in the wet sand with the incoming tide, burying a friend from toe to neck in the soft sand, floating on top of the peacefully calm ocean, creating faces of people and animals in the billowing overhead clouds, straining to see beyond the far-off horizon, where one knows there are beaches in far-off lands upon which there stand other children enjoying the wonderment of nature and the world around us, for it might just be that oceans and beaches were created especially for children, and, it is for certain that I, as a child, was created for the beach and ocean.

One of my favorite beach and ocean pastimes was to sit at the water's edge and create a sand castle by letting the wet sand drip out slowly from between my fingers, making spiraled towers for invisible knights in armor to climb as they look for invading armies, and fashioning windows, doors, moats, and wall-top walkways, building a stately and majestic monument to a long-gone era.

I remember the first sand castle I ever built by myself. I was seven years old. It was not as well designed or well built as my future structures were to be, but it was my first and I did it all by myself. It was the last day we were at the shore.

The following May, my father suggested that we take a ride to Atlantic City for the day. As soon as he parked I leaped out and ran full speed toward the boardwalk. I ran up on the boards, across them, down the wooden steps, and across the deep sand to the water's edge where I had built my first sand castle the previous September. It wasn't there. Not one trace of it. It had been so beautiful. I had spent so much time creating it. It had meant so much to me. I couldn't understand why it wasn't there. I still don't.

THE IOU

I had just finished playing a rough nine innings of hardball in Cobbs Creek Park and was leisurely making my way along the fifteen hot July city blocks away from my house. I was ten years old. I decided to cool off with a soda from the drugstore fountain in the Walnut Park Plaza Hotel, 63rd and Walnut streets.

"Help ya, kid?"

"Yeah, doc, I'd like a vanilla soda with lots of ice."

He put the soda in front of me and I slid my nickle across the counter toward him.

"It's six cents, kid."

"It's always been a nickle. I've had it here—"

"Went up last week. Let's have a penny. I've got work to do."

"I don't have a penny. I didn't know that—"

"Forget it."

"I won't forget it. As soon as I get an extra penny, I'll pay you back."

"Yeah, right. Good one, kid. Just finish and get out of here."

"I ain't conning you. Look, shake on it."

"Just shake your butt out of here."

He walked away from me. I gulped down the soda, filled my mouth with half the ice and put the other half in my pocket, and left the store.

I had an afterschool job for about a year, but, except for some necessary school money, I gave everything into the house. It was no big deal. Every poor kid did it. However, after a few weeks, I had an extra penny and walked up to the hotel and into the drugstore. The same pharmacist was on duty.

"Here's your penny."

"What penny?"

"The one I owe you for the vanilla soda. I told you I'd pay you back."

"I don't know what you're talking about, kid. Just take your penny and forget it."

He started to walk away but I yelled after him, loud enough for the customers to hear. "Look, mister, this is the second time you walked away from me and told me to 'forget it.' I told you

61

the last time, I wasn't going to forget it and I haven't. My word is gold. It's the way I was raised. Now, take your damn penny."

I left it on the counter, spun around, and left the store.

It's real tough to understand adults when you're a kid. Matter of fact, it's tough to understand most of them even after you've grown up.

THE NIGHT RUNNER

I hated being poor, especially not understanding why we were. Poverty is a life of "not." You're not able to do this or that or say this or that or go here or there or buy this or that or see this or that and a million other nots—not, not, not, not, not.

Poverty frustrated me and made me very angry. Oftentimes I'd vent this anger on the face of some innocent kid. Sometimes I'd express it through alcohol or drugs. Sometimes there were positive outlets, such as sports or dancing. But fights, drinks, drugs, sports, and dances come to an end. Poverty doesn't. It's with you when you go to bed and there to greet you when you wake up. It is a twenty-four-hour-a-day horror.

I tried to get out of it by doing that much spoken-about, poor person's pride—an honest day's work. But all I ever had was a bunch of shit jobs that paid shit wages, which didn't help get you out of your shit life. In spite of this, I never missed a day of work, never showed up late, and always worked as hard as I could. My friends used to think I was crazy, but I tried to explain to them that I was in training; that is, if I were able to do this with a job I hated, imagine what I'd be able to do when I finally got into something I loved. I was right in the long run. In the short run, it meant nothing.

When you are stuck in a poor neighborhood, it is not possible to forget how poor you are and what it's doing to you and the people you love; it is not possible to stop thinking about it, to stop feeling it. Poverty is omnipresent and, all too often, it is omnipotent.

Sometimes when I would go to bed in my unheated room at the back of our house, with the cracked ceiling, the windows whose stuffed rags didn't prevent the cold night air from whistling in, with the annoying dripping sound of the broken toilet in the bathroom right next door, sometimes when I was in this bed in this room, no longer hanging out on the street corner laughing with my friends, not at a neighborhood party dancing the night away, not making passionate love in the back of a car, not blocking and delivering punches in a street fight, not drinking cheap scotch illegally in a local bar, not hiding in an alley tooting some coke, I would lie there, hands behind my head, staring at the cracks in the ceiling, not able to fight off the thoughts of poverty, not able to stop my stomach muscles from tightening, not able to open my fisted hands, not able to figure out a way to get myself and my family out of it, and anger would well up inside of me. My leg and arm muscles would tighten, my head would throb, my stomach would stiffen like a snare drum, my breath would shorten.

When this would happen, and it happened way too often, I would slip silently out of bed, pull on my jeans and tank-top underwear shirt, step into my canvas high-top sneakers, and I would quietly move down the stairs to the first floor and out the front door, across the porch, down the front steps, and then I'd fly into space, running as quickly as my long legs could take me, across 58th Street, straight down Sansom Street to 52nd Street, full speed, seeing only the blur of row houses and parked old cars, the blur of poverty's evidence. At 52nd Street, I would stop, place my hands on my knees, take a few real deep breaths, and take off again at full speed for home.

When I reached my house, I would charge up the front steps, but stop to walk quietly across the wooden porch. I'd quietly open the front door, usually gasping silently for breath, and ever so quietly make my way up the stairs to the second floor, walking on the far sides of the steps so they wouldn't creak as they did in their weakened middles.

Every so often, my mother would be waiting for me at the top of the stairs, in her faded bathrobe. I guess she heard me leaving the house, or maybe it was just a mother's instinct to know when a child is leaving, when a child is tormented. She always spoke the same words to me, quietly and gently: "Were you running, again, David?"

"Yes, Mom. Everything is okay now. Go back to sleep."

That's all we ever said to each other. That's all we ever had to say. She knew I was hurting and why, and I knew she cared. What else was there to know? What else was there to say?

Then I would get undressed and flop back into my bed, dripping sweat, but I'd fall into a sound, peaceful sleep, until the next time the poverty monster would enter my room and sit on the end of my bed, glaring and laughing at me, pointing its finger at me, as though to inform me that he and I would be together all the days and nights of my life. Then I'd run again in the middle of the night.

Today I am not poor. I live in a magnificent town house in the heart of Manhattan, and on the shelf in my den are my original pair of canvas high-top sneakers. I hope I never have to put them on again. I hope my night runs are over forever.

CLENCHED FISTS

One of my favorite pleasures as a little boy and a teenager was taking a walk through the neighborhood with my mother. We were always such very good friends. I always loved her to my full capacity. For several reasons, some of which I detailed in my first book, *Soft Pretzels with Mustard,* including an insane grandmother, who had evicted us from her house when we had no money, forcing us to live without furniture for a year amid rank and tormenting poverty, at a time when a child's life should be filled with fun and security, mine was not. Oh, I had lots of fun, mostly made up by myself, but inside I was often tormented by the frustrations of where and how we lived, the constant battles between paying the bills and my father's meager income. I started working when I was nine years old to help out. My sister did the same. Life was a constant struggle.

I guess poverty doesn't bother some kids. I had friends who never minded it. Maybe they just accepted it as a way of life, as their lot. I didn't. Unlike those whom, you must understand and believe, I considered lucky to not feel the pain of poverty, I was aware of it, too aware. Being poor hurt me terribly.

One magnificent spring day, Mom and I were taking one of our walks together in Cobbs Creek, a park that acted as the county line between West Philly and Upper Darby, Pennsylvania. My mother loves nature. She absolutely adored caressing a leaf and telling me all about it. Before her eyes failed her, she used to paint the scenes of nature she so loved.

I wasn't as much into nature as my mother. I was a real city kid. I loved pavements, alleys, tar streets, empty lots, buildings, gutters, sewers. But I would always listen to Mom and act interested. As we walked through the trees on this particular afternoon, my mother asked me a question: "David, do you think you will ever walk with your fists not clenched tightly?"

"What do you mean, Mom?"

"Look at your hands, darling. Your fists are always clenched so tightly your knuckles are white."

She was right. I had never noticed. I guess that I was so angry, so frustrated, so uptight, so unable to relax, that I was constantly ready to spring into action, to fight an unbeatable enemy—poverty.

I looked at my mom, and without opening my hands, I answered, "Maybe someday, Mom. I hope so."

"I do, too, David."

I walk with my fists unclenched, today. My mom has never said anything about it, but I know that she has noticed.

THE FAMILY CAR

Like most young teenagers of my generation, I was car crazy. I could tell you the make of a car and its year from a distance or by just listening to its motor as it passed me on the street.

I worked very hard, saving whatever I could, so that when I turned sixteen and got my driver's license, I was able to buy my very own car—a classic 1941 Buick Roadster convertible, dual carbs, dual exhaust, black, with a silver swan hood ornament and thick black leather seats. The girls loved it.

Thanks to my black beauty, I was able to do what very few boys from my neighborhood had ever done—date a girl from the Main Line, the posh, stuck-up immediate suburb of Philadelphia. Blue-blood territory. Her name was Merle. She was pretty good-looking and we were hitting it off pretty good.

One day my beauty broke down. The car, not the girl. I borrowed my father's old, beat-up Chevy for my date with Merle. I picked up my friend Beb and his girlfriend, Lenore, and we drove to Merle's Main Line mansion. I parked behind the very tall bushes bordering the spacious lawn, which was still covered with white snow, unlike in the city, where the snow turned gray and black within hours of its fall. We walked up the winding path to the ten-bedroom estate. I felt like I was walking on the face of a Christmas card. One of the maids let us in. We sat in the living room, which was bigger than the houses in which each of us lived, and waited for Merle, uncomfortably. In a few minutes she came down the winding staircase, kissed me warmly. I introduced her to my friends. She handed me her coat. It was fur, real fur. Beb secretly gave me the sign you would give a pal who just hit the mother lode.

We left the house and started down the path to the pavement.

"Merle, my car broke down."

"I hope it's nothing serious."

"No, just some car trouble. Anyway, I borrowed my dad's car."

"That's fine, David."

As we neared the end of the path, she saw my dad's car parked at the curb. She stopped dead in her tracks. "You must be kidding. *That* is a family car?"

Her words hurt. They brought to the surface all the resentment I had always had for the rich and their spoiled offspring. As I always did—and still do—when livid and about to explode, I spoke very softly. "You're pretty, Merle. You're also intelligent. You got a lot going for you, but you have one major problem—you've got a dirty mouth that should be washed out."

I swooped up a handful of snow and deposited it in Merle's face. Beb, Lenore, and I got into my dad's car and drove back to where the streets were dirty but the minds were clean.

Years later, when I was attending Temple University, I saw Merle walking toward me. I hadn't seen her since that fateful night five years before. I smiled and called out to her, "Merle, how ya doing?"

She smiled a polite, automatic smile until she recognized me.

Then she hurried across the street. There wasn't even any snow on the ground. I got in "the family subway" and went home—to my same old neighborhood, for the time being.

NOBODY EVER SEES YOU EAT TUNA FISH

During my teens, whenever I would be in an expensive restaurant or nightclub in Philly or New Jersey with a date, eating steak dinners, drinking fine champagne, treating everyone I knew and liked to dinner or drinks, letting the good times roll and the money fly, someone would ask me what they so often would ask me: "Dave, I don't get it. This is about the tenth time I've seen you pouring out the big bucks in a place like this and we both have the same kind of shit jobs making the same kind of shit money. So, how come you can do it and I can't? What are you —running numbers or selling dope or something?"

I would always answer the same. "Nobody ever sees you eat tuna fish."

"What the hell you talking about?"

"Look. When's the last time you saw me on a big spree? A month and a half, two months ago, right? Okay. So, from the last time you saw me until tonight, I've been going out on real, real cheap dates, like a movie or a walk and eating a tuna fish sandwich at home, saving my money for another big splurge. Now, everyone sees you living it up real big but nobody ever sees you eat tuna fish."

P.S. I loved tuna fish. I still do. Only now I sometimes order it in very expensive restaurants.

I'LL BE BACK

Being denied is part of being poor. It is a painful form of rejection. Wrong-side-of-the-track boys can't date certain girls, are not served in certain restaurants, are not allowed to shop in certain stores, and so on. Whenever it happened to me, I'd always look the person who had rejected me right in the eye and say the same line: "My name is David Brenner and I'll be back!"

I had every intention when I was living on the wrong side of the tracks of "becoming somebody" and then returning to show them, to throw it in their faces. Well, I've made a good life for myself, achieved my goal. I guess you can say I "made it." It is time to go back. Well, although I can distinctly remember every person, every place, every time I was hurt back there in the neighborhood, I realized that what is more important than going back is living where I am and thinking of where I want to go. I really don't need to prove anything to those persons and places in my past, because attaining something in your life for yourself, your own form of success, is the purest way of getting back.

However, there is this one girl's parents . . .

PLAYING THE DRUMS

When I was ten years old, I had this tremendous urge to play the drums. One day it was announced in assembly (isn't that a wonderfully nostalgic word out of the past—"assembly"?) that students could sign up for drum lessons. I was the first one out the swinging doors and in front of the sign-up desk. The fee was ten dollars. That was a lot of money in those days, but I had a job in a grocery store, and by putting in overtime, I could probably raise it. I busted my ass running errands, working overtime, pitching pennies, doing anything to get the money, and I did it with enough left over for a hoagie.

The first day of the drum lessons I was so excited I couldn't concentrate on anything any teacher said. Not that I found it easy to do that even on normal days. I had this picture of myself in my head of me sitting behind this set of transparent silver-trimmed drums. I'd be wearing a black silk tuxedo, a black bow tie that I would eventually pull off and throw into the audience as I unbuttoned the front of my shirt to the screams of all the girls. I'm perspiring as I beat those drums, my long wet hair matted to my head, all the young girls pressed up against the front of the bandstand, cheering me on.

The lessons were held during recess in a basement room. I charged into the room. There were school desks, the same as in any other classroom. I sat at one in the front. Usually I tried to sit as far back as possible so the teacher wouldn't call on me.

On each desk top was a pad. The instructor came in and handed each of us a set of drumsticks. As soon as I put my hand around them, I felt my heart skip a beat. He then stood in front of the twenty-five of us who had signed up for lessons and began to beat his set of drumsticks on the same kind of pad we had on our desk, saying the same words over and over.

"Mama . . . dada . . . mama . . . dada . . . mama . . . dada. Now you try it. Left hand twice for 'mama' and the right hand twice for 'dada.' Hold the sticks like this. Let me see. Good. Now everyone—mama . . . dada . . . mama . . . dada . . ."

Everyone was hitting the pad on their desk except me. Finally I called out, "Yo, may I ask a question?"

The instructor and all the students stopped drumming.

"Of course. What's your name?"

"Brenner. David Brenner, and this is my question. When do we get the drums?"

"We won't be getting drums, David. This school cannot afford them."

"You mean to tell me that I just paid ten bucks that I had to bust my ass to make to sit in this basement room and play mama, dada on a desk? Well I didn't sign up to learn how to play a desk. I want to learn to play the drums, real drums."

"I'm sorry, David. I can teach you the basics and then someday, maybe when—"

"I've already learned that 'somedays' don't come. Give me back my ten-spot."

Do you know which of the students who took those desk-top drum lessons in my elementary school grew up to play real drums in a real band? No one.

I never pursued my early interest in the drums. Actually, I moved up in the musical world. I went on to not being able to afford to learn how to play the piano. However, I sort of got a chance to make up for it, sort of. . . .

My thirteen-year-old nephew, my brother's son, Eric, was sitting between my brother and me in the front seat of my brother's station wagon. They were driving me to the airport after my few-days visit with them in Madison, Wisconsin. Eric kept glancing fleetingly at the large cartons in the back of the wagon.

"What are you looking at, Eric?"

"Nothing, Uncle David. Just those boxes."

"What do you think is in them?"

"I don't know."

"Don't tell me the Brenners finally have a dumb member in the family. What is the picture on each of the boxes?"

"A drum."

"Very good. Now let's try some deductive reasoning. What would that indicate is in each of the boxes?"

"Drums, I guess."

"Brilliant. Moby, you can tell now that he is your son. Do you know why there is a complete set of the finest drums in the world sitting in the back of your father's station wagon?"

He shook his head.

"Because your father told me you want to learn how to play the drums. They're yours. Beat them in the best of health."

Eric didn't say one word all the way to the airport or, as my brother told me later on the phone, all the way home. He just stared out the window. He was in shock. When he and my brother were taking them out of the boxes and setting them up in the basement, Eric was excited.

Sure, he learned to play them. Very well, too. Even had his own group in high school. At least one Brenner got past mama, dada.

IV

THE BRENNERS

CHICKEN SOUP

I'll tell you how poor people make chicken soup. Well, at least, I'll tell you how my mother did it. She would toss some peas and cut-up slices of carrots, onion, and celery into a big pot of boiling water, and then she would think about a chicken. If company was coming over, she'd think about two chickens.

MOM'S EYES

When my mother's sight failed, the only one who knew about it was my father. In order not to upset us, my mother memorized every square inch of her apartment in Atlantic City, so that when we came down to see her she could maneuver around everything and we would know nothing of her problem. One day over the telephone, after keeping it secret for nearly eight years, my father confessed to me what had been happening and that the situation was getting worse. I sent my mother to the best eye specialist in Wills Eye Hospital in Philadelphia. Her diagnosis was a degenerative disease of the retinas, for which there is no known cure. My mother's sight continued to fail until she became legally blind. I had learned about Dr. William Feinbloom, who had developed a series of lenses that when attached to eyeglasses enabled some people with limited sight to see better. As a result of a series of tests, it was decided that my mother was one of the fortunate ones who could have her sight improved by the lenses. She had her eyeglasses fitted for reading as well as for distance. When she first put them on, my father telephoned me. He is usually an unemotional, stoic man, but this time he was all choked up.

"I wish you could have seen it, Kingy. Your mother read from a book."

I could tell he was crying now.

"We took a walk. She could see people crossing the street a block away and told me to look at a pretty red flowerpot on the second-story windowsill of a house across the street. I wish you could have been there, Kingy. You've done it. It's the greatest thing you have ever done for us."

My mother told me the humorous side of it. When she had her lenses fitted, she looked at my father, smiled, and said, "Oh, my God, Lou. You've gotten so wrinkled."

There is no guarantee that everyone can be helped, but if you know someone who has an eye problem, there is a chance that what has helped my mother can help. Contact the William Feinbloom Vision Rehabilitation Center at the Eye Institute of the Philadelphia Center of Optometry at 1-800-433-EYES.

VAS TUSTA DORTIN?

When my father was eight years old, in 1904, he sang in the synagogue choir where his father was the rabbi. One day he slipped away to satisfy a strong physiological need. The only bathroom was in the dark cellar, a single toilet behind a wooden door. My father had made the semi-darkened journey hundreds of times, so he knew every inch of the way by heart.

He threw open the wooden door of the pitch-dark stall and let the stream fly. From inside he heard, *"Vas tusta dortin?"* Translated from Yiddish, this means, "What are you doing?"

These words were followed by a giant of a man dressed in an ominous black frock coat and a soaking wet beard. He came charging out of the stall. My father spun around and began running through the underground passage, spraying the walls as he ran. The mad giant was closing in fast, hot on his heels, screaming Yiddish curses. My father luckily made it outside and home, didn't stop until he was safely hidden in his own home, probably being the youngest flasher in Philadelphia.

When I was a child, this was one of my favorite family stories. I made my father tell it to me hundreds of times. I still request it.

FALSE ALARM

As a little boy, whenever I would go into the bathroom in our house only to discover that nothing happened, that I really didn't have to go, my father would refer to it as a false alarm. One day in school a fire-department official spoke in our school assembly and informed us that a false alarm was punishable by a fine of $1,000 and up to two years in prison. From that day on, whenever I went into a bathroom, I got results. I guess you could say that what that official said to us that day scared the shit out of me.

PASS 'EM, LOU

My father has had a love affair with automobiles all his life. It began in 1904, when he was eight years old. Just recently, when he had a bit of a physical scare, which, thank God, turned out to be nothing serious, he told me that if he couldn't get in his car and drive, then life was all over. Or, as he so graphically put it, "It's time to take the gas pipe, Kingy."

Although he loved cars, he could never afford a good one, from the time he lost his money in the Great Depression, seeing a tristate vending-machine business stop dead in its tracks when no one had any spare money.

As a kid, I witnessed the worst cars no money could buy. We had an array of clunkers with problems and idiosyncracies that ran the gamut from fenders that flew off if you took a corner too quickly, springs that sprang out of the seats unannounced and painfully, steering wheels that came off suddenly in one hand, brake pedals that disintegrated under your foot, horns that played their own tunes whether or not you touched them or were even in the car, to headlights that blinked on and off when the mood struck them. You name an automotive problem and we had it. We had cars that had they been buildings they would've been condemned and razed. If you had a face that looked like our cars, you wouldn't go outside.

Besides the physical handicaps of the cars, we were also the unproud owners of the slowest vehicles on wheels. Kids on tricycles used to whip by us. With all the windows open, the gas pedal pressed to the floor, we never felt a breeze inside the car. You could have a cop walk up to you and hand you a ticket for a moving violation while you were still moving. In the Brenner family there were three absolutes you could count on—paying taxes, dying, and never getting a speeding ticket.

One of the great family thrills was sitting in the family car with my father at the wheel, either going to or coming from a day at the beach in Atlantic City, and as we approached another car on the highway, my father would jam the accelerator to the floor and all of us would scream, "Pass 'em, Lou! Pass 'em!" If we by some miracle even neared the car in front of us, we would go wild, applauding and slapping my father on the back. Once in a great while, we would pass a car. Usually they were either pulling off with a blowout or parking, but we counted them.

A few years ago, I was lucky enough in my career to be able to surprise my father with a brand-new car. Now, whenever he feels like it, he can whip by any car.

"Pass 'em, Lou! Pass 'em!"

ONE MILE

Another lifelong automotive dream of my father's was someday to watch the mileage counter on the speedometer of his car turn over to read "00001."

When I bought my father the brand-new car, it was a complete surprise for my parents. They thought they were going to have their old car inspected. I was hiding inside the showroom when they drove up. The salesman was showing my parents their car on the lot without their realizing that it was theirs. I then walked outside.

"So, get inside and start it up."

"Kingy, what are you doing here?"

"Taking pictures of you getting a new car."

"What the hell you talking about?"

"It's yours. I bought it for you."

My father signed the title and drove off, honking the horn. I got into my rented car and headed back to New York.

As I entered my apartment, the phone was ringing. It was my father.

"What's up, Lou? Something wrong with the new car?"

"Kingy, I got something to tell you that you're not going to believe. You remember how I always used to say that someday I wanted to watch the mileage in my car change to one mile?"

"Sure."

"Well, as we were driving it home, I kept my eye on the speedometer and watched that one come up."

"That's great, Lou. I guess—"

"Wait. You haven't heard the best part, Kingy. As we got closer to the house a few minutes later, I looked down and she was still on one mile. Kingy, it's stuck on one mile. Who says there's no God?"

He drove it that way for almost six months before taking it in to be fixed. Can you blame him?

WEATHER

Unless I'm going on a picnic or sailing, I couldn't care less about the weather. I don't allow it to postpone or cancel any of my plans. If it's raining wherever I'm going, then I'm going to get wet; if it's snowing, I'll be covered with snow; if it's cold, I'll be cold; if it's hot, I'll be hot. But, I'll still be where I want to be and still be doing what I want to be doing. The weather is here to stay. It's not going to disappear, nor will we, so why let it interfere with your life?

Actually, I should believe the opposite of this, because my father is addicted to the weather report. When I was a kid, not only did he listen to the weather report for Philadelphia and vicinity, but for the entire United States and most of the Free World. Even though he wasn't going anywhere, he was constantly checking the weather between Philly and other major cities. When he was listening or watching the weather report, no one in the house was allowed to talk. He would shush everyone so he could hear about the windstorms sweeping across Kansas. My father not only lived *with* the weather, he lived *for* and *by* it.

In between the hourly weather reports on TV and radio, my father would call the telephone company's local weather report. He called at least twice an hour, sixteen hours each day and night, seven days a week, fifty-two weeks a year for at least ten years that I could remember. My father was an incurable weather junkie.

One day on my beat-up tape recorder I recorded the telephone company's weather report off my phone. I rewound the tape, pressed the "pause" button and the "play" button. I called my father. When he answered, I released the "pause" and the weather report started playing. I heard my father scream out to my mom, "Stelle! They're calling me!"

He actually believed for one very brief moment that, because of his years of faithful calling, the telephone weather report was calling him. I know it was for only the briefest time, because the next thing I heard over the phone was his bellowing voice. "Who the hell is this? All right, who's the wiseacre?"

I couldn't stop laughing long enough to tell him, but he knew.

REVENGE

My father is a very vengeful man. Matter of fact, one of my mother's nicknames for him is "Revengeful Louie." My father believes that you should get even for every single wrong done, no matter how long it takes you or what you have to go through personally to do it. The New Testament reads "Turn the other cheek." The Old Testament reads "An eye for an eye and a tooth for a tooth." My father's testament reads "A head for an eye and a face for a tooth." He also believes that when you go after someone, don't leave him crippled—go for the jugular vein, because, if you do the former, "one day the son of a bitch will come wheeling out of a dark alley in his chair and get you in the back." My father didn't just believe all this, he lived it. He had a long list of names and got them all, except the one he probably talked most about getting.

My father came home from work one evening. He tossed his hat on an overstuffed chair and bellowed, "The son of a bitch died!"

Calmly, as always, my gentle mother inquired, "About whom are you raging, Lou?"

"I just can't believe he got away from me, that I never got him. All my life I've wanted to get my hands around his neck and watch him turn the color of a raspberry. But, no, my luck he died of natural causes."

"Lou, you'll have to tell me about whom you are speaking. If you expect me to guess which person on your list it is, I'll probably also die of natural causes before I finish."

"The main one, that's who. The top of the list. I'm talking about that son of a bitch who told me to get married."

He put his head back and roared with laughter. My mother only shook her head slowly side to side, trying to hide her smile. I laughed, too. The funniest thing is that it was true. The guy who advised my dad to marry my mother did die that day. Personally, I'm happy that he *had* lived long enough to give my father that advice, and I'm positive that my dad is, too.

I remember seeing a cowboy movie when I was a kid. It was one of those typical plots where someone's loved ones are brutally murdered and the man goes after the killers, catching up to them one at a time. Usually, when he is closing in on the last killer, a man of the cloth or his best friend or a child or his new girlfriend talks him out of the revenge and into bringing the killer into the court for justice under the law. I always hated that part of the movie. I am my father's son.

Well, in this particular film, the ending was heading that way. It was a best friend and a girl friend. However, there was a slight twist. You're not certain if he's going to complete his mission of revenge or not. However, when the last killer is sneaking up behind him, our hero spins around. He takes a bullet in the arm and does kill him, blowing the killer to kingdom come with the remaining five bullets. On his horse, with his arm in a sling, riding off with his best friend, he's asked the big question: "Well, now that you've killed 'em all, are you satisfied?"

I figured that here it comes, some kind of goody-goody-I-learned-my-lesson-revenge-doesn't-pay crap. They were going to ruin another movie. I wanted to clasp my hands over my ears. The cowboy touched his painracked arm. "I learned that revenge is not the answer."

Shit!

"But it comes so damn close."

Hooray!

The hero—my hero—kicks his spurs into the sides of his horse and rides off at full speed, leaving his friend to eat his dust.

I loved it. As soon as my father came into the house that night, I told him he must go see the movie. I'm not sure if he ever did, but I know that he "lived" the movie and so do I.

Over the years, people have done me wrong to different degrees and I have gotten even to different degrees, much different degrees than they got me, as I was taught by my father. There are still some people on my list. A few of them have betrayed and hurt me and my family worse than anyone has ever done. They know exactly who they are, and if they know exactly who I am, they will not sleep at night, because some-day . . .

You understand, don't you, Lou?

THE PUPPET

My father is eighty-nine years old. His spirit and mind are in their early twenties. One night he took my mother to see a live stage show where they live in Florida. They go often. Sometimes they even go because of the dancing. Because my mother is visually handicapped, my father always makes certain that he has a front-row seat so she can see the show.

On this particular night, the entertainer was a puppeteer. At one point in her act, she called for audience volunteers to come up on stage to be interviewed by the puppet. Whenever the volunteer was elderly, the puppet was insulting, making comments about senility, loss of hearing, lack of sex, and all the other cruel stereotypes we Americans enjoy inflicting upon our senior citizens.

All of us Brenners hate any form of prejudice and bigotry, whether it is toward someone's age, race, occupation, nationality, religion, *et al.* Watching the performance, my father was steaming, and my father really knows how to steam.

The puppeteer suddenly pointed to my father and asked him if he would volunteer to come up on stage. My father has never and would never turn down an opportunity to be in front of an audience, because in his youth he was a vaudeville song-dance man and comedian.

My father bounced up on the stage. As the woman turned her puppet toward him, my father grabbed the mike out of the puppet's hands. "Lady, let's get one thing straight right off the bat. I don't talk to wood."

The audience laughed and applauded. The woman dropped the puppet by her side and conducted a very civil, and thanks entirely to my father, a very funny conversation with my father.

Maybe it is true that you cannot teach an old dog new tricks, but an old dog can teach a young dog a trick or two.

THE PROMISE

When I was eleven years old, I made my parents a promise. "I'm going to send you two around the world someday."

"That's very sweet, darling."

"I mean it. Mom, I'm going to do it, around the whole world, all the countries, everywhere."

"Kingy, you can't even send us around the block."

"I don't mean now, I mean when I grow up and I'm rich."

"Okay, Kingy," my father said, "we'll add it to the long list of other things you've promised us. I can't wait till you become rich. I thank you, but for right now, I think you ought to put the world on the side and travel into your plate of hot dogs and

81

baked beans. After all, your mother spent minutes bent over a hot can opener just so you could have this dinner."

"I mean what I say."

"I know you do, darling, and your father and I appreciate it very much, but what we want most of all is that you'll be happy."

"I'll be happy the day I'm rich and you two are going around the world."

In January 1984, my mother and father boarded the *QE II* luxury liner to begin their ninety-three-day cruise around the world. During the trip, my manager and I joined them, and then my brother and sister went on board. We divided our visits that way so my folks wouldn't be without family for too long. They became such good travelers that in 1985, while they were cruising around the world again, this time aboard the S.S. *Rotterdam*, my manager, brother, sister, girlfriend, and I joined them in Greece and sailed with them to Yugoslavia, Italy, Malta, and Portugal, where we all got to spend some time in Lisbon. Mom and Dad sailed across the Atlantic again. In 1986 all of us joined Mom and Dad for their third world cruise. Why not? Now all of us can hardly wait for 1987—the next time that eleven-year-old kid's promise is fulfilled.

TREATING ATHLETE'S FOOT

When I was ten years old, while playing in an abandoned brickyard, I dropped a brick on my toe. I didn't go to a doctor, of course. Who could afford a doctor unless death was imminent? My big toe swelled, turning black and blue and looking real ugly. Part of life.

At this time, I slept with my very handsome, very popular with the ladies, very intelligent, very much older, very squeamish brother. I guess he believed he was close to perfect and wanted to keep it that way, and therefore anything, no matter how seemingly insignificant, that in any way violated his near-perfect standing was totally unacceptable and had to be dealt with posthaste.

I awakened one night to find my brother sitting up in bed, a flashlight shining on my foot.

"What are you doing, Moby Dick?"

"What the hell's wrong with your toe?"

"I dropped a brick on it. Thanks for caring. Good night."

I laid back to go to sleep but my brother shook me with his hand. I sat back up. He shined the light in my face. "Athlete's foot. That's what you got."

"What's that?"

"A disease. You've got a disease of the foot and it's contagious."

"It was a brick. Ask Dee-Dee and Beb. They were with me. Now, leave me alone. Good night."

"I'm not sleeping with someone with a foot disease."

"So, stay awake. Good night."

I laid back and dozed off. The next thing I knew I was being shaken awake again by my brother. "Okay, David, let's go. I brought up that old army cot that was in the cellar and put it next to the bed. You're sleeping in it until your athlete's foot clears up."

"I'm not sleeping in no cot. You sleep in it."

"David, I'm your older brother and I'm telling you that you are sleeping in the cot."

"Moby, I am your younger brother and I'm telling you there's no way I'm sleeping in a cot in my own bedroom. You're weird. Good night."

His legs were very strong. With his feet pressed against my back, he sent me rolling out of the bed and onto the cot. I tried to get back into bed, but I was no match for my brother. Strength wouldn't win the war, strategy would. I waited until he was asleep, and then I slowly started to slip back into the bed, inch by inch. The inches didn't even add up to a foot before a real foot came flying out from under the covers and rolled me back into the cot.

For the next two weeks, if I went to sleep in my bed, when my brother went out for the evening, he would force me into the cot when he got home. If I tried to get back into bed, he physically thwarted all my attempts. I was exiled to an army cot and that was it. A couple of weeks later, my sore toe cleared up, and after a close inspection, my brother allowed me back in my bed.

If you ever get athlete's foot, I would not suggest the army cot guarantee treatment for it, especially if it was caused by a brick falling on your toe.

THE CHAMP

My much older brother and I used to box in the living room of our house on Sansom Street in West Philly. Both of us were into the sport because our father was an avid boxing fan.

Because my brother was so much older and therefore so much stronger, he would box me while standing on his knees. Although he was still taller than I and still had the longer reach and much more powerful blows, I had the advantage of being able to move around faster and more easily. It wasn't an even match, but pretty close.

One afternoon, when I was around the age of twelve, after I had returned from my bag-packing job at the supermarket, my brother suggested that we box. We hadn't put on the gloves in quite some time.

I danced around him, throwing left jabs and ducking his, until I saw an opportunity to land an overhand right. I threw it; it landed hard. I followed it up with a set of combinations. Every punch was right on target.

My brother and I simultaneously were becoming aware of something that had transpired since last we fought—I was becoming a man. My strength and agility were developing in almost direct proportion to my brother's declining as a result of the inevitable aging process. I won my first bout with him. It was the last time my brother and I ever boxed. Another wonderful pastime of youth had ended.

THE WHITE CLIFFS OF DOVER

In 1981, my brother and I took a much talked about, much dreamed about "brothers'" trip. We decided on England. It was all it could have been and more. Two brothers frolicking about devil-may-care, having fun, sharing laughs. We had many wonderful experiences. The following is just one of them.

We stood looking up at the White Cliffs of Dover. We decided to take the tram up to the top. The view was magnificent. The only other people up there were an old man with a shock of white hair exploding from beneath the sides of his plaid cap, and a walnut walking stick in his bony hand. He was walking with his seven- or eight-year-old grandson and a white Scottish terrier. It looked like a scene from a wonderfully sentimental Greer Garson and Walter Pidgeon movie. My brother and I watched these people saunter off into the distance, and then we began walking through the short but thick green grass.

"Wait a minute, Moby Dick. I've got a great idea. Let's take off our shoes and socks and walk barefoot."

"Fabulous idea, David. I haven't done that since I was a teenager."

We whipped off our shoes and socks. The grass was velvety soft. You do feel an attachment with Mother Nature when you touch her with your bare skin. We had taken about twenty-five steps when I threw up my arms and called to my brother, about twenty feet behind me. "Don't move. Freeze! Not a single step."

We both stood frozen like soldiers who had suddenly discovered they were crossing a minefield.

"What is it? What's the matter, David?"

"You're not going to believe it, Moby. I don't know how we got this far. I can't believe it myself."

"Believe what? What are you talking about?"

"Look around you. No, not at the scenery. Down."

"Oh, my God. What are they?"

"Well, I'm not exactly the Great Outdoorsman, but I'd venture a guess that this is rabbit shit."

My brother and I started laughing. We have a contagious effect on each other, so should one of us collapse weakened from laughter, the other one would go down, too, which in this particular situation was the *last* thing we wanted to happen.

I knew I had to make a move, before the laughter sapped any more of my strength. My brother followed my lead. We each balanced on one leg like two storks, and in between painfully suppressed laughter, we managed to slip into our shoes and socks.

Once our feet were protected, we threw our arms around

each other, and shrieking hysterically, like two drunks, we staggered across the green grass of Dover.

On behalf of my brother and myself, I'd like to publicly thank the White Rabbits of Dover for all the great belly laughs that day.

WHO NEEDS A SISTER?

I guess everybody at one time or another feels that his sister is a giant pain in the ass, whether she is younger or older, maybe even if she is a twin. I was no different.

However, while I was in the army with plenty of time to think about my life, I noticed that whenever I peeked through a door into my past, to a more pleasant time, my older sister, Bib, kept appearing in the pictures of my mind.

Bib was the one who wheeled me around in my baby carriage, and later on, it was she who took me for long walks through the neighborhood. It was my sister who played imaginary games with me on the frayed rug in our living room. It was my sister who spent time sitting on the front porches and backyards of all the many houses in which we lived, listening to me.

When I was seven years old, my sister worked as a salesgirl and cashier in Dennier's, a small, privately owned five-and-ten. She used to babysit me by taking me to work with her. It was the only time I played with store-bought toys, instead of the homemade kind I had.

My sister took me to her high school gym and taught me gymnastics. She was a great gymnast and could have easily made the Olympics had she had the opportunity, but opportunity never came into our neighborhood.

When my sister got a job as the ticket collector at the Warner Brothers Movie Theater on the Boardwalk in Atlantic City, I would walk up and make believe I was handing her a ticket. She would make believe she was ripping it and handing the stub back to me. During the summer I saw all the movies I wanted to see for free. What a fabulous present.

Yes, my sister took care of me. And spent the time. She fought for me and she loved me. Looking back, she was everything a little boy would want for a big sister and then some.

The reason I am writing all of this is simply because I love my sister. She knows it, I am sure, but I want everyone to know it, too.

BIG LOSER

Saying good-bye to me after one of her many visits to see me in Las Vegas, my sister told me she had lost real big at blackjack. As I kissed her, I slipped some money into her hand. "This'll help make up for some of your losses."

She tried to give it back, but I insisted that she keep it. Later that night, after she got home, she called. "Are you crazy, David? You gave me two hundred dollars."

"I would've given you all your losses but my money was in a safe-deposit box downstairs and I—"

"I lost twenty dollars."

"—didn't have a . . . What?"

"I said I lost twenty dollars."

"I thought you said you lost big."

"I did. Twenty dollars."

I had forgotten that my sister still operated on the old money values of when we were growing up poor. She was right. She lost big.

PORTRAITS

There are two oil paintings hanging in my den: One is of my paternal grandfather, and the other, of my paternal grandmother. They are by two different artists. I don't know who painted my grandmother's portrait, but the story that accompanies my grandfather's is very interesting.

In addition to being the rabbi of a synagogue in South Philly and being one of the leading rabbis in the city, my grandfather was also the chaplain at the nearby prison, Moyamensing, known in the streets as Moco. He dealt with the religious life of the few, very few I might proudly add, Jewish prisoners.

As is common among prisoners, one inmate pleaded his innocence in the murder of a man. He was sentenced to die in the electric chair. He was a European immigrant who did not speak any English, only Yiddish. He claimed that his lawyer didn't understand him and he didn't understand his lawyer and that no one understood the others and it resulted as it did.

My grandfather believed this man. He got the case reopened, and prior to the second trial, another man confessed to the murder and the immigrant was set free. He had no money. Even if he had, my grandfather would not have taken it. An innocent man's freedom was pay enough. The man insisted upon repaying my grandfather in some way, so he painted the portrait of the rabbi who saved his life.

This has always been one of my favorite Brenner stories.

COUSIN JITTERBUG

When I was four years old, she taught me to dance. Thus the nickname "Cousin Jitterbug." Her real name was Nessie, although she called herself Nanette. She was one of the truly great characters in the Brenner family, possessing, like the others, an abundance of love of life, a great sense of humor, and an enormously kind heart. She was the oldest daughter of my father's sister, Lena. She was about twenty years older than I. Curvaceous and beautiful with a supersonic personality. My favorite cousin.

I had not seen Nessie for quite a few years. She had moved to Chicago and I lived in Philly. When I got a job working as a producer for WBBM-TV in Chicago, I called Nessie as soon as I got settled in. She suggested that we have lunch the next day.

The operator called my office the following afternoon. "Mr. Brenner . . . uh . . . there's a . . . a woman . . . who claims to be your—"

"Cousin. Tell her I'll be right there."

I hurried out to the reception area. As I pushed through the double doors, I saw her. Just as I remembered her. Thin, busty, and beautiful, but even more so. Her long hair hung down her back, her bright red lipstick accentuated her full lips, her heavily made-up eyes could be seen through extra-large glasses, whose frame had gold snakes entwined around them. Her skirt was micromini, her shapely legs were trapped inside black netting, her full bust was screaming hellos from the plunging off-the-shoulder red and black polka-dot blouse, her heels levitated her almost to the ceiling, and her ears managed to stay on her head in spite of the twelve-pound gold hoops that hung from them.

She sexily snaked and wiggled and shook and bounced her way over to me, grabbing me in a bone-crushing bear hug and planting a big red kiss squarely on my lips, nose, and chin simultaneously. She grabbed my arm tightly and wiggled and shimmied me out of the door.

When we were out of sight of all the people who witnessed the scene in the lobby, she turned to me. "They'll really talk about you now, my darling."

I screamed with laughter. She was such a wild character and she was also right. Not only did everyone talk about me from that day on, they never stopped. Nessie and I had a lot of wonderful belly laughs during the time I worked in Chicago.

When Nessie found out that she had terminal cancer, she called me in New York to announce her plans. "I'm going to leave in a few days, darling. It is absolutely unthinkable that Europe not be given one more opportunity to see me."

That's exactly what this brave soul did. In spite of her excruciating pain, she toured the Continent. Upon her return she called me from JFK Airport. "David, darling, I would just love to see you and trip the light fantastic in exciting and vibrant Manhattan, but I must return to Chicago as quickly as possible on a matter of urgent business. I love you."

She was so full of life on the phone, but . . . That was the last time we spoke. Nessie, Cousin Jitterbug, my sweet, sweet lady, returned to her home and died, and so did a part of me. I love you, too, Cousin Jitterbug, and I miss you so.

THE CIGAR BOX

As you might imagine, my son, Cole Jay, is not hurting for toys. I was buying him toys before he even entered the world. Today, if it can be squeezed, pushed, carried, turned, opened, closed, twisted, squashed, stepped on, rolled, lifted, tossed, built, put together, taken apart, drawn on, bounced, sat on, laid on, stood on, or tasted, Cole Jay has it.

One day Cole was visiting with my parents in Florida, and naturally brought a dozen or so toys to occupy his time.

"Kingy, I'm really surprised at you," my father said.

"Why, Lou? What's the matter?"

"Well, Cole brought a lot of his things and I noticed that he doesn't have one, and I'm shocked that you didn't get it for him."

"One of what? Cole has one of everything. Two of some things! What are you talking about?"

"He doesn't have a cigar box, Kingy."

"You're right, Lou."

You see, when I was a boy, I didn't have one of everything; I had none of everything. The toys I had were not store-bought but homemade: an old broom was a horse; a rope was a lasso or a snake; buttons were money; stones were gold; nails were bullets; skeleton keys opened magical doors; a broken piece of metal was silver, for which an owner would give a great reward. Yes, I had a lot of treasures, and I kept them all in the cigar box that my father had given me. The cigar box itself was a car, a speedboat, an aircraft carrier, a bulldozer, a tank, a house, a fort, a mountain, a spaceship—anything your imagination wanted it to be. It was one of my favorite toys.

I searched the Manhattan tobacco stores until I finally found a large cigar box. I took it home and I filled it with a stone, a string, a shoehorn, pieces of shiny metal, some stones, a few buttons, a small pencil, part of an eraser, a piece of rope, a used postage stamp, a foreign coin with a hole in the middle, some keys, a broken lock, a large rubber band, paper clips, and all kinds of wondrous, imaginative treasures. I gift-wrapped it and gave it to my son, Cole.

Today, it sits on a shelf in his room among the hundreds of toys. I've never seen him play with it, but my father is very happy that I gave it to him, and so am I.

SAY HELLO

When I was a little boy, my father taught me something that I have passed on to my son.

"Kingy, it doesn't cost you anything to say hello, especially to older people, because most of them are real lonely. So when you walk down the street do what you always see me do—say hello."

I always did it as a kid. I passed it on to my son, telling him to say hello to all the elderly people we saw.

One day, when I returned from a meeting, Cole's care person told me that my lesson had finally sunk in. As they were crossing Park Avenue, an elderly man was crossing the street toward them. As he neared, Cole smiled, waved his hand, and said, "Hello." The man walked by with no response. Cole looked up at his care person and said, "That guy was asleep."

When they reached the other side of the street, another elderly man approached. This time Cole took the advice of his care person and spoke louder, smiling and waving. Again his hello was ignored. Cole looked up and said, "That guy's asleep, too."

I haven't heard Cole say hello since and I believe it is a somewhat important lesson for him to learn. So if you are an elderly person and a little boy with blond hair, brown eyes, and a small nose (thank God) says hello to you, please say hello back to him. Thanks.

HOW CAN YOU WIN?

I bought my two-and-a-half-year-old son, Cole Jay, one of those plastic space guns that has twenty combinations of lights and noises, something I would have loved as a child. Actually, something I'd still like to have. Cole Jay loved the toy.

One day when I came home, Cole's care person told me that Cole had thrown his gun across the room and it broke. He did it after she had told him that he had to put away some of his toys before watching cartoons. He was in the dining room eating his lunch. I went in and sat down with him.

"Cole, I heard that you didn't want to put away your toys after you played with them and you broke your space gun. Now, Cole, you know that you must take care of your toys. Daddy has told you how many children don't have toys, that you're lucky. Daddy never had toys when he was a little boy. So, since you didn't put away your toys and because you broke your space gun, you can't play with your toys this afternoon."

He banged his little fist on top of the table and made this "angry face" of his in which he rolls his eyes to go as far up as they can go. It is so difficult not to laugh when you see it, but I was going to stick to my guns, no pun intended, really. I was going to keep control and establish discipline.

"Cole, are you angry with Daddy?"

"Yes."

"Well, it's okay to be angry with me, but would you tell me why? Let me guess. You're angry because I won't let you play with your toys. Isn't that right?"

"Yes."

"Cole, you're a good boy, but what you did was wrong. I think it is important that you learn to take care of your toys. Now, you can stay angry if you want, but no toys until tonight."

I stood up and started out of the room, so proud that I had conducted myself as a bona fide father.

"Daddy."

I turned around to face my handsome son, braced for his angry argument, maybe even a nasty word or two.

"What, Cole?"

"Daddy, I love you bigger than the sky."

I wanted to run over to him, give him a big hug, and kiss and tell him that he never has to put away another toy as long as he lives and he can break anything he wants, but instead, I held my ground. "I love you, too, Cole. See you later, kid."

I left the room and went upstairs to my office. Cole really won, but he didn't know it. When he reads this he will. Cole, you're probably no longer playing with toys, so now I want to talk with you about playing with girls and putting them away after you're finished. . . .

I love you bigger than the sky, too, Cole.

COLE'S COMPUTER

You never know how much is being absorbed by a child. You talk, read, explain to them, and play with them with absolutely no idea of how much, or if any, of it is registering, will be remembered, is understood, or will have any use to them. Sometimes, when I spoke to my son, Cole Jay, I felt like I was addressing a blob. At best, Cole would just look at me. One summer afternoon, when he was two and a half years old, he taught me something.

One of the guidelines I use in helping to raise my son is my own childhood. How did I feel about this or that? What did I like and dislike, fear and not fear? One of my favorite places was the Museum of Natural History in Philly, so I took Cole to the one in Manhattan.

We stopped at every single display. When I thought he was especially interested in something, I would explain it to him. What seemed to go over the biggest was the biggest—the whales, the elephants, and the dinosaurs.

The museum has the largest motion-picture screen in New York. That day the film was about flight. Cole sat on my lap and I whispered into his ear a narration in sync with the pictures on the screen. Who knew if it meant anything? He was very attentive though.

When the film ended, we went to the museum store, where we bought a book about insects for his pal, my manager's son, Zackery, who is three months older than Cole and has shown an interest in anything that crawls since he was crawling. Maybe he got that way watching his Daddy come into the house after one of our long one-nighter tours. Then I bought Cole a bag of little rubber dinosaurs. Cole did not say one word about anything he saw or anything I said.

We left the museum and went to an outdoor café on Columbus Avenue for lunch. Cole still hadn't said a word about that day's experience.

Suddenly I felt his little hand on my shoulder. He was shaking it to get my attention. I smiled and looked into his dark eyes. He smiled and said, "Daddy, you're nice."

"Thank you, Cole."

We went back for our hamburgers and glasses of milk.

Cole, I said "Thank you" not only for the kind compliment you gave me that day but also for teaching me that the little computer inside your head is working all the time and nothing is going to waste. It also showed me that your heart is working right, too. Thanks, Cole Jay.

V

BRENNER, DAVID N., PFC.

PRIVATE BIRDSONG

We just happened to be put into the same sleeping quarters of the army transport shipping overseas. His bunk was right above mine. The day we got aboard, I saw the name tag on his duffel bag—Private Birdsong. Birdsong? What kind of name is that? Birdsong? I couldn't believe it. In all my teenage years, the only names I had ever heard were those that ended in "stein," "berg," or "man," like Goldstein, Goldberg, or Goldman, or with a vowel—o, a, i,—such as Benedetto, Linsalata, Lamorgia, or names that began with an *O,* such as O'Reilly, O'Neal, O'Mally, or names in honor of presidents, such as Booker T. Washington. Normal names. What the hell is a Birdsong?

Well, a Birdsong was a tall fellow, taller than I, and with broad shoulders, the body of someone who worked out with weights to stay in shape. His physical strength was disguised behind a freckled face, capped off with blond hair that hung down in front of his bright blue eyes behind thick glasses; a face that had no nose and no lips. In other words, your average non-

Eastern, non-ethnic, non-urban American male. To me, he was a freak because, up until entering the army, I had never seen anyone like him except in magazine ads. On top of all this, Private Birdsong was a man of very few words. As a matter of fact, in fifteen days and nights I heard him speak only four words, the same four words, over and over and over, and if it hadn't been for me, he wouldn't've even uttered these.

I got on Private Birdsong's case before the ship even pulled away from the dock and continued on it through ten days at sea and five days in the de-embarkation center. This was all to the merriment of myself and the many fellow soldiers traveling with us, but not to Private Birdsong.

"Hi. I'm David Brenner. I've got the bunk right below you. Glad to meet you, Birdnest."

"The name is Birdsong." These were the four words. That's how it went all the time. I'd call him by the wrong name, and he'd correct me by simply saying, "The name is Birdsong." He said it quietly, not angrily, seemingly not caring about the laughter I evoked by fouling up his name. He just said it matter-of-factly: "The name is Birdsong." Over and over and over . . .

"You want to go to the show, Birdeye."

"The name is Birdsong."

"Oh, I'm sorry, Birdface. So whaddya say, Birdwhistle. If we leave right now, we can get in the chow line before it gets crowded, Birdbeak."

"The name is Birdsong."

"Say, Birdseed, they're showing a movie tonight. You want to go? I'll save you a seat, Birdhead. Tony, remind me to save Birdnose a seat, okay? See you there, Birdbath."

"The name is Birdsong."

"Beautiful on deck today, isn't it Birdfeed? I mean, it's really warm for this time of year, isn't it, Birdhouse?"

"The name is Birdsong."

"Right, sorry, Birdwing. Is it this warm where you live, Birdhouse? Where do you live anyway, Birdegg? I'm from Philly, Birddrop. You ever been there, Birddoo? Maybe when we get out of the army, Birdpecker, you'll come to Philly with me. I can just see me introducing you to all my street-corner friends.

" 'Stan the Dancer, Bebby, Dee-Dee, Big Micky, I'd like you to meet Birddip.' "

"The name is Birdsong."

"Yeah, guys, this here's my pal, Private Birdcage."

Well, the day came when we got our location assignments. The five days in the de-embarkation center were over. Birdsong was leaving. I was staying another week. He slung his duffel bag over his shoulders and headed for the door. I called out to him. "Good luck, Birddick!" Everyone screamed with laughter.

He turned and smiled. It was the first time in fifteen days I had seen him smile.

"The name is Birdsong. B-i-r-d-s-o-n-g. Birdsong!"

He turned and left amid the gales of laughter. After he was gone, I kept wondering why he had smiled. It was a strange kind of smile, like the cat who swallowed the bird. "Birdswallow"—I could've used that one, I chortled, but I was still bothered by that strange smile. Later that night I took my usual shower, wrapped a towel around me, and opened up my footlocker to take out a fresh pair of shorts, T-shirt, and socks. The locker was empty. Where all my underwear and socks had been was a beautifully painted sign in various colors: "My name is Birdsong."

Every day for the next week I had to wear the same set of underwear and the same pair of socks, and every night as I washed them out and hung them to dry, I laughed at the same thought: He's a good old bird-song!

THE GREAT TRAIN RACE

I really hated my two years in the army, but I must give it credit for helping me to unscramble my confused teenage mind and for helping me to become a man. What really helped me was my being able to travel throughout Europe from my post in Stuttgart, Germany. Whenever I had the opportunity, legal or illegal, I traveled. With a buddy in headquarters who was in charge of marking off allotted leave and pass time, it was simple to get extra time.

To add to what was already a fantastic adventure, I would

heighten the experience by showing up at a train station whenever I felt I had seen enough of whatever city I was in and buying a ticket to wherever the next train was going, provided that I had never been there before.

One morning I felt like it was time to check out of Austria. The next train was heading for Rome. I bought the ticket and then managed to figure out from which track it was leaving. None too soon either, because the train pulling out at the far end of the station was the Roma Express.

Holding my heavy suitcase in one hand and my stuffed gym bag in the other, I took off, racing across the station. I didn't get to the track until the train was already out of the station. Even though I had a three-pack-a-day cigarette habit, I was still a human bolt of lightning.

The advantage human beings have, for a short run, is they start out at full speed immediately; the advantage trains have, in the long run, is they gain speed up to their maximum and then maintain it. It was becoming a long run. I was going to lose, especially since I was lugging my baggage.

Standing on the platform of the last car, smoking a cigarette, a lightweight top coat draped over his shoulders, watching me with great interest, was a good-looking Italian man a few years older than I. He gestured for me to hand him my bags. Good idea. I tossed the smaller bag, and when I got close enough, he leaned as far as possible over the rail so he could grab my suitcase. As soon as I released it into his hand, I dropped back a few feet.

The train was gaining speed. I was growing weary. I looked at the Italian man. He had a smile on his face. No, it was more like a smirk. I realized that he had offered his help not altruistically but criminally. If I didn't make the train, he had brand-new clothes and possessions.

I kicked up my heels, giving it everything I had, my very best. I could feel my lungs filling, my heart pumping away like mad, the blood rushing through my veins, the muscles of my legs tightening. First with just my fingers, then with my whole hand, I managed to grab hold of the railing. With all the strength and determination I could muster, I swung myself up on the bottom step. I was on. I had won. I slowly walked up the next three steps, bent over, picked up my two bags, looked into the slightly smiling face of the Italian man, smiled slightly myself, and spoke: *"Grazie."*

"Prego."

I entered the car and collapsed in a seat.

Sometimes it's other people's lack of faith in you that gives you that something extra you need to help you reach your goal.

SO TYPICALLY ITALIAN

While on leave from the army, I had spent a lot of time visiting Rome, Venice, and Milan. I then boarded a train heading for Florence.

I was sitting in a compartment all alone, when the door slid open and seven Italian boys my age entered. They threw their bags up on the overhead rack and sat down. From the little Italian I knew, I understood that they were all university students going back to school after a holiday.

When I took out my pack of cigarettes, I noticed one of them looking at it. I offered him one. He smiled, took one, and offered me one of his. I accepted. I then offered cigarettes to the others. Those who smoked took them. The first one lit the cigarette he had given me. It was horrible tobacco, but I smiled.

They spoke no English, but we managed to talk through a combination of my limited Italian, some German, French, and Spanish. It wasn't easy, but it was interesting and helped pass two hours. They were very nice and very lively. We shared a lot of laughs. One of the first things I learned from traveling in foreign countries is that humor is international. I made people laugh in every country I visited except Germany. They have little sense of humor and I was not interested in making them laugh anyway.

When the students arrived at their destination, they stood and began removing their belongings from the overhead rack. In the hall outside our compartment, in order to maneuver past an overweight passenger, a gorgeous Italian woman in her early twenties pressed her huge, gorgeous tits against the glass of our door. All eight of us stared at this marvelous sight, or, rather, these marvelous sights.

When she squirmed by and had gone, the Italian youth who

had done most of the talking with me, smiled at me and said, in perfect English, "That, my young American friend, was the international language."

We all laughed at his line and the joke they had played on me. They shook my hand and spoke their good-byes in perfect English.

I'll never forget them and their great spirit of friendship. I'll never forget those tits, either.

THE BIG BATH

During a field exercise in Germany, I got hurt. It was nothing heroic. We had been living in the Black Forest for four weeks, playing the ridiculous war games. Once again we had helped to prove that no one knows what the hell is going on in the army and that battles are won by stupid luck. I was with my buddies in the back of an ambulance, heading back to our post in Böblingen. I chose the ambulance because it is the only army vehicle with a heater. I fell asleep and never saw or heard the truck that smashed into us. The accident report claimed it was doing eighty-five miles an hour. I had lacerations down my entire left side, from shoulder to ankle, and a brain concussion, which rendered me unconscious for twenty-four hours and semiconscious for seventy-two hours. I was in the hospital twenty-six days. I wouldn't have had to spend so much time in the hospital, except someone made a clerical error and released me too soon! My company commander who hated Jews put me on guard duty the night I got back to my base. The next morning, they found me in the snow unconscious and rushed me back to the hospital, where an idiot clerk apologized for releasing the wrong man. The right man was discharged from the hospital and I was sent up to a ward.

I was in pretty rough shape for about a week, and then in the middle of the night, I felt better physically but was restless. I got out of bed and shuffled slowly down the hall. I couldn't read because my eye focus was still off. I wasn't entertaining the most pleasant thoughts during this experience, so the walk through the darkened hospital hallways was a pleasurable way to spend the time.

I saw a swinging double door. I opened it. There it was, the most beautiful and biggest one I had ever seen in my nineteen years on earth—a steel-lined bathtub. It was at least eight feet long and six feet wide. The faucets (or spigots, as we call them in Philly) were almost as big as fire hydrants (or plugs, as we call them in Philly). Now I've got to explain why this was such an exciting, big deal to me.

All my life, I had only taken baths. There were no showers in any apartment or house in which I had lived. Because of a bad water heater and a lack of money, the five members of my family used to use one tub of water. My mother and sister would bathe first. I would usually go third, because of my status as the baby; my brother, fourth; and my poor father, last. Even by the time I got into it, the water was no more than lukewarm. It was for this reason that I had an undying appreciation of hot baths, even to this day.

In the army, they only had showers. I hadn't taken a bath for over a year and missed it terribly. Here was my opportunity to have one in the largest bathtub in the world.

I scurried as quickly as my weakened legs could take me back to my ward, grabbed a bar of soap, some shampoo, a towel, and scurried back to the room with the largest bathtub in the world.

I turned on the faucets, which gushed the hot water out like giant fire hoses. It took no time for even a tub that big—and it was so big you could actually swim in it. With steam rising from the surface of the water, I climbed in. I lay back, floating in the extra-hot water. It was Utopia, Valhalla. It was so restful, so peaceful, so womblike. I dozed off.

The crash of the swinging door flying open awakened me. I looked up to see a black man in a white hospital attendant's uniform standing behind a large hamper he had obviously pushed in. It was piled high with bloodied sheets.

"What the hell you doin' in my washtub, man?"

It was not a bathtub. It was a washtub for the bloodied operating-room sheets. I never knew that it was humanly possible to reenact the cartoon characters' ability to physically lift themselves into the air, freeze in space, and then shoot off like rockets, but that is exactly what I did.

I hurried back to my ward as quickly as possible, got into the shower, and scrubbed myself with soap until the bar disappeared. I then took another long, long, long, hot, hot, hot, long, long, long, hot, hot, hot shower.

About a year later I was discharged from the army. One of the first things I did when I returned to the comfort of my parents' home in West Philly was get into a bathtub filled with hot, hot water and take a long, long bath and try to forget all memories of the biggest bathtub in the world.

KOSDICK THE CLOWN

"Beaver Falls, Pennsylvania? Where the hell is Beaver Falls, Pennsylvania?"

"It's near Wilkes-Barre."

"Near Wilkes-Barre? I never heard of the town and I'm from Philadelphia, pal. What's in Beaver Falls, Pennsylvania?"

"Joe Namath is from there."

"Oh, yeah? You mean you actually had a famous person come out of Beaver Falls, Pennsylvania?"

"Yeah, it's a great little town."

"Did you hear that guys? It's a great little town. The recruit here said Beaver Falls is a great little town. Let's take off our hats and have three cheers for Beaver Falls, Pennsylvania. Let's hear it. Hip-hip hurray! Hip-hip hurray! Hip-hip hurray!"

We threw our hats into the air, screaming wildly. Danny Kosdick, the newly arrived kid to our barracks in Germany, walked over to his locker and finished unpacking. Turned out he was a terrific guy, and very funny. We used to kid around a lot. Matter of fact, whenever people saw Danny and me together, crowds would gather because they knew wildness was about to happen.

Whenever most of the company went out on maneuvers, a few of us would be left behind. It was easier to keep this skeleton crew in a few rooms rather than scattered throughout the billets. Kosdick was assigned to my room. When we were going to sleep that night, Kosdick called over to me from the other side of the darkened room, "Good night, Brenner."

"Good night, gorilla gonads," I replied.

"Sleep tight, turtle tit," he answered.

"I will, anteater anus."

"Glad to hear it, bird balls."

By this time the giggling had started. In the next half hour, we built it up to uncontrollable hysterics. Kosdick and I wouldn't stop. We couldn't. We were out of control.

"Okay, Kosdick, I'll see you in the morning, monkey mucus."

"Right, ape ass."

"Maybe we'll do something tomorrow, dog dung."

"I'd love to, horse hemorrhoids."

"How about a movie, tarantula twat?"

"Could be, orangutan uterus."

"We'll decide tomorrow, viper vagina."

"That's a deal, snake snot."

"Maybe we'll even have dinner, camel come."

That did it. The "camel come" broke the straw. The guys had been up too long, laughing too hard. They screamed for us to get the hell out of the room. Kosdick and I left. We went down the hall. There was a lister bag there. It contained salt water. For some reason, whenever the troops went out on field maneuvers, the company commander thought that we should share the experience of not being able to drink tap water and should drink salt water, the water with salt pills in it to keep men from becoming faint from the heat. A stupid idea, but, then again, almost every idea in the army is stupid. Kosdick and I slipped underneath the lister bag, leaning against the wall. I turned to him. "What a bunch of bad sports, huh? Rhinoceros rectum?"

"They sure are, cockroach clit."

This went on for several hours. Kosdick and I were hysterical. I don't think either one of us ever stopped. I think we just eventually passed out.

I was discharged from the army about six months before Danny Kosdick, and we lost touch with each other. Several years later, I was walking with a date on Market Street in Philadelphia. Coming toward me was Danny Kosdick and his wife. After introductions, Danny and I started to catch up on what had happened to both of us.

As I talked to him, because he was shorter, I got down to his height. He continued talking and got lower. We both continued talking as I got lower. He got lower, I got lower. He got on his knees. I got on my knees and leaned forward on my arms. He got on his stomach. I got on my stomach. He pressed his chin against the pavement. I pressed my cheek against the pavement. He pressed his cheek against the pavement. There we were, two grown men in the middle of the pavement, lying face to face, with people going by. Years had disappeared but not our madness.

If you happen to read this, Danny, I want to thank you for all the great belly laughs. You know what I mean, dinosaur dick?

JOHN KEARNEY

I hated the two years I spent in the army, but it's a good thing I went in, because it gave me the time I needed to think, and there was a lot to think about—the rest of my life.

I was mixed up after high school. Actually, I was mixed up most of my life. I never knew what I wanted to do. All I ever knew was that I wanted to make a lot of money and take care of my family, but I had no idea in the world how to do it. I longed to get us out of the neighborhood without an inkling of how to do it. I was still hanging out on the street corner and started to get into bigger trouble than the little trouble I had been getting into most of my life. At least I had enough sense to know that I was heading up Trouble Alley. The army took me away from the streets but not entirely away from the street guys.

I hung around with fellas from the big cities back in the States, guys very much like I had known all my life, for big-city streets produce pretty much the same kinds of guys. However, because of my work as a cryptographer, a code specialist, I was also associating with a group of fellas a few years older than I who were all college graduates. I lucked out on the aptitude test and that's how I got the job.

One of the college boys was a red-headed Irishman from Wilkes-Barre, Pennsylvania, named John Kearney. He was a few years older than I and a lot wiser. We became steadfast friends. I used to talk candidly to John about my indecision about the future. Sometimes, I'd leave our heart-to-heart talk to go with the "wild bunch" into town, where we'd drink, fight, and whore. John was always critical of that side of me and some of my friends.

One night, as I was on night duty in the barracks, which consisted of sitting at a desk outside the commanding officer's office and doing absolutely nothing for eight hours, John walked in and threw some papers on the desk top. "I filled in all the facts about you that I know or could find in the company records, David, but there are some only you know."

"What is this, John?"

"It's an application for Temple University. Fill it out, mail it, and get your ass into college. It's where you belong."

He walked out.

I graduated from Temple University with a degree in mass communications, television writing/producing and directing, which was my first career. I might not have gotten there were it not for John.

We lost contact after the army. A few years ago, I heard that John Kearney passed away in the prime of his life, leaving a wife and two children. I was so sorry to hear that. He was a terrific guy and a good friend. He cared about me at a time I'm not so sure I even cared about myself. Thanks, John.

(*Above*). Mom at age seventeen. One of the great beauties of Philadelphia. (*Right*). Dad at age fourteen. One of the most popular guys in Philadelphia.

Some of the Brenners way before I was born celebrating a Passover dinner at my rabbi grandfather's house in South Philly. Mom is standing. Dad is missing.

These pictures are the only proof I have that my sister and brother were ever children. By the time I remember seeing them, they were two more grownups to boss me around.

(*Left*). My first appearance on camera. Also my first hat, or maybe I had natural white wool hair. (*Right*). Starting to realize that I'm cute as hell and how to take advantage of it.

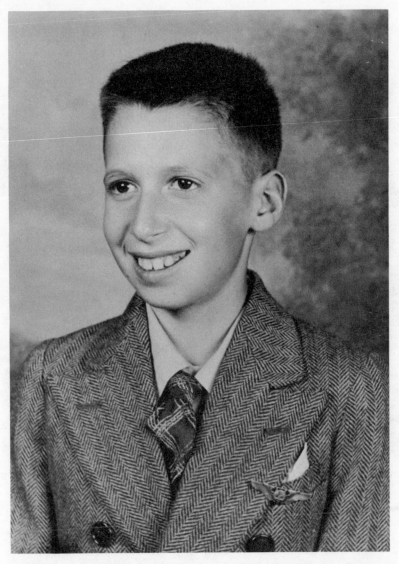

Me at age nine and a half when my teeth began growing before I did.

Brother Moby Dick (top row center) was a real hero—just like in the movies.

(*Above*). Mom, age twenty-one, and Dad, age twenty-five, on their wedding day, June 26, 1921. (*Right*). Mom, age eighty-four, and Dad, age eighty-eight, holding hands and still in love.

In 1964 Dad revisited San Diego's Balboa Park where he had entertained sailors with his jokes, songs, and soft-shoe dancing during World War I. The fleet threw my parents an onboard luncheon and Dad later duplicated a pose he had taken nearly fifty years previously.

(*Above*). Here I am at age fourteen (at right), poor as hell, with a lot of hair and a lot of dreams. Only difference today is that I'm not fourteen and I'm not poor as hell. (*Left*). You can tell by this photo that as a teenager (top row, third from left) I was very, very serious.

As a poor kid of fourteen in Atlantic City I never realized that the hotel behind the light pole would someday be called the Sands Hotel and Casino and I'd be its spokesman and making six figures a year for doing it.

When I wanted to play the drums as a kid they had me beat a school desk. When my nephew Eric had the same dream, I got him a set of drums. That's what family is all about.

(*Above*). Art Fisher (left) was a sensational television director and a great friend. A faulty helicopter rotor ended a great career and a great friendship. (*Left*). One of my favorite people in this whole world is Dr. Milton Reder (middle). Seen here with his son, Dr. Milton Reder II, and Steve Lawrence and his son David.

Taking a last picture with my mom the day I was shipping overseas for the next year and a half. From boy to man.

(*Top*). Danny Kosdick and John Kearney, who helped me straighten out my wild life but didn't live long enough to see the results. (*Bottom*). Directing my first documentary TV series. For you film buffs: the reason we're shooting into the sun is to silhouette the prisoner so he couldn't be identified.

The special lady in my life, Victoria, who accomplished the impossible—
becoming the special lady in my life. Personal love and happiness at last.

The family aboard the S.S. *Rotterdam* somewhere between Dubrovnik, Yugoslavia, and Venice, Italy. The guy with the mustache is my manager, Steve Reidman.

VI

HAVING SOME LAUGHS

JANE WYMAN

Every once in a while, I would ride back to West Philly after a day of classes at Temple University with my childhood friend Joe Podolsky. One day, just to pass the time on the subway, I created different actors and actresses in different movie roles who would be absolutely horrendous in the parts. For example, instead of Burt Lancaster playing the role of the famous Olympic Gold medal winner Jim Thorpe, I cast Orson Welles. Or instead of the gorgeous and sexy Jennifer Jones in *Love Is a Many-Splendored Thing*, I substituted Kate Smith. Then, rather than the wild and sexy actress in a certain role, I told Joe I would have cast the quiet, sedate, ladylike ————. I forget her name. This wasn't uncommon. There were people with whom I worked and shared an office every workday for two or three years at whose mail I had to peek upon coming in in the morning so I'd remember their names when they showed up. It is a terrible affliction. I think it is simply some part of the brain that doesn't work. However, for some unknown reason, I am great with nicknames. I'll never forget Moose, Thin Legs, Double Chin, Knuckles, Death, Double Douche, or Pimples, but it isn't often that one meets an adult with such a name. Thank God, doctors and dentists have their names on the windows of their office doors, and secretaries have nameplates on their desks.

Sometimes, while out on a date, I had no idea what the girl's name was and lived in fear that we would run into someone I knew and would have to introduce them. I used to repeat over and over my date's name to myself all night. I'm talking about the tenth or twentieth date. I'm serious.

Now, don't write me all the remedies you've heard of for such an affliction. I've tried them all. Nothing works, from repeating the person's name in conversation to associating a person with an object. The latter has only lead me to embarrassing myself by calling people Bed Pan, Enema Bag, and Vibrator. A piece of my brain is missing and that is that.

Anyway, I kept trying to remember the actress's name that day on the subway with Joe, but it was hopeless.

"Come on, Joe, you know who I'm talking about. Short, cute, usually wears her hair in bangs, great actress. She played the part of the deaf girl in the movie called . . . Wait, the title was the name of a woman. . . . Damn, I forget. She was deaf. Jesus, I can see her face in front of my eyes. . . . Dark hair . . . You've seen her a million times. When I tell you, you'll say 'of course.' Damn, this is going to drive me crazy all night. Short, dark, bangs . . ."

Joe couldn't think of whom I meant and neither could I. I was too stubborn to look her up in the library or search through movie magazines for the next few days. I tried desperately to think of the actress's name but couldn't. As time passed, I thought less and less about it, but I never stopped thinking about it.

The following year, Joe graduated from college, becoming a schoolteacher. We had lost contact with each other. About a year and a half later, out of absolutely nowhere, for no reason, the actress's name popped into my mind. I got out my old phone book and dug up Joe's phone number. I dialed it. I hadn't spoken to Joe for almost two years. He answered. "Hello."

"Jane Wyman."

"You have the wrong number." He hung up. I redialed. He answered again.

"Hello, Joe? David Brenner.... Fine, man. How are you? Yeah, it has been a long time.... Listen, Joe, that was me who called a minute ago.... Yeah, because that's the actress whose name I couldn't think of for the movie on the subway. Her name is Jane Wyman, and the mute part she played was in the movie *Johnny Belinda*.... The game we used to play on the subway, coming home from Temple.... Come on, you've got to remember. Think. I used to make up ridiculous castings for major films, like Paul Lynde as Moses instead of Charleton Heston.... Yeah, very funny.... You still don't remember? Come on, Joe, I made you laugh a lot with this bit. I've been racking my brain for almost two years for Jane Wyman's name and now you're telling me you don't even remember.... What the hell am I talking about?... Angry? Of course, I'm angry.... Because I've spent two years of my life trying ... Yeah, I know it wasn't every minute of the past two years, but it ... Yes, of course I've got something better to do with my time than think of an actress's name. Matter of fact, I've got something better to do right this second than to stay on this stupid phone talking to you. I've got to take a shit!"

I slammed down the phone. Man, one of my pet peeves is people who forget the important things in life. That's why I never talked to Larry after that day. Larry? Who the hell is Larry?

SKYDIVING

Whenever I stand at any great height that is in the open, such as the roof of a tall building or atop a cliff, I get this queasy feeling in my stomach, a tingling sensation on the backs of my hands, and a desire to jump off. I thought everyone felt this way. I had no idea that I had acrophobia, a fear of heights. Now, no one likes to discover one has a phobia of any sort. Personally, it would bother the hell out of me if I found out that I had a fear of Afghan hats, even if I knew I was never going to Afghanistan. I decided to overcome my phobia by performing some sort of heroic act at a great height. Getting married atop Mount Everest was too heroic, so I settled on skydiving. I knew myself well enough to know that I could never do it alone, so I called upon my supermacho friend, Bob "Moose" Caruso, a former Green Beret, great outdoorsman, sailor, and Italian. I knew he would say yes. We located a skydiving school in New Jersey and were accepted.

I invited Moose to have an early breakfast at my place the morning of the jump. As he sat there chattering away excitedly about the upcoming event, I opened my refrigerator, removed four eggs and some bacon, and then got some bread out of the cupboard, opened the refrigerator and removed the butter and put back the bacon, closed the refrigerator and put the butter on the kitchen table, opened the cabinet over the sink and took out a frying pan and put the eggs in the cabinet, opened the refrigerator and took out the milk and put the pan in, closed the refrigerator and put the milk on the table, and then opened the refrigerator and put the bread in it and removed an old chicken breast, closed the refrigerator, opened the floor cabinet and took out some jelly and put in the chicken, and then opened the refrigerator and put in the jelly and removed the bread, closed the refrigerator, opened a cabinet and took out some dry cereal and the eggs, broke the eggs into the bowl of dry cereal and poured orange juice over it, and then turned around to face Moose.

"I'm too fuckin' nervous to make breakfast, Moose. Let's eat on the road."

"You little chickenshit. I knew you weren't going to go through with it."

"Listen, don't go swinging your big elephant balls around. I admit I'm scared, but I'm going to do it."

"We'll see. We'll see."

"That's right, you'll . . . What's that around your neck?"

"What are you talking about? Nothing."

"That."

"What?"

"Don't close your shirt, Moose. I saw you got some kinda pouch hanging around your neck. What is it?"

"It's just a leather pouch, that's all. Now let's—"

"What do you mean 'just a leather pouch'? How many people walk around with a just a leather pouch hanging around their necks? What's in it, Moose?"

"It's just something I took with me for today, that's all."

"Oh, so you have something with you while I have nothing with me. Even up, Moose. Whatever you have, I want some, too. Let me see it."

Moose embarrassingly opened the pouch and dumped the contents on my kitchen table—a piece of garlic, a cross, a crucifix, a Star of David, a mezuzah, a St. Christopher's medal, a Buddha, an Indian charm, and a bat-hair ring. Moose was taking no chances.

We got into Moose's Volkswagen and drove to a diner in New Jersey. I was too nervous to eat. Moose put away his breakfast and mine. Nerves of steel. We got back into the car and started driving again. I was getting cold feet. Let me be honest—my feet were frostbitten. I didn't know how to get Moose to turn around and go home without spending the rest of my life hearing about it. The station wagon on the other side of the road approaching us was filled with nuns.

"Moose, look. A sign from God that we shouldn't jump. Make a U-turn, follow the nuns back to Philly. Don't disobey God's wish."

"What are you talking about? Man, you call *me* superstitious."

"It's not superstition, Moose, and as a Catholic, you should know better. It's religion. Since the beginning of time, it's written in the Bible, both Old and New Testaments, that a station wagon filled with nuns means 'Turn around. Don't do what you were going to do. Go home, brethren.' "

"Very funny, Brenner. A station wagon—"

"Oh, my God, look at that!"

A hearse passed us.

"Come on, Moose, what more do you need? God is screaming at us. There's probably a dead skydiver in there. Maybe a dozen of them. Listen to the Lord. U-turn. U-turn. U-turn sayeth the Lord."

"Look, if you don't want to jump because you're chicken, just say—"

The car began to sputter.

"What's wrong with your car, Moose?"

"Feels like it's running out of gas, but that can't be. I just filled it the other day. Besides I've got an emergency tank. Damn, that seems to be empty, too. How can—"

"A third sign. What more do you need, Moose? You want God to fly in front of your windshield wearing Groucho Marx's glasses and nose and hold up a picture of your apartment? Let's get out of the car, make a U-turn by foot, and walk back to Philly."

Moose turned off onto a side road and we coasted downhill.

"Moose, it was my idea so I'm allowed to cancel it and I'm canceling it. I just realized that I have a bigger fear than heights—death. Let's just—"

"Ha. You talk about signs from God? Look at that sign."

"That reads 'ESSO,' not God."

"Exactly. God had me turn off the main road so I would coast down to that ESSO station and get gas, so we could continue to the skydiving school. Thank you, God. Come on, Brenner: 'Thank you, God.' "

"I'll talk to Him when I get home. If He let's me get home."

There were no more signs. When we entered the skydiving school, a very good-looking woman in her midtwenties was behind the counter. I couldn't resist acting real macho.

"Hi. We're signing up for jump school. Brenner, that's me, and Caruso, that's this scared guy. We're going to jump out of a plane. Ever think about trying it yourself?"

"Well, I've made two thousand two hundred and seven jumps so far and will be doing five or six this afternoon. Here, fill these out and don't forget number seventeen—next of kin."

After filling out the forms, we were led into a classroom where another six students were seated. The lights were turned out and we were shown a color film of the best American and Russian skydivers. The purpose is to psych you up. Well, the men and women in the film are amazing. As they are flying through space with unopened parachutes, they hold hands, play cards, eat a sandwich, drink vodka, read a newspaper, do fancy acrobatics, take a nap, and then they spin away from one another and open their chutes and land like slow-motion feathers.

They make it look so easy and like so much fun that when the lights come on, you are ready to run into a plane and jump even without a parachute.

Next came outdoor instructions. Our luck we got one of those dumb, retired army sergeants. I spent two years wondering how nature had mistakenly not made them the grapefruits they were meant to be. You know the type—a waistline that is twice the number of his IQ and a speech that is peppered with "dese," "dose," "dem," "dat," "dey," and "dis." The first day I was in the army one of these white gorillas with three stripes on his arm said, "I had a mens who wouldn't do what I tol' 'im to do and den I tol' the CO and youse better believe dat dis mens done did dood it." I thought he was joking and fell to the ground laughing. I spent the next twenty-four hours on KP duty. Yes, I done did dood it, too.

"Okay, youse mens and youse lady [there was one woman in the class and one man seventy-five years old], when youse jumps you will be hit wit a combined wind force of seventy-five, so youse got to jump hard in da spread-eagle position, like dis."

He demonstrated but was so fat, he looked like a spread ostrich. Then he led us over to a platform with three steps leading up to it and a couple of stadium benches on it.

"Dis here's a mock-up of an airplane."

"Looks more like a mockery."

The class laughed at my comment. The sergeant glared at me. I remembered that look from my army days.

"Now, I want a volunteer to jump. You."

He pointed right at me. I knew I had gotten myself in trouble with this erect baboon.

"I'm not good at platform jumping, Sarge."

"Dis is a plane and don't youse forget dat."

"Oops, I must've left my boarding pass in my other jacket."

The class laughed. The sarge reddened. "Move it!"

The old stimulus response took over and I walked up onto the platform and sat down on a bench.

"Okay, now remember, youse is goin' to be hit by a seventy-five-mile-per-hour wind, so go into a strong spread eagle. When I say 'Jump,' jump. Okay, get ready."

I didn't know what 'get ready' meant but I got off the bench and made believe I was standing in the door of an airplane, that I was Richard Conte in a 1940s war movie.

"Jump!"

I felt so stupid, but I jumped the two feet down to the ground in an awkward spread-eagle position. As soon as my feet touched the dirt, the sergeant ran into me full force, with his arms extended, knocking me down hard.

I got to my feet, brushing the dirt off me. "What the fuck's wrong with you? Why the hell did you knock me down?"

"I'm the wind."

"First you tell someone you're the wind, or do what they used to do in school plays—paste cotton balls all over your face and have a sign around your neck that reads 'Wind'—and then run around and knock people down."

We spent the next three hours learning how to fall, pull the rip cord, work the emergency chute, check for problems, how to do everything there is to do. It was an excellent course. No detail was left out except how to keep from making a ka-ka in your pants.

"Okay, youse mens and youse lady, if youse look up, you'll see our best skydivers, our cream of the cream. No one up dere has less dan two thousand jumps."

Way up in the sky, we could see these eight black dots leaping from a small plane. They joined hands and did all sorts of maneuvers, just like in the film we watched. It seemed as though they were never going to pull their rip cords.

"Moose, aren't they waiting too long to open their chutes? I mean—"

"Come on, Brenner, these guys are the best. I'm going to be like them someday."

"Today is not your someday, Moose."

The chutes opened. Moose gave me that told-you look of his that I hated. I gave him the big-deal-who-cares look that he hated.

"Moose, aren't they sailing too close this way? I mean—"

"Brenner, these guys can land on top of a hummingbird's ass if they want to."

"Why would they?"

"What?"

"Nothing. It's just that it seems to me that the wind is blowing them too far this way and—"

"You know what your problem is, Brenner? You're so nervous, you can't see or think straight."

"I am not nervous, Moose. I'm scared shitless. However, that has nothing to do with my calculation that they are drifting too far this way."

"Brenner, do me a favor. Just watch them and learn."

"Okay."

I watched them as they crashed onto the rooftops of buildings, the hood of a car, a tree, a telephone pole, the benches of our meeting place, the roof of the building directly behind us, and down to the ground in front of our feet.

The crème de la crème, the pros, the 2,000 and more jump experts had miscalculated. That helped me calculate—I was not going to jump. However, since I had already paid for everything, I figured I'd go up in the plane, sit out on the wing, look at New Jersey, then get back in the plane, and fly down with it to a safe, happy landing. I was looking forward to a lifetime of acrophobia.

They put the parachutes on our backs. Now, in class I was doing great spread eagles. With the weight of the chute, I was lucky to do a spread sparrow. As a matter of fact, Moose had to lift me into the plane.

We drew numbers out of the Sergeant's helmet to determine the jump order. Moose drew seven and I drew eight, so I had to sit there and watch everyone else go out. If there was any chance of my jumping, it would have been only if I had drawn first or second. Watching everyone else would unnerve me, not that I wasn't already unnerved. The benefit of drawing the last number was that only the sergeant would be on the plane when I didn't jump and I couldn't care less what that peabrain thought of me. I even thought that what I might do after I landed with the plane was get out, open my chute, and run with it over to the rest of the class.

Moose insisted that we bet one dollar on who in the class landed closest to the target bull's-eye that was on the field. Great—another dollar blown.

The first student climbed out on the wing. That was enough

for me. I didn't watch him jump or anyone else until it was Moose's turn.

"Yo, Brenner, watch me and learn something."

The plane flew a wide circle to return to the target area. It took about five minutes to get there. I noticed that with each passing minute Moose's normally swarthy Sicilian skin was getting paler and paler, until it was bleach white. He was staring straight ahead, his eyes bulging. You could see his heart beat in his throat. The veins in his forehead were protruding and pulsating, like a road map coming alive. He whitened more. He became transparent. You could see what he ate for breakfast. I tried to comfort him, shake him out of it. I had never known him to show any fear about anything.

"Yo, Moose, have a good jump. Hey, hey, hey, this is the big moment. You're going to do it. Have a great jump, pal."

He didn't look at me. I don't think he could look at me. He couldn't hear either. He stepped out on the wing, stiff-legged, like Dr. Frankenstein's monster, and just fell off the wing. I watched him spin out of sight. I thought, There goes my friend, Moose. I lost my pal. A gruff voice shook me out of my thoughts.

"Okay, number eight. Let's go, Brenner. Your turn."

I stood up and weakly moved toward the door. I was determined to at least stand on the wing of the plane. It was really the least I could do. It was actually the most I could do. I very gingerly made my way out onto the wing. I held onto the braces as tightly as I could grip them. The sergeant was giving me my last-minute instructions, but I was so scared it sounded like this to me: "Zuba mugga huggy. Zuga mugga huggy."

I turned to him and yelled, "Don't 'zuga mugga huggy' me. I'm coming back in. I'm not jumping."

I still don't know to this day why he did what he did. He hit me on the top of my helmet with the bullet end of his officer's swagger stick. I still don't know why I did what I did—I jumped!

Now, you're supposed to yell "Geronimo" when you jump. Forget what I yelled. Mothers on the ground were cupping their hands over their children's ears and looking heavenward. I also didn't jump in the spread-eagle position. I jumped in a prenatal position, sucking my thumb and yelling, "Mommy, mommy, mommy . . ." I looked like a giant baby sailing across the sky.

The strangest thing was that my fear was not that the chute wasn't going to open but that, instead of coming down, I would go up. A giant hand would come reaching out through the clouds and as an organ and harp played a voice would boom, "I've been waiting for you, Brenner."

But I did go down, and down and down and down. Now, the next thing you're supposed to do is count to ten and pull your rip cord. I was so petrified, I could not remember what came after one. There I was, screaming, "One . . . imblick . . . one . . . imblick . . . one . . . imblick . . ." Finally I decided to just repeat one until I felt like ten of them had passed. I did just that, and then pulled the rip cord. Nothing happened. The chute didn't come out. I pulled it again, and still nothing came out. The third time I pulled a little piece of it—about the size of a hand-kerchief peeked out a little bit. I was in very big trouble.

I went into the emergency procedure. Now, let me tell you something here and now. It is nothing like in the paratrooper movies. You remember how it is there: Someone's chute fails to open. A nearby paratrooper yells over to him, "Excuse me, Bob, sorry to interrupt you, but your chute didn't open."

"Oh, thanks a lot, Jim."

Then Bob pulls this little handle, and, poof, his emergency chute billows out like a gentle summer cloud.

That's not how it works in real life. What you got to do first is pull the cord. Then, as you are plunging to your death—for the first time—you open this little door on the emergency chute, which is on your chest, punch it with your fist, gently take out the chute with your calm little hands, and then throw it out away from you and fluff it. Who can think of all that? I fluffed everything. Finally, the emergency chute opened.

Next, you turn on the radio that is strapped to your waist so you can be guided down to earth from ground control. I turned on my radio and got static. I turned the dials. Nothing but static. I punched it and punched it and punched it. No help. I shook it real hard and a rock and roll song came in very clearly, followed by an obnoxious DJ telling me to get Clearasil. At that moment I couldn't care less if a pimple popped out on my cheek bigger than Mount Fuji. I smashed the radio with my fist. I heard a voice. Ground control.

"All right, Mr. Gorman, you're looking real good. Just turn a little to your right."

I pulled the cord and turned a little to my right.

"A little too far, Mr. Gorman. Go a little left."

I pull the other cord and turn slightly "to the left."

"Perfect, Mr. Gorman, now just bend your knees, look at the horizon, and prepare to land."

I bend my knees and look. There's no horizon, because I'm not Mr. Gorman. That was the guy who jumped before Moose.

Well, they finally guided me down to the ground and I landed, right on the target, believe it or not. Now, what you're supposed to do is get up, run around to the back of your chute, and cave it in, or it will fill with air and drag you. I'm down on the safe ground. I just dug my nails into the earth and called out, "Go ahead. Drag me."

Now, if you want a short cut to drive from New Jersey to Florida, just follow those two irrigation ditches I dug that day.

My acrophobia? Oh, the jump didn't cure that. As a matter of fact, after I skydived, I developed this fear of silk. Then I tried hypnosis, which gave me a fear of eyes.

Heights—I can live with it.

There are two follow-up ironies to this story. One is that on his eleventh jump—oh, yeah, Moose lived—Moose's chute and emergency chute did not open. About 400 feet above the ground, which is only about a half second before contact, his emergency chute did open. He hit the ground very hard, but Moose's legs are like redwood tree trunks. All he did was wrench both legs. He was very lucky. He knew it and never skydived again.

The second twist of fate was really unbelievable. After our first jumps, we stopped in a nearby gasoline station to make a phone call back home and let everyone know we were okay. A young attendant, about seventeen years old, was working at the station. He overheard us talking on the phone. When we hung up, he spoke to us. "Man, you guys are crazy. I watch the people jumping out of them planes all day. You can see them from here. Not me. I like keeping my feet right here on the ground, nice and safe and sound."

Three days later, in a Philadelphia newspaper, I saw a photo of that same young boy. Somebody had robbed the gasoline station and shot and killed the kid. I guess there is no such thing in life as playing it nice and safe and sound.

NO GARBAGE, PLEASE

When I was a kid, the only time we ever ate out, which was rarely, was at the neighborhood Horn & Hardart Automat. Now don't misunderstand me. I loved H&H and still do. Nothing can beat their hamburger, home fries, baked beans, and creamed-spinach platter. However, I think even the president of Horn & Hardart would agree that his establishment was not exactly five-star gourmet dining. I swore to myself that when I became a man and made some money, I would never eat at home but would eat every meal out. It was a priority. To me, food in the refrigerator is a symbol of poverty. When I see an empty refrigerator, I know I've got some bucks. Not everyone is the same. My friend and ex-manager, Rick Bernstein, grew up as poor as I, but to him, if he sees one millimeter of space on any shelf in his refrigerator, he must immediately rush out to a store, regardless of the time of day or night, and buy some food item to fill in that gap. He has spent half the night in Beverly Hills searching for a thin bottle of gherkins. Spaces remind him of his poor boyhood, when the refrigerator was sometimes bare, as his mother and grandmother struggled to raise him without male help. We're both right, even though we're both crazy.

As soon as I became a television documentarian and moved out of the old neighborhood, I began eating every meal out, every day and night. A date, not knowing about my eating-out phobia, meant well but made a mistake.

One night, when I opened the door of my apartment, she came bouncing in, both arms loaded with large paper bags. "Kick off your shoes, David. We're not going anywhere tonight. I'm making us dinner. I never told you I was a gourmet cook."

Now on TV or in the movies, the man smiles ear to ear, winks into the camera, rips off his shoes, and flops down on the sofa, happy as a bull on the first day of mating season. Not me.

"Thanks a lot, but, without going into a long explanation, which will only seem highly neurotic to you, let's keep our reservations at Geno's. I really appreciate your gesture very, very much and know you don't understand, but try to understand without understanding. Maybe I'll explain why no dinner over dinner. I'm going to shave, then we'll leave."

Later, over a great dinner at Geno's, I explained my neurosis. As expected, she stared at me like I had weeds growing out of my face.

About six weeks later, on a particularly hot August night, as I was sitting in my apartment, putting on my shoes to go out for dinner, I smelled something awful. Now, I must explain to you that, in spite of my rather large nose, I have a terrible sense of smell. The equipment is mammoth but it doesn't work. It's a diesel truck with no diesel engine. All the football games and street fights as a youngster closed the right nostril and left me with little sense of smell. If you tied a mackerel to my nose, I wouldn't smell it and probably wouldn't feel it either.

Now that you understand my nose, you can imagine how horribly pungent the odor was in my apartment. It was a familiar odor, something from my past, something from the old neighborhood, familiar and yet . . . Wait a minute, I recognized that odor—garbage.

I rushed to the window and looked outside, expecting to see mounds of garbage piled up because of a garbage strike, or a garbage truck overturned in the street below. Nothing was there.

I ran to the door and swung it open, expecting to see a pile of garbage as a Halloween prank. When there was nothing in the hall, I realized that Halloween was still two months away and rehearsals for it are rarely held.

I closed the door and pondered the problem. The smell was definitely stronger inside my apartment than outside. How can that be? I never had food in this place and never even boiled water. Then I remembered the aborted home-cooked meal. She probably put all that food in my refrigerator before we went out to eat. From this moment on, you will probably not believe a word I write, but it is the absolute—if sick—truth.

I had lived in this one-room apartment for three years. I paid a woman to clean it for me once a week. The place came furnished. I remember the landlord showing me a small refrigerator but had never used it and had forgotten where it was. Yes, that's right, I was living in an apartment for three years and didn't know where the refrigerator was. I'll take a pause here so you can laugh your ass off and call friends and tell them about it. . . .

Okay, had a good laugh? Now I can continue my story. Logic told me that the little refrigerator must be concealed behind a cabinet door or under the sink or in a cupboard. I opened all the cabinet doors, only finding a broken stereo of mine, and under the sink I found my typewriter. I spent the next thirty minutes opening everything that could be opened, feeling inside places, looking in dark places with a flashlight, sniffing like a basset hound, thinking and reasoning, searching and pondering. Nothing produced results. No refrigerator. I plopped down on my sofa bed completely frustrated.

What's that? That small, silver button off the floor, next to the sink, under that cabinet. I leaped off the sofa and pressed the silver button. What appeared to be a solid side of a cabinet, suddenly swung open. The stench that emanated confirmed that I had found my refrigerator and the food. The smell was so bad I gagged.

I had to act quickly. The refrigerator was jam-packed with two bags, which, among the jungle weeds, had fungus and penicillin growing out of them. Inside the bags, I could see strange-colored items, most of which were shining in the dark.

I ran and got a large Hefty bag. I know what you're thinking. If I didn't cook, how come I had a Hefty bag? To carry my dirty clothes to the laundromat, of course. I held my breath as I threw the two bags of food into the Hefty bag. Then I tied a knot in the top of it and charged out of the apartment. My idea was to put it outside for collection. There was one catch. Although I had lived there over three years, I never had garbage, so I didn't have any idea where to put the garbage for collection.

I stopped on the third floor of my building. The young married couple who lived there was strange. They were absolutely straight. WASP, on their way up. Prototype Yuppies. I was a wild bachelor, ghetto Jew, a nocturnal soul who stayed up all night and slept during the sunlight hours, who was seen tramping up and down the stairs with strange-looking people. To them I was a Martian. I guess that's why they not only never said hello to me but went out of their way to get out of my way. Weird ducks. They were so straight that when they walked you could hear their asses squeak. It takes all kinds, right?

I knocked on their door. I could feel the eye peeking through the peephole. The door opened, only as wide as the protective chain would allow. The husband peered out.

"Hi, I'm David Brenner. I live in the back apartment right above you. Sorry to disturb you at this late hour." (It was only seven in the evening, but I figured to these bores this was late. Besides, I had heard that line so many times in so many movies it came out automatically.) "I wonder if you could tell me where to put my garbage and when they collect it."

Now, I want you to do something I never thought of doing at that moment and should have. I want you to put yourself in my neighbor's place. You hear a knock on your apartment door, look through the peephole, and open the door slightly to a man you already believe is mildly insane, at best, who is standing in his stocking feet (Remember that I was about to put on my shoes when I first smelled the garbage? Well, I never got around to putting them on.) with a large Hefty bag slung over his shoulder, like Santa Claus, that smells god-awful (one must assume that my neighbor's small Protestant nose worked perfectly well, having never been subjected to street fights, unless it was damaged in a polo match), who then asks you, after having lived in the building for over three years, when they collect the garbage and where to put it. Of course, the logical conclusion is that your upstairs neighbor had been saving his garbage in his apartment all this time, which is probably why he slammed the door in my face. I heard all his bolts turning and what sounded like a chair being dragged across the floor and propped up against the doorknob. Can't say I blamed him.

My landlord lived across the street from me. He was a young Italian guy who was a lawyer for all the nonrepresented peoples of the world—blacks, Puerto Ricans, peaceniks, socialists, etc. I walked across the street to his apartment. There was a handwritten note attached to his door: "Marching in Washington to Ban the Bomb."

Great, I've got a bomb slung over my shoulder and the one man who could help me is about to get arrested in the nation's capital. I decided to go back into my apartment and think things out. There was only one problem. When I had rushed out with the garbage, I had not taken my apartment key. The duplicate was—right you are—with the marching landlord.

I decided that the first thing I had to do was to get rid of the garbage. I walked a couple of blocks up Spruce Street, where I recalled seeing a big litter basket on the corner. I was right—it was there. Just as I lifted the Hefty bag above my head to dump it in the basket, a police car pulled up right in front of me. I smiled, tried to ignore my shoeless feet, hoisted the bag on one shoulder, and crossed the street. The cops kept watching me, so I kept walking. A few blocks away, the same cops pulled up alongside me. I turned toward them and smiled. "One of these days, I'm going to shove the garbage right up my old lady's ass!"

They laughed, being husbands and understanding. I crossed the street and walked into the lobby of the TV station where I worked. The receptionist, Maggie, looked at me.

"Lots of paper work, Maggie, lots of paper work."

I sat at my desk, no shoes, my socks almost worn out, a big bag of stinking garbage under my desk, locked out of my apartment. An idea struck me. There was a producer no one liked. He was a short, bald, Elmer Fudd–type guy, with a Napoleonic complex and a totally negative personality. He was King Schmuck. His office was directly above mine and he always left it unlocked.

This guy had a hand-tooled leather desk top, which he crowed over. Bought it with his own money to impress the company. He once fired a friend of mine while sitting behind it. He spent all his spare time kissing the ass of our boss, another putz, and once conspired with him to get me fired. His desk still smelled new. But not for long.

So no one was on the fourth floor when I got off the elevator with my Hefty bag and no one was in King Schmuck's office when I dumped the garbage on top of his desk.

I walked out of the studio, down the street, bought some

socks and a beautiful pair of leather shoes, asked the salesman to please throw away my folded black Hefty bag, and returned to my office, a very happy man.

Revenge is sweet, especially when it stinks like hell.

FASTEST RIDE IN NEW YORK

I sat in Rick Newman's old Cadillac shivering with pain from the subzero weather. We had just left his nightclub, Catch a Rising Star. It was a few minutes after three in the morning. Rick suggested we grab a bite to eat. I said I felt like Italian, so we decided to go to Little Italy.

"Damn, Rick, turn the heater on. My lungs are getting frost-bite."

"It's on full blast."

"Full blast? I don't feel anything."

"Has to warm up."

"What are you saying? We got to drive to Miami before it'll work?"

"No." He laughed. "It'll get going when the car moves."

"Then move it or the headlines in the *Daily News* tomorrow will read " 'Two Jews Found Frozen in Cadillac on First Avenue. One had his hands wrapped around the other one's neck as though he were choking him.' "

Rick laughed and pulled out of the parking space. We were going to make a right turn at the corner on 78th Street, another right on York, pick up the Drive, and head down to Mulberry Street. The streets were still covered with snow from a recent storm. When we got to the corner, the car died. Rick tried over and over to start it. Nothing.

"Rick, my testicles are reduced to the size of BB's. I'm catching a cab and going home to soak them in a teakettle. *Ciao.*"

"Wait, David, it'll start."

"The same day the pope auditions at your club."

"If I could just get a push, I know she'll start."

"After I get out, I'll give her a little push. Good night."

"Wait, there's a car waiting behind us. I'll ask him to push us."

"Better yet, Rick, ask him if he wants Italian food."

Rick got out of his car, ran to the car behind us, ran back, and got in. "He said okay."

"Must be an out-of-towner."

I felt the bump as the guy's bumper hit ours. He started pushing us. When we got up to about thirty miles per hour, Rick tried to kick her over, but nothing happened. Rick tried again and again. Nothing.

"Rick, she's not even making a clicking sound. The battery is as dead as my feet are right now. Tell the guy to stop pushing us. Put her on the side of the street and let's share a cab home."

"Okay. Damn, she started this morning."

"A lot of people who started this morning are dead tonight. Signal the guy."

Rick opened his window and signaled the car pushing us to stop. We kept going. I looked out of the windshield and noticed all the traffic lights up ahead were red.

"Rick, signal him to stop or we'll run a red light."

"I'm signaling but he ain't stopping."

We went roaring through a red light and were speeding up for the next one. I looked out the window next to me and saw the buildings flying by. I looked at the speedometer.

"Jesus, Rick, we're doing seventy-five!"

"The guy won't stop!"

"Where's the guy from —the Twilight Zone?"

I turned around and looked out our back window. "Rick, the fuckin' guy's sound asleep or dead!"

Rick turned and looked out the back window. "I smelled whiskey on him. He must've passed out."

"You let a drunk push us? Don't you know to give a guy a sobriety test before you let 'em push you? Look, we're doing ninety! Blow the horn!"

Rick kept his hand pressed down on the horn, although it didn't blow as we roared through one red light after another at speeds exceeding one hundred miles an hour.

"Rick, if we don't stop by plowing into a truck or something, you know what's at the very end of First Avenue where we're heading—right off the Willis Avenue Bridge."

"Great night for a swim."

"At least I'm not cold anymore. I always sweat right before I die. Every time."

There was no way we could stop being pushed. The guy was still in a stupor or dead. The scenery outside the windows had become a long blur. Then, as quickly as he fell asleep, he awoke and, through the stupor while waking up, slowed down. We coasted to a stop, and the other car pulled up beside us. Rick rolled down his window. The drunk was leaning out, looking at us through the open window on the passenger's side.

"Okay, boys," he said with a slur, "say hello to your Aunt Margaret for me."

Then the drunk drove off, still leaning across the passenger seat.

"Who the hell is Aunt Margaret?"

"I got a better question for you, Rick. Where the hell are we?"

Rick looked at the street sign. "I don't believe it! One hundred and Thirty-seventh Street! We're lucky we're still alive."

At 137th and First at four in the morning our chances of staying alive are slim to zero.

"Look, there's a phone booth outside that luncheonette. We can call a cab."

"Why don't we call the *Guiness Book of Records.* I'm sure no one's been pushed fifty-nine city blocks by a sleeping man."

We got out of the car and entered the luncheonette. Rick called several cab companies. A few wouldn't come out, and the shortest time in which one could get to us was in at least an hour. We settled for that company and Rick hung up. "Well, look at the good side. We can eat as planned."

"I don't think this place is famous for its scungilli."

When we sat in the only available booth, I peeked around the luncheonette. There were about twenty customers, each meaner-looking than the next. Faces like these are usually seen with prison-cell bars in front of them. The guys had scars on top of their scars. They were all staring at us. Rick finally noticed them.

"Oh, God," he whispered, "what do we do?"

"Well," I answered, "normally, in this kind of situation, I'd say we should just act like we come in here all the time, but I doubt if anyone is going to believe that."

Rick laughed softly, very softly. No one was saying a word. The place was deadly silent, like right before a tornado, and I was afraid there was going to be one any moment. The waitress came over to the booth. Everyone was still staring. It was a chilling scene.

"Whaddya want?" the waitress asked.

"I'll have everything on the menu," I answered in a loud voice, "because I know I'm not getting out of here with any of my money!"

Rick, the waitress, and everyone in the place broke up. We had a wonderful breakfast and didn't even notice the cab was a half hour late.

A BIG HELLO FOR A LITTLE GUY

Morty "the Bird" Hoffman and I have known each other since we were little. Actually, he is still little and always will be. When I shot up at age fourteen to my present height of six foot two, Morty shot up to his present height of five foot two. Shot out of a cannon and a BB pistol, respectively. However, when you measure him by how kind, generous, and warm he is, and by his friendship, Morty is twenty feet tall. I love him. All the old gang love him.

If you didn't grow up on a big-city street corner, there is something I've got to explain to you. When a bunch of kids hang around with others in school and then on the street corner at night, putting one another down for anything is great sport. The verbal attacks covered the gamut of life, including ethnic and racial slurs, report cards, mistakes in sports, losing bets, tripping on the sidewalk, girlfriends, dates, and physical handicaps, such as big noses, fatness, thinness, bad hair, tallness, and shortness. It is all done with love and, in the long run, helps you overcome any hangup you may have about yourself. It was a very healthy form of humor.

Anyway, I hadn't seen the Bird in a couple of years. He had become a successful executive in an engineering firm. I was in Philly from New York to tape the *Mike Douglas Show,* and as was customary whenever I came in for the show, I was taking a nostalgic walk through the streets of my hometown.

About a half block in front of me, heading in my direction, I spotted the Bird, walking in the middle of what were clearly four top executives of his firm. As we got closer to each other, the Bird saw me. He smiled and waved. I did nothing. When he was within a few feet, he reached out his hand to shake mine, a big smile on his face. "Dave! How are you?"

I slapped him across the face and kept walking, disappearing into the lunchtime crowd. It took him a week to track me down by phone.

"Brenner, you sick son of a bitch. How could you do that to me? They were all my bosses. I've been telling them for years how we grew up together, that we were best pals, and then you humiliate me in front of them. Now they think I made up the whole story about us. I still can't believe you did that to me. You're sick. You always were sick and you always will be sick. You're a real sick, disturbed person. A mental case. So when are you going to be in Philly again. Marsha and I would love to see you. We can go to dinner together, my treat."

We see each other a lot and it's always great. We'll always be the best of friends, even if some business executives in Philadelphia will never believe it.

Oh, please don't get the idea that I'm no longer a disturbed person. For example, whenever the Bird and his wife, Marsha, come to Atlantic City to see me perform, or to my hotel room in Philly or to my home in New York, I always make him jump. Let me explain. Let's say I'm in my room in The Sands Hotel in Atlantic City and I hear a knock on the door. I look out the peephole. The Bird and Marsha are standing there. I call out, "Who's there?"

"The Bird."

"I can't see anyone. Is anyone there?"

"Come on, Brenner, don't putz around."

"I think I hear a little voice but I can't see anyone. If anyone is out there, please jump up and down so I can see you."

"I'm not doing it this time, you sick son of a bitch. Open the door."

"Jump, jump, jump."

"We're leaving, you crazy bastard!"

"Are you a little child? Is that who is out there? If you are, please jump up so I can see you."

"That does it, Brenner, we're not coming to your show and we're not having dinner with you. Go to hell!"

"Jump. Jump. Jump. If not, I'm walking away from the door."

"Goddamn it, you bastard. This is the last time I'm going to do this. I swear it. Here, I'm jumping, I'm jumping."

This is when I throw the door open and grab the Bird in a tight bear hug, his face in my stomach.

"How you doin', Bird. I'm so glad to see ya. Hi, Marsha. Come on in. Gee, I didn't know it was you or I would've opened the door right away. So, tell me—"

"Sick bastard."

I really love that small giant of a friend.

WALKING TOUGH

Whenever I work anywhere near my hometown, I get together with my childhood friends and hang out. I guess it's our way of trying to recapture a piece of the past, a moment from yesterday, when we stood as youths on a street corner, when responsibilities consisted mainly of making a few bucks to help out at home and getting through high school, a time when most of life was the future, when the unknown that lay ahead could be anything we wanted it to be, where all the values in life were so clear and understandable, when life was still black and white and not a confusing blend of all kinds of shades of gray, back in a time when friendships were made of steel and dreams were made of glorious hot colors, when all was solid, anything could be achieved. Living through these feelings together bound us in a lifetime of friendship. These childhood friends were people you could count on to come through for you no matter what your needs, no questions asked. You need, they deliver. This has been tested throughout the years and there's never been one failure. We can count on one another as one can count on the moon and sun rising and setting, except in these friendships there is no setting.

I was working the Valley Forge Music Theater for a week, so I had an opportunity to see my street pals. A group of us got together for a "walk and talk" through the streets of Philadelphia.

There was Stan the Dancer, Morty the Bird, Beb and his wife, Lenore, and my manager, Steve Reidman. A friend of mine from New York, Irwin, a diamond merchant, had come down to Philly to spend a few days. He was what we called a rich boy when we were growing up in the poor streets of our neighborhood. You know the kind of kid—never has to work but may take a summer job just to pass the time and get laid, which he rarely does because he hasn't got that cocky street attitude; a fellow who only has to ask, and Daddy buys him the new sweater or the new car; a kid who enjoys the soft life and ends up paying for it by becoming a soft man.

Irwin, like a lot of men who grow up in such a bland environment, was striving to be one of the boys. He was attempting to become a street guy by hanging out with the real thing. He was trying to become through osmosis what he could never become. Irwin was to learn this lesson on this particular day.

We were walking around South 10th Street, which is still part of South Philly even though it is on the borderline. South Philly is everything people have heard it is—a very tough, mainly Italian, neighborhood. It is comparable to the Italian section of Brooklyn. I started out there before moving to the West End, which is pretty close to being as tough, except most of the tough guys were Jews. Even though my friends and I had gotten out of the neighborhood and were no longer hanging out in the streets, we had our roots back there and were still capable of leaping back in time.

As we walked, we occasionally passed some "neighborhood toughs," mostly young Italian kids who wore the South Philly uniform: tight, white strapped underwear shirts, jeans, and canvas high-top sneakers. When two particularly rough-looking teenage boys passed us, Irwin turned to me. "Wow, there are really a lot of tough-looking fellows around here."

"Killers, Irwin, killers!"

"Really? Wow! They are really frightening-looking. I mean, like they can scare the hell out of someone."

My friends looked at me and smiled. None of us was scared or ever would be, because we had been these guys what seemed like only a few years ago. We had always enjoyed intimidating and scaring rich boys like Irwin in those days.

"Not if you scare them first, Irwin."

"What do you mean?"

"Simple. You got to look tough, walk tough. Then they leave you alone."

My friends held back their laughter. They knew I was going after a joke with a soft boy as I had done when we were kids on the corner.

"What do you mean 'walk tough'?"

"The way you walk. Like you walk . . . well, you walk . . . kinda funny for down here. You'd be in a lot of trouble."

"What do you mean? What's funny about the way I walk?"

"I don't mean 'funny' in the sense of ha-ha. I mean 'funny' like in growing up in an upper-class neighborhood such as yours. You can tell by the way you walk that you always had money."

"What are you talking about?"

"Well, look at the way you walk. Look at it."

"What? I walk normal."

"Exactly what I'm talking about. You walk 'normal.' You've got to walk like a street kid—tough."

"How do you walk 'tough'?"

"I'll show you. Do exactly as I do. First, you got to bend forward. A little more. That's it. Now, as you walk, you move one shoulder forward and then the other one, like you're throwing punches with them. Try it. Good. Now extend your arms to your side like you're carrying an invisible watermelon under each arm. That's right. Make it a bigger watermelon. Perfect. Now take long, deliberate steps. Swagger. That's right. Swagger, left, right, left, right. Like you own the world. Okay, now put a real mean expression on your face and turn your head from side to side as you walk. A little meaner in your face. Make believe Gucci has revoked your charge card. Good, that's it. Growl a little, sort of under your breath. Good, good. Now you got it. You're now 'walking tough.' The next time we see some South Philly tough guys, we'll all 'walk tough' together and you'll see how they react."

About ten minutes later, we turned down South Street. It used to be one of the most dangerous streets in Philly when I was growing up, but it has since become a great shopping area, with wonderful boutiques lining both sides of the street where the whorehouses and bars used to be. Coming toward us, down the block aways, was a group of five South Philly teenage boys. They were obviously street kids.

"Okay, Irwin, here comes your first chance to 'walk tough.' See these guys coming toward us? When I give the signal, we'll all walk tough. Okay . . . get ready . . . okay . . . now!"

Irwin was in front of all of us. He snapped into his newly learned tough-guy walk, resembling a small ape who had thumbtacks rolling around inside his underwear shorts. Irwin swayed and hobbled down the street. The rest of us just stood still watching him. We never took a step. He was all alone and didn't know it. We were hysterical. When he got within twenty yards of the approaching teenagers, they took one look at him and crossed to the other side of the street. A lot of other people did, too. Everyone was carefully watching the semihuman, distorted form swaggering down the street.

Irwin turned to look at the "street gang" he was leading down the street. No one was there. He had been walking, if you want to call that walking, all by himself. We couldn't even catch up to him if we wanted because we were too weak from laughter.

Irwin and I both learned a lot from that incident. He learned that you got to be born and raised with the streets in you. It is something you can't learn. It is something that is just a part of you.

I learned that just as effective as really being tough is being a lunatic. No one wants to get involved with someone who is crazy, not even the muscle-shirted South Philly kids.

There is something else I learned: Street people are special, real special. When I ran into one of the worst problems in my life—my fight to have visitation rights with my son—all my lifelong street friends volunteered to do anything, and I mean anything, to help me. Irwin, who knew the people with whom I was battling for my son, and could influence those same people and be a big help to me, not only did nothing to help me, but joined the other side.

I guess someone who has to fake being tough also has to fake being a man. I'm glad I grew up in the streets, and although my son will never have to go through the hell I did, I'll bet you he's going to have a lot of the streets in him. I'm going to see to it, and I know that if anything ever happens to me, my friends will see to it that he does.

PIGEON ISLAND

Garfield's job is business investments, getting people to invest their money in projects he recommends. Through a mutual friend I invested a good sum of money in Garfield's latest find—natural-gas explorations in Pittsburgh, Pennsylvania, a "sure thing," according to Garfield. A total fiasco according to reality. I lost most of my money. I would have lost nothing, or very little, if Garfield had told me the bad news when he learned of it, but he just pulled his own money out and let everyone else take a bath. Not exactly the most kosher thing to do, but, let's admit to one thing—no one twisted my arm to invest in the first place. In the end, it was my decision, based entirely on Garfield's expertise, but still my final say. That's what investing is all about. However, I'll tell you what really bothered me, besides Garfield not warning anyone and saving his own wallet, was the big kick he got out of telling everyone what a jerk I was to invest in such a wild scheme. He constantly mocked me to others, enjoying great peals of laughter while relating how stupid I was to put a lot of money into natural gas in Pittsburgh. I figured that I'd get even with him—and I did.

Before telling how I got back at him, let me give you some background about Garfield for those of you who might still feel sorry for him, in spite of what you already know. Garfield is the kind of guy with whom you want to get even, even if he never lost you a lot of money. He is one of those superstraight, superboorish "Muppies" (middle-aged urban professional) who even wears a gray suit, white shirt, and maroon tie to bed, has cuffs on his white boxer shorts, and makes love only in the total dark with a Mantovani album playing on his stereo. Ho-hum time. The only aspect of Garfield that is the least bit interesting, although highly neurotic: He has begun a mail-order collection of dildoes. You get the picture, right? Good. Now to getting even.

Sometime after the gas loss, I met Garfield on a Caribbean

sailing vacation. Of course, he just couldn't wait to relate the story of my Pittsburgh investment to everyone aboard, squealing with delight at every telling. Well, he who squeals last, squeals best.

I had learned that Garfield had a morbid fear and disgust of city pigeons. I'm the first to admit that pigeons are not among the most beautiful and desirable of our fine feathered friends, considering them to be the bag ladies of the bird world, but when I see one, I don't break out into a cold sweat, go pale, and faint. This information afforded me the opportunity to avenge Garfield's humiliating comments about me. The captain and his wife, who were not too enamored with Garfield in the first place, primarily because of his better-than-thou attitude, were more than delighted to help me with my plan, which we initiated one early morning when Garfield appeared on deck, wearing his Playboy Club bathrobe.

I approached him. "Good morning, Garfield. Beautiful day. If this great weather keeps up and the seas remain as calm, we should be at Pigeon Island by noon tomorrow."

"What do you mean 'Pigeon Island'?"

"Come on, you know all about Pigeon Island. That's where all the pigeons originated. You know, the prototypes of the pigeons we have today. Of course, these are much bigger, the size of full-grown turkeys and can't fly, but they look the same and are delicious to eat. A big delicacy in these parts."

"Come on, David, don't jest with me. Don't try out one of your TV comedy skits on me. I'm not a fool, you know. I am the owner and president of a Manhattan, New York, investment company, with only one partner, whom I'm already working on moving out."

"Hey, don't believe me, Garfield, but it's the truth."

"David, I'd bet all my Gucci loafers and belts that you are wrong."

"I don't wear Gucci, Garfield."

"Why not? Everyone does."

"You just answered your own question, Garfield."

"I don't understand."

"Of course not."

That evening, as we all sat around on deck relaxing, except

for Garfield, who was reading *The Wall Street Journal* and complaining that the night sea air was ruining his ascots, the captain called his wife over to him at the helm. "Well, Grace, the wind is strong, the seas are becalmed, so we should make Pigeon Island by noon tomorrow easily. Get the big pot ready for the pigeon roast."

Garfield put down his financial section, removed his thick horn-rimmed glasses, and said to the captain, "Did you say 'Pigeon Island,' Captain?"

"Yes, why?"

"Well, I . . . that is . . . I mean . . . is this the same Pigeon Island about which I know?"

"Well, there is only one Pigeon Island, Garfield. Probably the one you know about. The place where the pigeon originated, where they are as big as . . . well, say turkeys or wild geese. Of course, through evolution, like so many other living species, they have shrunk in size and migrated throughout the world. However, on this one little island in the middle of the Caribbean, practically in the middle of nowhere, there exist the survivors. Thank goodness there are so many of them that they are not on the endangered species list, because they are absolutely delicious to eat and no one prepares a giant pigeon better than my loving wife."

Grace hugged and kissed her captain husband. The captain did such a wonderful job that, even though I had originated the story and rehearsed him telling it, I was almost convinced these birds actually existed. Garfield was definitely convinced.

"Of course I heard of Pigeon Island, Captain, and knew the story, but, to be honest, I would have bet my Club A Original Member membership that the prototype pigeons were really extinct."

"Well, if we're lucky enough to catch a few tomorrow, you'll learn quickly how nonextinct and tasty they are."

"Captain, if it meets with your approval I'd like to lead the hunting party for the giant pigeons tomorrow."

"That'll be fine, Garfield, but take David with you. He's had experience hunting them."

"Well . . . okay."

The next afternoon we dropped our rusty anchors off the island we were making believe was Pigeon Island and swam ashore. Like a miracle, there were large bird tracks on the beach, probably from very large pelicans. I pointed them out to Garfield, who was already holding a hunting knife in one hand, a handle of a plumber's helper in the other, and looking nervously around.

"Look, Garfield, prototype pigeon tracks."

"I know prototype pigeon tracks when I see them, Brenner. You don't have to point them out."

I suggested that all of us follow the tracks into the jungle. Garfield agreed and suggested that I lead the way and he bring up the dangerous rear. When we were working our way through the thick underbrush of the jungle, I threw high into the air a handful of pebbles and shells I had picked secretly off the beach. As they came crashing down through the trees and bushes, Garfield leaped a foot into the air.

"Wow, did you see that? Giant pigeons on the move. Careful everyone."

I threw more stones and shells. Garfield panicked. "It's a pigeon attack. Everyone for himself."

Only the heels of his Gucci loafers could be seen crashing through the underbrush. The rest of us calmly walked back to the beach. When we got there, Garfield was telling three scuba divers who had just come out of the water about the giant pigeons and asked them to return to the wild jungle with their spearguns to help him hunt down the winged killers. The divers looked at Garfield for what he was—a putz.

We returned to the boat and Garfield spent the remaining afternoon hours on deck, binoculars glued to his eyes, scanning the shoreline for a sight of those dangerous giant pigeons.

While we ate our roast beef dinner that night, I let Garfield in on the joke. Of course, he tried to scream above the laughter that he had never fallen for my joke in the first place but only went along with it for laughs. Well, I had my motion-picture camera with me and recorded Garfield on deck with his binoculars and his comments about his search for the prototype pigeon, just in case anyone needed proof that the only giant pigeon that day was Garfield.

The only thing I have trouble understanding to this day is

that whenever anyone brought up the story of Garfield and the giant pigeons living on Pigeon Island, everyone laughs except Garfield. I just don't understand why he found natural gas that doesn't exist so funny but saw absolutely nothing humorous about giant pigeons that don't exist.

A NEW PATIENT

Eighty-six-year-old Dr. Milton Reder is the man who kept me from being in excruciating back pain since 1972. He is also one of my all-time favorite human beings and one of the funniest men I have ever met. Had he gone into show biz instead of med biz, he would have become one of our classic comedians. Personally, I'm glad he didn't.

I have had millions of laughs in his office. Every day I am in New York, I get my back treated and my spirits lifted at Dr. Reder's.

One of the funniest moments was the day a new patient came into the doctor's inner office. He had had only three treatments and already was free of a back pain that had been nagging him constantly for a dozen years. The man was bubbling over with happiness and excitement.

"Dr. Reder, it's amazing. I feel so much better."

Dr. Reder looked at the man who was seated in a raised examining chair across from him. "What did you say?"

"I said that I feel much better. It's amazing."

"Could you say it louder. I didn't hear you."

"I said," the man called out louder, "that it's amazing how much better I feel."

"Say it again. Louder."

"I feel one hundred percent better! It's amazing!"

"Again. Louder."

"I feel much, much better!" the man screamed. "It is really amazing!!"

Dr. Reder smiled. "Thank you. I have two new patients in the waiting room and I wanted to give them confidence."

VII

WOMEN

GIRLS VS. BASEBALL

I can remember the exact millisecond I first looked at girls and appreciated them. Until that moment, I was like every other preteenage boy: I thought girls were a giant pain in the rear end, with their stupid giggling, the silly games they played, the way they always had the right answers in class, their constant roles as teacher's pets, their joy at squealing on you (except my sister Bib), getting one hundred on tests, having superneat composition books and beautifully neat handwriting, never getting thrown out of class or expelled from school, always wearing clean clothes, never having scabs, never blowing their noses real loud, sneezing so softly they sounded like ants, being afraid of bugs, threatening to get their big brothers after you all the time, getting angry when they heard cursing, sticking their noses in the air when they walked by a group of us, never spitting in the street, never urinating up the alley, never having a fistfight, and always telling all of us that we were disgusting. All in all, girls were just totally sickening things to be around.

Anyway, we were playing a choose-up sides game of softball in the William Cullen Bryant Elementary School yard. We were in the first half of the fourth grade. As always, a group of girls was standing along the first-base line, watching us and giggling. I came up to bat. There was a man on second. The score was tied. The pitch was just where I liked it—low and on the outside. I smashed it over the second baseman's head for a double, scoring the runner.

The girls were jumping up and down, squealing, cheering, and applauding. For some strange reason, I liked it. I liked it a lot. It made me feel good, real good. Kind of warm inside. I smiled at the girls. They smiled back. A few of them waved. I waved back. I walked off second base toward third. My teammates yelled at me.

"Where you goin', Brenner?"

"Get back on base."

"What are you doin'?"

"Count me out, guys," I called back without taking my eyes off the girls. "I'm out of the game."

"What do you mean 'out of the game'?"

"What the hell's wrong with you?"

"The sides aren't even now."

I walked right up to the girls and put my arms around two of them. "What's happening, girls?"

They giggled and blushed. We all walked away together. I paid no attention to all the cursing coming from my friends.

That was the exact moment I noticed ladies, gave up playing softball, and took my first steps toward becoming a man.

SLOPPY PARTY HUMOR

One of the nicest girls in my class when I was in elementary school was Michele Weinstein. She was always the proper lady, nicely dressed, clean, and quiet. On top of that, she was very pretty. Everyone liked her. I know I did.

To celebrate her eleventh birthday, she invited the whole class to a party in the recreation basement of her row house. Her mother had prepared a wonderful deli spread on a long table, including corn beef, pastrami, roast beef, turkey, sour pickles, sour tomatoes, cole slaw, and potato salad.

Someone suggested we play some stupid party game where you turn out the lights and have to find someone. I always hated those kinds of games. Anyway, we chose up sides and the lights were turned out. I decided to liven up the party. I took a handful of cole slaw and hung a few strands of it off my own shoulder. Then I flung the remainder of it through the darkened air.

Kids screamed. The lights were turned on. Cole slaw was hanging off faces, clothing, and in kids' hair. I complained as loudly as the rest, brushing it off my shoulder. We all confirmed angrily that it was a very juvenile thing to do and not funny. The lights went out again. The Deli Killer struck again. This time it was pickle slices. More screams, more curses, lights on and then off again. Flying potato salad ended the game forever. The Deli Killer was never identified or captured. The perfect crime had been committed. Almost . . .

When I appeared on my first *Tonight Show*, I received a lot of letters. One of them was from Michele Weinstein, whom I hadn't seen since we graduated high school. She congratulated me on my appearance on the show and wished me the best of luck in my career in show business. There was a P.S. to her letter.

"P.S. David, I still have my childhood blackboard with the stains on it from the pickles you threw at my birthday party."

She knew all the time. I told you she was a classy lady.

MANNEQUINS

All my life I have felt sorry for store mannequins. They're usually so beautiful, so handsome, so young, and so full of life. They are always dressed so magnificently, ready to step out and enjoy all the wonders and excitement of the world, but instead, they stare without seeing, appearing so lifelike but without feelings, looking so active but not moving, frozen in motion. With so much to do, to see, to hear, to touch, to taste, to feel, they do see, hear, touch, taste, and feel nothing. Dead life. As a little boy, when I looked at mannequins in store windows, I used to wish I could say the magic words that would bring them to life, that would free them. I still do. I'd also like to have a magic word that would turn real people into mannequins.

BECOMING MEN

The legal age for drinking alcohol in Pennsylvania used to be twenty-one. In New Jersey it was eighteen. Now, every teenage boy knows he is not a man until he sits in a bar or nightclub and orders drinks.

Twelve of us guys walked into this bar in Jersey that was known for having the sharpest and the easiest-to-pick-up chicks in the area. The older guys reveled in their stories about the girls from this bar they met and laid.

Now, I must take a moment to explain that Jewish guys know very little about hard alcohol. We are given holiday wine to drink from the time we are infants, but there is not too much hard liquor drinking among Jews. If we buy ten quarts of beer a year among the six and a half million of us in America, it is a lot. Jews are rarely found hanging around bars with the guys bending elbows. It is just not our thing. I've always been glad that it isn't, too. Maybe that is why we are second only to the Chinese Americans in our low rate of alcoholism. Crime, too, by the way.

Anyway, as we sat at our table, we decided that in order not to look underage and inexperienced, one of us should order the drinks for all twelve. For some reason, I was selected. Someone said it was because I had once dated a girl who was in her twenties. Very logical, right?

I looked over the drink menu, as though I understood it. When the waiter came over to our table, I looked him right in the eyes, and, in my deepest and most mature voice, ordered the drinks. "Twelve pink ladies, please."

Man, did we feel like twelve pink assholes when we got those long-stemmed glasses with the pink gook in them, the paper umbrella with maraschino cherry on top. Did we pick up any older women that night and get laid? Are you serious?

CROSSROADS

Although she was only fourteen years old, she already looked like a mixture of Susan Hayward and Rita Hayworth. I was a year older and had a crush on her. She had a crush on a friend of mine and had virginal sex with him in the backseat of a car one night at a drive-in theater. My friend could never resist bragging. By the following evening everyone in the neighborhood knew every detail of it. She was branded. After high school she disappeared. The rumor was that she had gone to New York and had become a hooker.

Six years later, I and my date were with two other couples. We had just come out of the movies and were trying to decide where to eat. A loud, course voice bellowed into our conversation. "Come on, baby, let's see this one."

The guy was in his late fifties, wearing the uniform of the upright American businessman—blue suit, white shirt, maroon tie, brown oxfords, big belly, name tag, alcohol breath, and slobbering mouth. With him was a woman in her early twenties. The too-tight, too-short dress revealed a gorgeous body, and under the thick, bright makeup there was natural beauty.

She was trying to pull him away from the movie line. He tugged her arm, forcing her to spin and almost lose her balance. Our eyes met. She stared at me and then smiled warmly as she walked over to me. We hugged tightly.

"How ya doin', Stephanie?"

"Great. How you doin' David?"

"Terrific."

"I heard you're doin' documentaries. I'm so proud of you."

"Thanks. I've been lucky."

"No, it's not luck. Even when we were kids you said you were going to be somebody, and you did it. You even got better looking."

The drunk had purchased the movie tickets. He waved them in the air, screeching like a wounded elephant. "Come on, Melody, baby, let's go."

"Stage name. You like?" She half smiled.

I nodded.

"You comin', bitch, or do I have to drag you by the hair?"

"You okay, Stephanie? You want me to take care of that loudmouth for you?"

"No, I'm fine, David. Thanks. Well, it was good—"

"Listen, Stephanie, when we were kids . . . I mean like . . . I . . . What I mean is . . . Shit, I had a big crush on you when we were little kids and thought you were beautiful. You still are."

"Melody, goddamn it."

Her eyes filled with tears. I could hardly hear her voice. "Thank you, darling David."

"Melody, you better get your ripe ass over—"

She turned toward him. "Hold your goddamn water, putz."

She turned back to me. She didn't say anything, just looked deeply into my eyes, as though she could see a wonderful scene from the past that never happened but could have, and then touched my cheek gently with her small delicate hand. She spun around and with great, lively, sexy bouncing steps approached the drunk, throwing her arm around his bloated neck. As they entered the theater, she whispered something into his ear and he roared with raucous laughter.

Some people should remain just memories.

THE HONEYMOON SUITE

I took off in a friend's convertible from Philly to clear out my head. I needed a few days away from everything and everyone. I drove sleeplessly down Route 1. Outside of Daytona, Florida, the driving finally got to me, and exhaustion set in. I pulled into a motel. It was after midnight. I entered the office and spoke to the clerk. "A room, please."

"No rooms. Sorry."

"You've got to have something. I just can't drive another foot."

"Wish I could help you. Honest. But everyone's here for the races."

"Listen, I'll take anything, a sofa in the back room, a cot in an office, anything, and I'll pay."

"You married? With your wife?"

"No, I just look this way 'cause I've been driving without sleep. What's that got to do with a room anyway?"

" 'Cause we got a honeymoon suite, and—"

"I'll take it."

"But it's a real honeymoon, honeymoon suite."

"I don't care if it comes with a honeymoon couple. I'm exhausted. I'll take it."

"Well, you may change your mind when you see it. Tell you what. I'll only charge you for a regular room."

"Thanks."

"That's easy for you to say now. Here's the key."

He wasn't kidding. Everything in the suite was either pink, purple, gold, or all three. A monster round water bed was the main piece of furniture. Above it, hanging on the thickest fake gold chain the size of the *Queen Elizabeth II* anchor, was a purple-encased color TV. On pedestals around the room were large plaster of Paris nude statues. The ceiling and walls were mirrored, some with murals of naked women holding urns on their shoulders. At the foot of the bed, sunken in the purple rug, was a huge round pink Jacuzzi. The words "gauche," "gaudy," and "disgustingly ugly" would not do it justice. If people could throw up a room, this would be it.

I laughed as I quickly peeled off my clothes and flopped into the bed. The bed probably stayed up all night waiting for the other person to join me.

When I awoke the next morning, peeked out the window, and saw the beautiful swimming pool and the Florida sunshine, I decided to spend the hot daytime hours relaxing there and finish the drive to Miami in the cool night.

When I walked out of my pink, purple, and gold door, everyone sitting by the pool looked at me and started to whisper and giggle. Of course, they were witnessing a newly married man on the morning after his honeymoon night. The idea rocketed into my head.

I walked somewhat laboriously to the pool attendant's desk for the morning paper, then to two lounge chairs, one for me and one for my newly wedded wife, of course. I smiled at the curious onlookers and slowly sat down in my lounge and began reading the paper.

Periodically, I'd glance at my watch and look back at the honeymoon suite. After about a half hour, I folded my newspaper, sprang out of the lounge, and briskly walked over to my suite and entered. When I peeked out, I could see everyone was chattering, laughing and pointing toward my suite.

After a half hour I sluggishly opened the door of my suite and stepped outside. I turned and looked into the darkness of the room. "Honey-love, I'll see you by the pool. Okay, sweetie pie? Bye, sugar lips."

I turned and ever so slowly, with legs parted slightly, made it back to my lounge chair, where I flopped down, my motionless head flattened, my droopy eyes looking toward the heavens. I ignored the giggling.

After not moving for about twenty minutes, I struggled up on one elbow, looked at my watch, peered toward my suite for a few minutes. Then I gingerly rose and slowly, legs farther apart, waddled my way back to my suite and entered.

After sitting on the unmade bed for a half hour, I staggered out into the bright sunlight. Leaning against the frame of the open door, I called inside: "Honey, I'm going back to the pool. It's a beautiful day, sweetie pie. You should get out of bed, tulip face. See you out here, sugar-plum darling."

I staggered weakly to my lounge chair and crashed into it, where I remained dead to the world for twenty minutes. The muted voices and laughter of the poolside crowd was continuous. When I propped myself up on one elbow and strained to see the dial of my watch, the laughter was thunderous. I ignored it and, with great physical strain, managed to get to my shaky legs and, only through great tenacity, work my way back to my honeymoon suite. Loud laughter accompanied every painful step.

Twenty minutes later, I opened the door an inch at a time and came outside like a butterfly working its way out of a cocoon. My bathing suit was on backward and very low. The roar of the poolside spectators was deafening. I propped my limp body against the wall until the laughter subsided, then called into the suite: "Honey babe, darling duck feathers, please, my pussy willow, you must come out. For both our sakes, my sugar lump. Get out of bed, my evergreen tree. Pleeeeeeze."

I then weaved like a drunk to my lounge chair and collapsed across it, motionless, ignoring the explosion of laughter. After about twenty minutes or so, my broken neck rose, my squinted eyes tried desperately to focus on the hands of my watch, my tortured body inched its way to a seated position until my wobbly legs could support my body weight. Like the last thirty feet of pavement for a dying marathon runner, I miraculously made it back to my suite.

After about fifteen minutes inside, I threw open the door to my suite but didn't come out for several minutes. Then I fell out. From the pavement, I gasped into the darkened room, "Please, pumpkin pie, come out, come out, come out, please, please, please."

I feebly swung the door closed and crawled back to poolside, resting one arm on my lounge chair, my limp body draped across the ground. I spent the next half hour using whatever energy remained in my body for climbing onto my chair. The crowd at poolside had tripled, as had the volume of laughter. As soon as I got all my body on top of the lounge, I looked blindly at my watch and then toward the suite.

With the greatest effort and personal perseverance, I literally belly-crawled back to my suite. From the prone position, I reached up and opened the door, and crawled inside. I then leaped to my feet, took a long hot shower, dressed, packed, made a few phone calls, and with my small overnight bag in one hand, I opened the door ever so slowly. I could see that every poolside eye was on the door. I put out one leg, then the other, then the rest of me. I leaned my back against the wall. I turned my head toward the open door. "I'm giving you one more chance, my peanut-butter cup. Get out of bed. I can't do it anymore. I'll die, my rose petal. My dick is not made of stainless steel, my apple dumpling. . . . What? I said my dick is not made of apple dumpling, my stainless steel. Meet me in Miami. *Adieu, ma cherie.*"

I staggered a few steps and then collapsed to the ground, raised myself up, and repeated the performance all the way to my car.

I laughed continuously all the way to Miami. Not only at all that I said and did but at the image of all those people waiting for my wife to exit, possibly even sneaking up to the suite to try to peek inside. And, wherever you may be my nonexistent, invisible honey cup, pumpkin-pie sweetheart, come join me anytime, anywhere. I'll never forget all those hours we never spent together.

GUTEN NACHT, FRAULEIN (GOOD NIGHT, MISS)

A friend and I were double dating in a small, intimate, dimly lit disco in the basement of one of New York's best Fifth Avenue hotels. The crowd was always mostly European. My friend's date was also European, a German girl who was a flight attendant for Lufthansa, the airline of Germany.

The evening was going along just fine, until the flight attendant began belting down shot after shot of straight cognac. The more she drank, the more she talked. The more she talked, the more anti-Semitic she became. As soon as she uttered the first nasty remark, I was on her case.

"*Bitte, Fraulein.* Your anti-Semitism is showing at the wrong time with the wrong person. I'm Jewish. *Ich bin ein Jude.*"

She just stared at me through her mouse-sized blue eyes, sipping her cognac and uttering more insults about Jews. As time and alcohol progressed, her words became slurred, her German accent thickened, and her hatred became more obnoxious. I turned to my friend. "If you don't put a cork in her mouth, pal, I'm going to shove her cognac bottle up her Nazi ass."

"Come on, David, she's drunk."

"What the hell does that have to do with it? Next you'll tell me Hitler was tipsy when he ordered everyone into the ovens. Muzzle her or get her out of here."

He did neither. She kept drinking. By the end of the evening, we had a ranting Nazi concentration-camp commandant with us. I knew that given the opportunity, she would blow my brains out. Finally, she just passed out. We had a pleasant time the rest of the night. At closing time, my friend went to the men's room and I paid the check. When he returned, he looked around. "Where's Ursula?"

"I stuffed her under the booth. Let's go."

"Seriously, David, where'd she go? The ladies' room?"

"Seriously, I stuffed her under the booth. Here, look."

I lifted the leather cover off the floor. Her arm fell out. I pushed it back and let go of the cover.

"Christ, is she . . ."

"No, unfortunately. Just drunk. Let's go."

"But, David, she's got an early flight out of JFK. If she doesn't show up, she'll get fired. You can't leave her there. She'll wake up in the middle of the night and not know where she is. You can't just—"

"Let me tell you something, pal. I've never turned my back on anti-Semitism, no matter how small or how big. If everyone had done that in the 1930s, there'd be six and a half million more of us. It's your choice. Me or the Nazi."

As the three of us were leaving, I heard the manager close the big lock on the large metal gates that separated the disco from the stairs leading up to the hotel lobby. I smiled and walked out. I don't remember the New York night air smelling so pure and clean. I took a real deep breath and felt real, real good.

NEVER AGAIN!

ONE DISADVANTAGE

There is a small spot on a person's back about the size of a quarter that is unreachable, regardless of what contortions you go through, how flexible you are, even if you're double-jointed. This is a real annoyance, especially when that is exactly where you have an itch or when you want to apply suntan lotion.

Well, by putting one hand over the opposite shoulder (say right hand over left shoulder) and the other hand up the back from the base of the spine with the palm facing outward, you can come pretty close to the target. The only way of hitting a bull's-eye is to ask a female companion to help you. This is the only disadvantage I have ever found to being a bachelor, so it is true that the life of a single man is not all bliss.

THE GREATEST SOUNDS

The two greatest sounds on earth that you can hear when you first open your eyes in the morning are the gentle lapping of ocean waves upon a still white sand beach and "See you in a couple weeks, honey."

THE YOUNG OLD LADY

I was waiting among the crowd on the corner of 57th Street and Madison Avenue when I heard the sweet, old voice. I looked down at one of the most angelic, sweetest faces I had ever seen. Inlaid in this eighty-some-year-old face, like a beautiful jeweled mosaic, were sparkling, bright blue eyes, perfectly chiseled features, and a warm smile. Still beautiful.

"Young man," whispered the soft voice, "would you like to help an old lady across the street?"

"I'd love to help an old lady across the street." I smiled, offering my arm, which she took gently but firmly. The light changed to green and we began our walk.

"You know, young man, I used to be able to get around just fine by myself, but last year I fell and broke my hip. Since then, I've had to use this cane, and it is still difficult to maneuver without assistance."

"Look at the bright side. Think of how many young men's arms you get to hold."

We reached the other side of the street. She looked at me with a sly sort of smile on her face. "Young man, in my day, I did more than just hold their arms. I did it all. I did it all."

I laughed. "Are you going to be okay, now?"

"Of course, young man. Thank you."

"No, thank *you*."

I stood there watching her amble her way slowly but proudly up Madison Avenue, until she was lost in the crowd, but never from my memory.

I thought that I wish I could've pressed a button and viewed the highlights of her life. She must have been someone very special. It was easy to tell that because she still was.

THE FIRST CARTOON

I thought of a cartoon that I think would be funny. You see
Adam standing in the Garden of Eden. He is holding a cigarette
in one hand, a dry martini in the other. He is peering into the
far distance as though looking for someone, and pinned to the
skin of his chest is a plastic badge that reads "Hello, my name is
Adam."

Maybe you have to be a nonconventioneer to see the humor
in it.

LOOKING FOOLISH

I never want to look foolish, whether it be in my career or in my
personal life. If the day comes when I no longer draw the
crowds I draw today, and I can't think of a way to rejuvenate
my career, I shall bow out. I'll never play bars and grills. I won't
look foolish.

In my personal life, I always thought that the one drawback
to bachelor life is someday getting to an age where dating
young women would make me look foolish—for instance, being
in my fifties and being with women in their late twenties or
early thirties. I never would want to overhear someone remark,
"God, Barbara, look at that young girl with a body like a brick
shithouse with that old guy who looks like his body was hit with
bricks and shit."

"Obviously, she's young and foolish enough to think that only
money matters, and he's old and foolish enough to let her spend
his."

"Foolish."

"Foolish."

Get my point?

One lovely spring afternoon, I was walking down Third Avenue. Coming toward me was a man about fifty-eight or sixty
years old. He was dressed in a contemporary way, but not too
youthful. His hair was white and well cut, his face tan, his back
straight, his walk bouncy, his eyes alive, his laughter contagious.
A happy, happy man. Holding onto his arm was a fantastically

beautiful Eurasian woman about twenty-six years old. She, too, was laughing and happy. You could tell they were crazy about each other.

Walking about ten feet behind this vivacious couple was another man and woman. The man was the same age as the other one. Only he was wearing a baggy pin-striped suit, and a white on white shirt and a wide tie, both of which had gone out of style in the 1960s. The uniform of his generation. His hair was also gray, but it was slicked back, parted on one side. His face was big-city white. He shuffled slowly, not lifting his feet, his eyes were dull and dreamy, and there was no laughter. An unhappy, unhappy man. Walking with him, but not holding his arm, was a female version of him, with some exceptions. Her hair was bleached blond, her clothes were well tailored and expensive. However, their facial expressions were the same. They didn't talk. They didn't look at each other. They just shuffled along together and alone.

It was at that moment that I realized that the man with the young woman didn't look foolish; the other one did. Why the hell did he let himself grow old? While he was schlepping in and out of the front door of his house, his spirit for life was climbing out the back window. Foolish.

I am no longer worried, for I know that I'll never look foolish.

STILL CHUGGING AFTER ALL THESE YEARS

I started "taking out" girls at a very young age—nine. Two years later, I had already developed a philosophy about altering one's life to accommodate someone of the opposite sex. I first expressed it when one of my childhood dates complained about something or another that may or may not have been valid. I really didn't care.

When she finished, I spoke softly but deliberately. "I heard everything you said, but you've got to think of me like I'm a train. I'm going in a certain direction, toward a certain place, at a certain speed. Don't try to change the direction, the place, or the speed. If you don't like anything, then, as the train slows down a little, jump off and get on another train, because I'm not going to change—for you or for anyone, only for myself."

I never thought that not only would I be saying these lines again, but that I'd be saying them over and over and over again my whole life. I still most definitely and emphatically feel and believe as I did back then.

Nowadays, there is only one passenger on my train. She got on not too long ago. So far she is enjoying the ride and I love having her, so open up the throttle, full speed ahead. David and Victoria have a lot of track to cover.

THE LONG WAIT

We are spoon-fed a dream world when we are children about love and romance. While we are being told and reading about great love affairs, about men and women willing to throw themselves over cliffs for each other, no personal sacrifices being too great, we are witnessing the world of reality around us in which men and women tear out each other's hearts, dampen each other's dreams, and destroy each other's futures, while not caring for the feelings of each other, and apparently living solely to torment each other, as they live in relationships that are dead. As we go through life, we witness romance and marriage as it really is, seeing close up the horror of two people who act as though their assignment in destiny's logbook is to be bitter enemies, and yet, in spite of seeing all this happen, we cling to the man and woman world we are told about and read about, hoping that our lives will be different. That we will be the exception to the rule, that we will be truly happy.

I have gone through two marriages, a long relationship, one live-in girl friend, an out-of-wedlock child, numerous romances, lots of affairs, and many dates. I became what I am—a typical jaded, cynical, sarcastic, know-it-all with the full intention of slip-sliding from one affair to another until my last breath, totally convinced that true love, paying-off profitable love is no more than an elusive butterfly that, should it even actually exist, would never fly within my grasp. Then came that night in Dallas, Texas.

"She's cute."

That's how my manager described the friend of his Westport, Connecticut, neighbor's daughter, whom he had asked to join us for drinks in the disco in the Registry Hotel, where I was performing. We were having drinks and relaxing with friends.

"Oh, there's Cathy's friend, near the dance floor," my manager said, pointing.

Cute? She was gorgeous. Statuesque. Blond-streaked hair, perfect features, fantastic figure. When she joined our table of friends, I noticed her warm smile and captivating green eyes. I also noticed that she did not choose to sit next to me, but across from me. I wasn't used to such treatment. I figured that she didn't like me and that I should just forget about her, but I couldn't. I asked her to dance. We did. She was so sexy and sensuous but in a totally classy way. When the disco closed, I suggested that she and Cathy have coffee with me in the all-night restaurant. That's what we did—had coffee all night, coffee and talk.

It went from coffee, to friends, to lovers, to love. Her name is Victoria. She is my girlfriend. Because of her, I have dusted off old dreams. Because of her, I am happy. Because of her, I am. I love you, Victoria.

Some special moments aboard the *Rotterdam* for Victoria and me.

This is the man after whom I named my son, Cole Jay. He was a great rabbi and a super human being. I can only wish that my son takes after his namesake.

However, here's evidence that my son has little chance of being normal.

This is why I play shuffleboard with Victoria. Great form, huh?

Sometimes history repeats itself. I made it happen because I remembered how happy I was when I asked my daddy to lift me up into a tree and he did it.

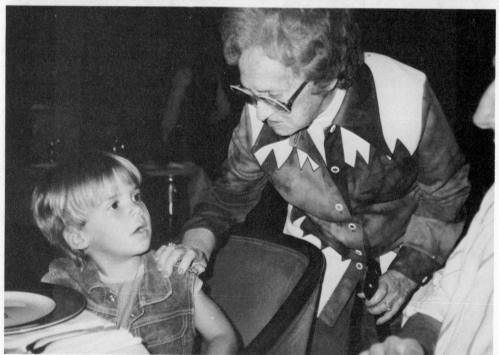

(*Top*). Three generations of Brenner fathers and sons. (*Bottom*). Cole receiving advice from one of the two people who gave me most of mine.

Cole Jay and I work some jokes into the act at the Sands in Atlantic City.

A moment that can only happen between a father and son

(*Top*). My two best friends in first grade were Edward "Dee-Dee" Romoff and Barry "Beb" Black. They still are. With them are their wives Mim (whom I met at the ripe age of nineteen) and Beb's Lenore, whom I can remember seeing in her kindergarten class. (*Bottom*). Brother Mel. No other explanation necessary.

(*Above*). The first night in the castle I rented in the south of France in May 1985. The reason we are so happy is because the day before we left New York, my brother was relieved of a medical scare and I won visitation rights for my son. (*Left*). My good pal from way back and the man who makes me laugh the most, Steve Landesberg, drops by to see me and my family. Not a big drop—we only live four blocks from each other.

(*Top*). Another neighbor—only around the corner—is my old pre-comedy friend and a true one-of-a-wonderful-kind, Bill Cosby. (*Bottom*). A big fight fan since my father got me into it at age four. Here I am with_____: Need I say more?

As a guest during one of my weeks as the co-host of "The Mike Douglas Show," Joan Rivers tried out an audience-directed question—"Can you talk?" Heeding my advice, she changed the "you" to "we" and the rest is history.

Even though Freddie Prinze and I were best friends, we never took a picture together. There were so many things we never got around to doing and now never will. I miss him a lot.

(*Top*). Read "Co-host Catastrophes" for the full story. (*Bottom*). Dad, Mom, and Moby surprise me by showing up on "The Phil Donahue Show." It was a great family moment. By the way, Mom stole the show.

In 1985 my hometown made me Grand Marshal of the annual Gimbel's Thanksgiving Parade, and the mayor, W. Wilson Goode, made me wave to his constituents even though *I* don't need votes. P.S. The guy waved back to us.

What is going on here? To be continued . . .

VIII

ON STAGE

WHO'S CRAZY?

In a performer's beginning days in show business, you accept almost any job, anytime, anywhere, for just about any amount of money. You need all the experience you can get and you certainly always need the money, however little.

Danny Aiello today is a star of Broadway, television, and motion pictures. A terrific actor. When we met, Danny was the combination master of ceremonies/singer/bouncer of a small workshop club on the West Side of Manhattan. The owner didn't like me, so he didn't let me go on stage until near closing, at which time I had to try to elicit laughter from two hookers who came in from the cold, a drunken sailor passed out on a table, and a dope addict shooting up in the men's room. Not easy. However, whenever the owner took a night off, Danny would give me a prime-time spot and I would "kill" the audience. Danny was a friend.

One day Danny called to tell me that he had a job for me, himself as a singer, and another new comedian, Jimmy Martinez. The pay was great—fifty dollars apiece. That's all I had to hear to say yes.

Danny drove us to the gig. It was in an old building on the lower West Side. We entered a side door in the alley and were led backstage. There was a small stage with lights, a microphone, and an audience. All that was needed. Someone shook our hands enthusiastically, thanking us profusely for coming and saying how much it meant to all the people. Whatever that meant.

Danny opened the show with a few remarks and a couple of songs, which were enthusiastically received. Then he introduced Jimmy Martinez, who charged onstage wearing his long, white doctor's coat and carrying his suitcase of props. Jimmy was going to do his sure-fire never-miss routine—The Mad Inventor. In between weird and funny chatter he would introduce inventions and then demonstrate them. Each invention was zanier than the previous one. For example, he would talk about this important invention, then search through his suitcase and pull out a man's dress shoe, announcing that he called it a shoe horn, at which time he would put the shoe to his mouth and do perfect trumpet sounds. This would be followed by a light bulb, which he would hold to his ear, saying "Hello." The act ended with his final and finest invention. He would take a small white pillow out, ask someone in the audience first to touch it and then yell for him to smell it. Jimmy would then proudly announce that he called this invention a chicklet. He would then try to get it into his mouth and would smother himself, falling dead on the stage. The act never failed, except this night.

I couldn't believe it when I heard no response to Jimmy's first invention. I figured it was just a fluke. Maybe he had said it wrong. However, when the second invention laid an egg, I peeked through the curtain at the audience. Something must be wrong, but everything seemed all right. The audience of about 500 was dressed nicely, male and female, young and old, all races. They were sitting in folding chairs and . . . Wait a minute, there was one man sitting with his back to the stage, and another man was sitting *under* his chair, and a woman was wearing her chair on her head like an Easter bonnet. I went looking for Danny.

164

"Danny, what the hell is this place? Jimmy's Mad Inventor is bombing and the audience looks kinda weird."

"It's a halfway house of sorts."

"Halway from where to where?"

"For inmates of the asylum. They come here before being released back into society."

"If these are the ones they're letting out, I'd hate to see the ones they're keeping. You should've warned Jimmy. The reason they're not laughing at his Mad Inventor is because they understand him. They think he's one of them."

After Jimmy finished, Danny announced me. As I was going onstage, I passed Jimmy.

"Watch it, David, they're crazy."

"Truer words were never spoken, Jimmy."

How'd I do? I killed them! Best response I had had in my young career. I said, "Good evening," and they laughed. I said, "I'm from Philadelphia," and they roared. I said, "My mother," and they screamed and applauded. When I said, "She's a bad cook," they leaped to their feet and gave me a two-minute standing ovation and a roll of toilet paper.

For the next fifteen minutes, I just said whatever word, phrase, or sentence popped into my mind. Every syllable I uttered was met with enthusiastic laughter and applause and a few foreign objects flying up onstage and one person from the audience doing a breast stroke across the stage behind me.

Never in the history of show business have so few words done so much for so many for so little reason. It was truly my finest quarter hour.

THE PLAY IS HALF THE THING

During my first month as a comedian, I met a young man who was a brilliant comedian and was to become one of my best friends. He is still both. In those early career days, Steve Landesberg, like the rest of us, was most often low on funds—broke. He loved the theater but never had the money to enjoy this luxury. What he used to do was put on a suit and tie and show up at the theater at intermission. He would mingle with the crowd outside. When the bell rang to announce the start of the second half of the play, Steve would move inside with everyone else. There is almost always one empty seat at every performance of every play, no matter how popular and how in demand. It just figures statistically that in any crowd of a few hundred persons, someone is going to be sick in bed with the flu or something else. Steve would sit in the sick person's seat and enjoy live theater.

Steve Landesberg knows more about the second half of more Broadway and Off Broadway plays than any other man in America. Of course, today Steve is now able to pay for the best seat for any play on Broadway. He is able to but I'm not sure if he does. What a funny, strange, and wonderful guy.

THE HUMAN PRETZEL

It was so difficult to get paying jobs as a new comedian. One place that afforded us an opportunity to work on our craft and get paid while doing it was the Cellar Door in Georgetown, outside of central Washington, D.C. Not only was it a good comedy room, you also got reviews in the newspaper, saw your name printed on a card in the window, and were paid up to $600 for the week, out of which you had to pay 25 percent to manager and agent, your air fare, hotel room, transportation to and from the club, food, drink, gratuities, rent for your apartment for the week, plus city, state, and federal taxes. It doesn't take a mathematical genius to figure out that each week worked at this club cost the entertainer between $100 and $200. It doesn't take a genius to also figure out that anyone who works at this big a loss is a schmuck. Well, no one ever said that comedians aren't schmucks. Maybe "schmuck" isn't the right word, maybe "strange" is better. Yes, it is for certain that we comedians are a strange breed. We are people who see the funny side of everything, who escape the oddities and inequities and hurts of life through the sound of laughter and take strangers along with us. Actually, it is a wonderful way to be strange.

One of our dreams, of course, is that we are going to "make it," become a star, and once that happens, you won't run into the red every week and every year. You run so far into the black that you are constantly looking over your shoulder to see if anyone is sneaking up on you to take it all away. But, then again, if anyone ever did take it away from you, you'd probably think of a great joke about it, and that would help you start your comeback.

The story I started to tell is not from the so-called in-the-black days, but from the very lean times. I had returned from the Cellar Door after doing my second show. The manager of the Georgetown Inn, where I stayed, was an early fan and gave me a suite for the price of a room. I had a bedroom, living room, full bath, and kitchen. On the money I saved cooking and eating my meals in, I cut down on my losses.

I had just prepared a late-night snack and poured myself a glass of milk and was about to settle down on the sofa for the late, late show when the night manager called. "Hi, David. There's a beautiful young lady in the lobby who is persistent about talking with you. She's a big fan."

"Oh, man, all I want to do is watch Bogey. All right, put her on."

"Hi, David. Sorry to bother you. I know how tired you must be, but my fiancé and I were driving by after seeing your show for the third time this week—we're really big fans—and we saw you walking in and just wanted to say hello. My fiancé is a foreign diplomat and we would just love to say hello in person. For two minutes."

"Well, I appreciate you being fans, but I just—"

"It would mean so much to both of us. We would remember it forever."

"Thank you, but I only want to—"

"When you become the giant star you're going to definitely become, we can tell everyone we met you and how sweet you were. Please, a minute and a half."

"Okay, but I really want . . . Hello . . . Hello . . ."

The hotel manager got back on. "Hi, David. I never saw a girl run so fast. She's a real beauty. Do you—"

"Listen, if you don't hear from me in five minutes, call my room so I can say I have a call. Just in case they stay too long. Just . . . Oh, they're at the door. Remember, five minutes. Bye."

He was right. She was a real beauty, very tall, very dark. She burst into the room like a cyclone. I looked in the hall for her fiancé, but he wasn't there. I figured he was parking the car and would be up any second, so I left the door ajar.

She was wearing one of those tentlike dresses that neutralize all bodies, but from her ankles and wrists I could tell she was thin.

I sat on the sofa. She sat on a chair opposite me. As she talked about which of my jokes were her favorites, I kept glancing from my sandwich to the door. I wanted her fiancé to enter and then leave with her, so I could get to my food. After a few minutes, I asked her where her fiancé was.

"Saudi Arabia."

"I know parking is tough around here, but don't you think going all the way to Saudi Arabia is a little extreme?"

She laughed. "That's funny. I must tell him what you said when he gets back. Anyway, are you—"

"Get's back from where?"

"I told you. Saudi Arabia. He's in the diplomatic corps there. Loves it. Anyway—"

"But, you kept saying 'we' and 'us' on the phone."

"Oh, that's probably from habit. We've been engaged for four years, so I guess I'm just used to saying 'we' and 'us.' Anyway—"

"Listen, I appreciate your saying hello but I really am starving. Haven't eaten this month, and the late show has a personal friend of mine in it—Charles Laughton—so—"

"Are you into yoga?"

"Only on a bagel with lots of cream cheese. Now—"

With the swiftness of a gazelle she was on the floor going through various contortions. I excused this rather bizarre behavior as part of the phenomenon of people saying strange things and behaving strangely in the company of so-called celebrities.

"Oh, I'm not free to move properly."

With this announcement she swiftly whipped her dress off. I was right. She was thin. I was wrong, too. She was crazy. I immediately had the thoughts any red-blooded American Jewish boy and so-called celebrity would have: lawsuit.

"Thank you very much for this splendid yoga demonstration,

168

but I must get over to see the president on an urgent matter, so if you'll just—"

She was paying no attention to me, continuing her exercises. Now, you're probably disbelieving that I or any male could resist a beautiful woman rolling around naked on the floor, unless she's epileptic, but, any body, no matter how curvaceously gorgeous, when its legs are knotted behind its head intertwined with mangled arms, and it is being rolled and bounced, has as much sex appeal as moose vomit—maybe less. Add to that a male who is highly, naturally paranoid, firmly believing that a tabloid photographer and/or a jealous fiancé brandishing a sawed-off shotgun is going to burst into the room at any second, and you'd understand why even the male's fingers would get soft.

"Miss, or Ms., you'll have to untwist, unfold, get up, get dressed, and get out. Otherwise I'll have to have someone come up and escort you out."

She answered by putting both legs straight up in the air next to her head and applauding her ears. I dialed the night manager. She went into a human crab position.

"Hi, David Brenner. Send security. I've got a human pretzel naked in the middle of my living room."

He laughed and hung up. I redialed. "Look, I'm serious. No joke. Right now, her ankles are behind her head and are rubbing together. She's propped up on her hands and is beginning to spin. Get the guard up here immediately."

"David, you're the funniest, man, but you're also the weirdest. Good night."

I redialed. "I'm going to get shot and you're going to read about it in the papers and cry because you could've saved my life. I swear to you that there is a human pretzel right in front of me. Oh, now she's spinning on one hand. She doesn't even look human anymore. I've got a raving loony bug on my hands, actually on my rug. Help!"

"You're serious, aren't you?"

"Any more serious, I'd be a banker in small loans."

"Charlie'll be right up."

"Thanks. The door's open."

She was now folded up like the Gordian knot. I could've put a sticker on her, taken her to the airport, and checked her as luggage on a flight to Cincinnati. I considered it.

Charlie, the night watchman, knocked and entered. He must've been a retired D.C. cop, long retired. I'd say he was in his early eighties. He was carrying a lighted flashlight. When he saw the bundle on the floor, with a tit here and a tit there, here a vagina, there a vagina, everywhere a vagina, his mouth dropped open and his eyes expanded into two golf balls. Finally he spoke. "Did you do this to her?"

"Are you crazy? Just get her out of here."

"How?"

"I don't care. With a meat hook. I don't care."

I knew I'd have to take the initiative, so I took the watchman by the arm and led him over to the body. When I was finally able to locate her eyes, I looked into them and spoke softly. "How ya doin'? This fine old gentleman, who has been the personal bodyguard for every American president since Lincoln, which was his only mistake by the way, is going to escort you to your car so you don't get attacked. You can either unravel yourself, as I would suggest, or he can roll you there. I want to take this opportunity to thank you for all your compliments and your stimulating demonstrations of the finer angles of yoga."

From somewhere inside the glub on my floor, a mouth spoke. "I hope that what you have learned will profit you in the future."

She actually sprang open, stood, dressed, and left. I tossed my sandwich into the wastepaper basket and went to bed.

As I made my way through the empty tables of the Cellar Door, after the third and last show that Saturday, I heard an all-too-familiar voice: "Hi, David. I'd like you to meet my fiancé, who has just returned from Saudi Arabia."

It was the human pretzel. Only this time she was dressed in a conservative gray business suit, her long black hair pulled back into a schoolteacher's bun, no makeup. Seated next to her was Mr. Wasp, perfect white teeth, no lips, tiny nose, blond hair, blue eyes, three-piece suit and tie, brown oxfords. He looked like he fell off the cover of *Esquire* magazine. I shook his hand.

"I understand you were very gracious to my lady. I thank you and would like to buy you a drink. We're big fans."

My curiosity was too much for me to say no. For the next half hour I listened to the most normal, if boring, conversation from the most normal all-American couple. All I kept thinking about was how this Peter Perfect had no idea that his woman was a raging lunatic. His future wife was a diplomat's wife by day and an inside-out fruitcake by night.

Every once in a while since then an image flashes through my mind. I see a sheik's tent in the desert of Saudi Arabia. Arab men in sheets are sitting in a circle. In the middle is a human form, bent, twisted, contorted, and on top is this young, innocent camel. An Arab-American arms deal is in the making.

A SIGN FROM GOD

The first comedy showcase in America was Pips at 2005 Emmons Avenue, Sheepshead Bay, Brooklyn, next to Joe's Clam Bar. It was the first place that paid me as a comedian. I got thirty dollars for an eight-show weekend. The owner was George Schultz, a former stand-up comedian whose stage name was Georgie Starr, a comedic genius who allegedly gave Rodney Dangerfield the premise and image of "no respect." George Schultz was my mentor, helping me with the construction and sequential order of my first twenty-five *Tonight Show* appearances. He's also been one of my best friends for the past sixteen years. A fabulous human being. The best.

Anyway, in the early days of my career, especially after my debut on *The Tonight Show* opened up the whole world for me, jobs kept pouring in left and right. George traveled on the road with me, both as a comedic consultant and as a friend.

One job at the Shoreham Blue Room in Washington, D.C., Dean Martin's Golddigger Girls were my opening act. They convinced George that he should go with me.

Because my pay was still far from great, George and I shared a room in the Shoreham Hotel. Although only in his late forties, George wore flannel pajamas. He was the only person I knew other than my grandfather who wore pajamas. I hated George's pajamas. He also wore those bedroom slippers you see in the Christmas Sears and Roebuck catalog. I thought that only gentile men wear slippers. Jews either go in stocking feet or put on their shoes. I couldn't believe that I had a Jewish friend who wore flannel pajamas and bedroom slippers.

One night, George was in our bathroom, in his pajamas and slippers, brushing his teeth before retiring. I called to him from my bed. "George, what are you doing on the road? I mean, at your age, it must be exhausting. Why are you doing it? Did you get a sign from God?"

"What the hell you talking about, David? Did God give me a sign? What kind of sign?"

"You know, God gives people some sort of a sign as to what direction in life they should go, what they should do in a certain situation. It's called a sign. Did you ever get a sign from God?"

"A yield right of way once, but that was it. What the hell you talking about, David? Look, I never heard from God, not even a postcard, let alone a sign. I opened Pips without a sign. I got divorced without a sign. I came on the road with you without a sign. God gave me no sign. No one ever gave me a sign. Does that answer your stupid question?"

"Hey, don't get angry with me, George. I just thought that maybe God gave you a sign indicating why you should be on the road with me, that's all. You see, I just can't believe that with all your responsibilities of running Pips and raising your sons that you'd be bouncing around the country with me unless God gave you some sort of sign."

George came out of the bathroom in his robe and slippers, a towel draped over one arm and a bar of hotel soap in the other.

"Do me a favor, David. Knock it off about God and this sign business. For the last time, I'm telling you that God gave me no sign. He didn't give me a bagel with cream cheese and lox. God never lit my cigarette for me or gave me an onion or asked me how business was at Pips. God has never given me anything."

"Don't say that, George. What about your two sons?"

"All right, God gave me two wonderful sons. Are you happy? Now, will you cut out this crap about God? Look, man, I hate discussions about religion. I'm here on the road because I like you and you make me laugh and I dig show biz, that's it—no God, no angels, no devil, no nothing, no signs, no nothing. Now, let me go to sleep, for God's sake."

"See, you are religious."

"Very funny. Good night, putz."

George slipped out of his slippers, pulled back the covers, and swung his pajama-covered body into bed.

"Signs from God," he murmured as he laid his head back on the pillow. "Ow. What the hell is that?"

George reached under his pillow and pulled out an opened Bible. I screamed at him, pointing to the book. "Look, George, a sign from God."

"Holy shit, David."

George threw the Bible into the air and leaped out of bed. He was so frightened that he didn't even put on his slippers.

"God gave me a sign. I don't believe it. This is terrible. It's wonderful. It's terrible. Oh, God."

I cracked up, unable to contain myself any longer. George looked at me, doubled up on the floor in the corner of the room. "You stupid, tall son of a bitch. You dumb Jew bastard from Philadelphia. You and your stupid juvenile jerk-off sense of humor. Sign from God. Very funny, you demented putz. I'm going to bed—again. Don't say one word to me and don't start with any of your stupid shit."

George picked the Bible off the floor, where it had landed when he threw it up in the air, and put it back in the end-table drawer where it had originally been. He climbed back into bed, pulled the covers up to his neck, and turned out his light. "Don't talk to me, David. Not one word, religious or secular. Good night, you demented Philadelphia putz."

I know that God gave me a sign—George Schultz.

A HORSEY COMPLIMENT

In 1972 I did a show for the National Harness Racing Association in the banquet room of the Liberty Bell Race Track in New Jersey. The show went very well, and as I was walking off stage, the MC, who was a charming southern gentleman reminiscent of the late Senator Ervin of the Watergate hearings fame, drawled over the microphone: "You know that boy is going to make it real big. Look at him. He has a mohair suit and a pawn-shop mind."

I thank you, suh.

SOMEBODY

A fan called out loudly across a crowded restaurant. "David Brenner, how's it feel to be somebody?"

I replied, "Everybody is somebody."

I believe this and so should you.

FRANK PALUMBO

The oldest continuously operating nightclub in the country is Palumbo's, on South 9th Street in South Philadelphia. It's been there for more than one hundred years. I used to go there as a teenager and in my twenties. It was always one of the in places in the city.

In 1974, I had an idea. I thought that my career was at a point where I could begin to headline rather than, or in addition to, being an opening act for other performers. I figured I could move from the smaller clubs up to the bigger and biggest ones. My plan was to do a heavy television blitz, appear on more TV shows as a guest than any other performer in history. I thought that if I appeared in front of the public continuously and constantly changed my comedy material, this would either escalate the career or cause it to fail, thereby showing me that I had reached my peak.

I explained my game plan to my manager at the time, Rick Bernstein. He believed that it was worth a shot, so he contacted the owners of what were considered "B" nightclubs. These are nightclubs that don't necessarily hold the largest number of persons, sort of like the Triple A minor-league baseball teams. They turned me down. No one felt that I was ready to take on the responsibility of bringing in the audience, or that I could turn a profit for the club owner. Rick then called Frank Palumbo, who said he would take a shot. He signed the contract and sent it right back. Rick then used that signed contract to get the other clubs to sign me to headline. I then began my TV blitz, appearing on every talk show on every channel I could and never repeating a joke. Palumbo's sold out all ten days— twenty shows—in a matter of a few days. My hometown was turning out for me. The other cities responded likewise. We were playing to standing room only. My plan worked.

Frank Palumbo and I had signed a contract that had to be lived up to by both of us. Neither one of us had to do anything more than was written on those legal pages. But Frank was from the old school. On opening day he showed up at my hotel with a few assistants. He had already arranged for me to be in a suite, although my contract called only for a room. He introduced himself and had his assistants pile the gifts he had bought me on the sofa—a hand-tooled leather attaché case with matching toiletry kit and calendar book, a beautiful 14-carat gold Star of David with my name on it and a gold chain, and various other expensive and tasteful items: Frank's way of thanking me for a successful engagement before I ever even stepped up on his stage.

Frank Palumbo was the first rung on my ladder of success. I never forgot what he did for me. I never will. Every year I played Palumbo's. It was my small way of thanking Frank.

Frank Palumbo was more than my employer, more than a nightclub owner. He was much more. Frank Palumbo was a rare and very special human being. I joined the thousands of Philadelphians who mourned his death. We lost a real man, a *mensch.* They hardly make 'em like that anymore. It's a damn shame such good guys have to die.

PLEASE BE NICE

"Brenner, I love her."

"Richard, you always love them."

"I'm telling you, this time it's the real thing."

"Richard, it's always the real thing."

"Brenner, I'm going to marry her."

"Richard, this time it's serious. I think it might be the real thing."

My comedian friend Richard Lewis is always falling in love, always having long love affairs that always end up the same— tragically. But this time he was serious enough to contemplate marriage.

"Brenner, I'm going to be bringing her with me when I do the Letterman show in three weeks. Can we get together?"

"Richard, you got it. Name the night."

"I'm doing Letterman on Thursday. How's Friday?"

"Friday? You've got it."

"Are you really going to show up?"

"Richard, if I say I'm going to show up, I'm going to show up. See you in three weeks."

The following week Richard called again, several times. The conversation always went the same.

"Brenner, you're really going to show? You're not going to let me down right?"

"Richard, I told you I'd be there. I'll be there. We'll have dinner; we'll go someplace for dessert. Maybe even hit a couple of discos. I'll be there."

"You won't let me down?"

"Richard, I won't let you down. I'll be there."

"Brenner, I mean it. This time it's serious. I love this girl. I'm going to marry her. You can't disappoint me. Don't let me down."

"Richard, I won't let you down. I'll be there. See you in two weeks."

The following week, I received a few calls from Richard. Just read the preceding lines because they were a repetition of them. Then came the week of the get-together.

"Brenner, Richard."

"Richard, Brenner."

"I'm coming in, you know."

"Oh, really?"

"Oh, no, you really didn't forget? Remember, we're supposed to get together Friday? You know I told you all about it."

"Richard, I'm only kidding. I'll be there Friday."

"I love her, Brenner."

"Good, Richard. I'm glad you're in love again."

"This time it's different. I'm going to marry her."

"Good, Richard."

"You want to know her name?"

"It would help, especially Friday night when we are out together."

"Her name is Arin."

"Richard, are you sure it's a woman? I went to school with an Aaron."

"It's spelled A-r-i-n."

"Don't believe everything you spell, Richard. Have you checked?"

"Of course. She's beautiful. I love her. You'll love her, too."

"I'm sure I will, Richard."

"But are you going to show Friday?"

"Richard, would I spent four hundred and seventy dollars for a gorilla costume if I wasn't going to show up?"

"What gorilla costume? Come on, don't mess around this time. This is serious. None of your damn practical jokes. Be nice. Please. Be nice, for once in your life. This is special to me. I love this girl. I'm going to marry her. Her name's Arin. She's from Texas. I met her there. I love her."

"Richard, I'm going to be there Friday night. I won't mess around."

"Don't mess around. Be nice."

"Richard, I'll be nice. I'm going to bring George Schultz with me."

"Great. That'll be great. You're really going to show?"

"Yes, Richard, I'm really going to show. See you Friday."

He called Wednesday and Thursday. Same thing, so no use telling you about it. You understand. Same thing. Only difference was he emphasized my being nice, and not playing practical jokes on him. I had no intention of playing a practical joke on him. I knew it was important to him. I wanted to be nice. He just bugged the hell out of me by telling me that I *had to be* nice. So here's what he did. Picture this scene. George Schultz, the owner of Pips in Sheepshead Bay, 2005 Emmons Avenue, 1-718-646-9433, and I are sitting in the backseat of a black stretch limousine, parked in front of the apartment house where Richard and his fiancée are staying. It's on West 73rd Street, off Riverside Drive. Richard and his fiancée exit the building. The blackened window of the limousine slides down about four inches. I stick only my hand outside, waving Richard and Arin toward the car.

"Over here, Richard. Over here."

I pull my hand back into the limousine. The black window glides up. Richard and Arin cross the pavement. They step off the curb between two parked cars. They are only a few feet away from the door of the limousine. The blackened window slides down again and George Schultz, armed with a blue plastic German Luger water pistol in one hand and a blue plastic U.S. Army forty-five water pistol in the other hand, and I, with a long black plastic machine-gun water gun in my hands, lunge out of the window. I scream, "Death to the Jew comic!"

We fire, soaking both of them. The guns are pulled quickly into the car as the window slides up and the limousine speeds off toward Riverside Drive.

Yes, of course, we made a U-turn and came back for them. We had a lot of fun together that night. Richard looked like he's in love. It looks like the real thing. It looks like he's going to get married. This is August of '84. I'll update this before publication. After all, I told Richard I'd be nice.

Mid-September 1984. Richard and Arin broke up. It ended tragically—again—still . . .

June 20, 1985. Richard called. Having an affair with a waitress. It could be serious.

August 13, 1985. Richard footloose and fancy free. No special woman in his life. It could be serious.

November 21, 1985. Richard in love again. Didn't tell me her name but said he might be getting married.

February 4, 1986. Richard broke off with above but met someone with a lot of potential.

HOT CHOCOLATE WITH MILK AND SNOW

The telephone in my apartment rang. It was a winter morning in 1974.

"Hello."

"Helloooooooo, Brenner. Come over. Let's talk."

"Cos, how ya doin'? Where are ya?"

Bill Cosby and I have known each other from before either one of us was a comedian. Back in the neighborhood streets of Philadelphia.

"The Sherry Netherland Hotel, man. I'm here to talk to some TV people. Come on over, man."

"Cos, I'd love to see you, but didn't you look outside? It's a blizzard out there. A foot and a half already. Nothing's moving, man. The city is shut down. It's so bad even the parochial schools are closed." (When we were kids, the parochial schools would always stay open, even when the public schools shut down. It was as though they were trying to prove that Catholic boys and girls could take more than others.)

"Brenner, it's only a flurry. We'll sit and talk. Got lots to tell ya."

"Cos, you would've told Noah it was only a shower. I'm telling you, man, it's a full-blown blizzard. I'm like twenty blocks from your hotel. Besides, I've got a lady with me who only has high heels. The storm was unexpected."

"Let her wear your galoshes."

"I don't wear galoshes anymore."

"You shouldn't have thrown 'em out, man. Should've kept 'em like I did."

"Well, I still got my Keds canvas high-top sneakers, but they aren't good in the snow."

"Brenner, put her into a pair of boots."

"Cos, I'm not with a seven-foot woman. She'd swim in my boots."

"Stuff the toes with toilet paper like we did with hand-me-downs as kids."

"Cos, I'd love to see you, but let's make it in a few days."

"Hot . . . chocolate . . . made with . . . milk."

"What are you talking about, Cos?"

"I've got hot chocolate made with milk, man, with milk."

"Nice try, Cos, but you can't con me with that one. Nobody today makes hot chocolate with milk. It's water and it tastes like crap. I ain't walking through a blizzard for a cup of watered down—"

"Milk, man, homogenized milk, fort-ti-fied with vit-ta-min A. Just like our mothers used to make."

"Quit trying to con me, Cos."

"Milk, milk, milk, milk, milk, milk."

"Cos, you're bullshitting me."

"I swear to you, Brenner. I got the hotel to give me a full pitcher of hot chocolate made with milk. It's waiting here for you."

Cos knew my weakness. I hadn't had a hot chocolate made with milk since I lived in the old neighborhood. Cos and I had shared cups of it in our college cafeteria.

"Cos, I'm going to come over, but I'm warning you, man, if you're bullshitting me, you're going out the window headfirst with a pitcher of watered down hot chocolate in your ass."

"Milk, man, milk. See ya."

I stuffed toilet paper in the toes of one of my pairs of boots for my lady friend and bundled up. I hate the cold. Anything below seventy-five degrees Fahrenheit is winter to me. I pulled on a wool ski mask that covered everything except my eyes. I covered them with thick ski goggles. As we left my apartment building, I turned to my friend. "You know when I'll know I'm a star? If one day I'm dressed like this and someone recognizes me."

"David, don't get your hopes up. Even I'm having trouble recognizing you."

With heads tucked in against the wind, we pushed our way up the twenty city blocks to the Sherry Netherland Hotel. I spun around the revolving door like a frozen robot, unable to bend my leg or arm joints. I managed to crash my way into the hotel elevator. My friend pushed Cosby's floor number. The doors closed.

"If there is one ounce of water in the hot chocolate, I'm going to kill that son of a bitch."

"David Brenner, my whole family loves you. We think you're the greatest."

I couldn't believe what I was hearing. There I was, face completely covered, crunched into the corner, and this woman recognized me?

"How did you know it was me?"

"Your voice. You have a distinctive voice. Besides, the mask . . . well . . . your nose is sticking out of your mask."

The woman got off at her floor.

"Well, David, looks like you're a big star."

"A frozen star who is about to murder a superstar, if I ever thaw out enough to close my finger on a trigger."

Well, Cosby is still very much alive. The hot chocolate was made with milk, just as he promised. It was worth the trek through the Yukon. Cosby is always worth the trip. He's a special kind of person, hot chocolate or no hot chocolate.

TOM, DICK, OR HARRY?

In 1972, I was the opening act for Sonny and Cher at the Sahara Hotel in Las Vegas. One late afternoon, as I passed by the window of the coffee shop, Sonny and Cher signaled me to join them for something to eat. They were sitting in a booth with Cher's sister, Georgeanne, their manager, Denis Pregnolato, the record producer David Geffen, and a fellow wearing dark sunglasses whom I didn't know. As soon as I slid into the booth, I cracked a few jokes about my horrid gambling experiences of the previous night and then turned toward the sunglassed stranger, who was enjoying a bowl of cold cereal. "Hi. I'm David Brenner. Are you in show business or do you have drops in your eyes?"

Everyone laughed. I assumed at my joke.

"I mean, are you a manager or something?"

They all cracked up again. I didn't think it was nearly as funny as my first line. Matter of fact, I didn't even think it was funny.

"No, I'm not a manager," he answered in a soft voice, a slight smile on his lips.

"I knew it. You're too artistic-looking to be a manager and not wearing enough gold to be an agent."

More laughs. Deservedly so, I thought.

"Too relaxed to be a promoter."

More laughs. I was on.

"What do you do?"

Without taking his face out of his cereal, he answered, "A little bit of this. A little bit of that."

Everyone laughed again. I didn't get it.

"In other words, you're Mafia."

Everyone laughed. I got it.

"I wouldn't say that."

He finished the last spoonful of cereal and lifted his sunglasses. My mouth fell open. Everyone laughed except me.

Later that day, as he and I sat by the pool for a few hours talking, Bob Dylan didn't mention a word about my making an ass of myself. I would've never thought that I could've become a bigger fan of his than I already had been, but I did.

MY WORST JOKES

In 1972, I was working Mister Kelly's in Chicago. One night, during my set, I ad-libbed several new jokes. That's where I do my writing—on stage. It doesn't mean that I am more creative or a better joke writer than the guys who pound away at home on their typewriters. It's just a difference in style, that's all. Anyway, I thought two jokes were very funny, although neither one got a laugh. I tried them again during the second show and again they bombed. I listened to the tapes of both shows over and over and couldn't hear any difference in delivery or wording.

For years, I would periodically slip those two jokes into the act and not once, anywhere, did either one of them get a laugh, even a snicker. Zero batting average. I could never understand it.

One night, when I was working for a spectacularly hot audience that was literally screaming and applauding at just about everything I said, I figured it would be the perfect test for the two jokes.

"You know, folks, I never tell an audience how I rate them, but I've got to tell you that you are one of the best audiences in front of whom I've—"

Before I could finish, they were applauding and whistling. When they quieted down, I continued.

"I didn't say that to get applause. You've given me more than my fair share of that tonight. The reason I told you how good you are is because I have two jokes that have bombed every time I've told them and I don't understand why. I figured that the best test I could give them is in front of you. If you don't like them, then I'll just have to admit that they aren't funny and forget them. Okay, here goes the first one."

182

Both jokes got the same raucous laughter and resounding applause as everything else I had said that night. After the concert I listened to the tape of the show. I had told them exactly as I had been telling them over the years. Somehow they worked this time. I was right. They were funny.

The next night, in a different town, I slipped the two jokes into the act, saying them exactly as I had the night before, and they bombed. Over the next week, in every city, they bombed. The following night I went up on the stage and explained to the audience about how I had two jokes that were bombing. At the end of the explanation, I told the two jokes and they killed the audience.

I figured out the answer. The two audiences that laughed weren't laughing because the jokes were funny, they were laughing *at me,* for thinking that they were funny. That's what was so funny.

I've never told these jokes again . . . until now.

WORST JOKE NUMBER 1:
When I was a little boy, we were very poor. The only toy I had was a dead cat, . . . which I had to share with my cousin on the next block. . . . He was always breaking off the whiskers and ruining it.

WORST JOKE NUMBER 2:
When I was a kid, we had a girl in our class, Fat Shirley. I always felt sorry for her, because she was too fat to play in any school-yard games, like hide-and-go-seek. She could never find a place big enough to hide in . . . except once. She hid inside an empty warehouse . . . but, we found her. Her arms and legs were sticking out the windows.

I don't care what you think. They knock me out.

CO-HOST CATASTROPHES

Whenever you were the co-host of "The Mike Douglas Show," his staff would try to fill the week of programs with your favorite entertainers as well as come up with personalized segments, in which your hobbies or likes would be dealt with in some way. It was very thoughtful of them, but sometimes their ideas backfired.

I was one of the best street roller skaters in West Philly. I could make moves on roller skates that most kids couldn't do in their shoes. The Douglas staff found out about this and designed a surprise tease opening for one of the shows.

On a side street behind the studio they put a helmet on my head, roller skates on my feet, and a rocket pack on my back. The plan was to have me jet-propel down the street. The rocket expert instructed me on the operation of the backpack. He forgot only one small detail—that the accelerator should be pulled back slowly. The red light on top of the camera went on, the stage manager cued me to start, I pulled the accelerator handle, and instead of rocketing down the street, I shot twenty-five feet straight up into the air and then came crashing down about twenty feet up the block.

Mike Douglas was the first to reach me. He pulled open my helmet visor. "Are you all right, David?"

I looked dazedly into the camera and slurred, "Is this Camden, New Jersey?" and fell back into a fake faint. Everyone laughed and we had a great tease opening for the show.

Another one of my loves from childhood to this day is boxing. I go to as many fights as I can. I've seen some of the greatest over the years. It was a thrill when Mike brought Muhammad Ali on the show one day and "Smokin' Joe" Frazier the next. We had a lot of fun with both of them. Great sports. The next day the staff came up with another boxing segment, another surprise, another backfire. Actually, it was more of a frontfire.

They built a boxing ring in the studio. I was told to change into professional boxing trunks and gloves. I even had a robe made up with my name on it. I stepped into the ring and waited in my corner for my opponent. In he hopped. Yes, hopped. A boxing kangaroo.

The bell rang and we both came out of the corners swinging. I never realized that kangaroos were so fast. I also never realized that they have pride in what they do. This animal wanted to win. He took a shot at me with his hind leg, and if I didn't move as quickly as I did, instead of pounding into my thigh, it would have sent my testicles up to my brain. As someone who had been in many street fights, I reacted automatically, and instinctively threw a left jab and an overhand right, both of which caught the kangaroo square on the nose and sent him flying across the ring. I could see his legs buckle and knew I had him in trouble. I charged, ready with a combination of punches that would have put him down for the count, when his manager came flying over the ropes and into the ring screaming that I was trying to kill his fighter. Bedlam ensued. The kangaroo got a second wind and was trying to get at me. I was trying to get a clear shot at him. His manager and some staff members were holding the kangaroo back and some people were holding me back. They quickly went to a commercial break, during which they got the kangaroo back to his dressing room and me back to mine.

To this day I'm sorry they didn't let us go at it. I know I would've kicked that kangaroo's ass from Philly to Sydney.

DEDICATION

It was one of those obnoxiously early flights. I had to leave the hotel by five-thirty in the morning. As I stepped off the elevator, I saw her curled up in an overstuffed chair. Sound asleep. She couldn't have been more than eight years old. In her hand she held an autograph book and pen. I kneeled down next to the chair and gently tapped her on the shoulder. Her eyes fluttered open.

"Are you waiting for me?"

Her eyes exploded open like two searchlights. Her mouth dropped open. She nodded.

"You're very lucky, you know. I have an early plane to catch. Otherwise, I might not have come down here until noon or one o'clock. What would you have done then?"

Her meek voice said, "I would've waited forever."

"Do your parents know you're here?"

"Yes. They said it would be all right, if someone from the hotel kept an eye on me."

"Is that an autograph book? Is that what you want?"

"Yes, thank you."

"You're welcome. Now, what's your name?"

She told me and I wrote her name and the following words: "And I would wait forever for you, too. Big hugs, kisses, and love."

You can't ask for a better fan than a child, and you can't ask for a better human being than a child.

PASSING BEFORE YOUR EYES

Steve Reidman started working with me as a road manager on October 1, 1976. Today he is my personal manager. He is still with me every time I go on the road. It is not easy for two human beings to get along twenty-four hours a day for weeks at a time, especially under the high pressure that show business brings about. However, Steve and I get along great. In all these years, we have never had a personal argument. The reason is mainly because Steve is an easygoing guy. As a matter of fact, I never met anyone easier going. As a further matter of fact, I never met anyone as easygoing who was still alive. Let me put it this way. Steve Reidman makes *The Tonight Show*'s Tommy Newsome look like a hyper bon vivant. Great joy and excitement to Steve are the following:

1. Book reading
2. Watching TV
3. Watching sports on TV
4. Reading about sports
5. Sleeping

If Steve were ever able to find a way to read a book, watch a basketball game on TV, and fall asleep, he'd have an orgasm. But to each his own.

On one of our thousands of airplane flights, we ran into a major problem. As we were about to land, the large jetliner suddenly jerked violently and shot back into the air. The noise inside the airplane was horrendous, and the plane felt like it was going to fall apart in midair. I looked at Steve. He was ashen.

He was no longer reading his book, which lay open on his lap, but was staring straight ahead into space.

I spoke to him as the airplane went through more convulsions. "You know what the worst part of this is, Steve? I'm seeing your life pass before my eyes. Didn't you notice that I was dozing off?"

Steve didn't laugh, nor did he comment. He was too scared. After we came back to the airport and made a successful emergency landing, Steve turned to me. "Very funny, Brenner, very funny."

When we got to our hotel rooms, Steve watched the Dodgers play, read some of his book, and fell asleep. I went into town and raised unholy hell all night. Everyone has a different way of celebrating the gift of life.

THE GREATEST BENEFIT

I was sitting behind a small desk in a San Francisco bookstore autographing my first book when a young man handed me his newly purchased copy. As I started to sign it, he spoke, softly. "I want to thank you for saving my life."

"That's okay," I replied flippantly, hardly looking up at him.

"No, I really mean it."

I stopped writing and looked at him.

"My father died," he said quietly. "He was my best friend. I loved him and couldn't stop crying for weeks. I decided to take my own life. The night I was going to do it, I happened to have the TV on. You were hosting *The Tonight Show*, doing your monologue. Next thing I knew I was watching you and laughing. Then I started laughing hysterically. I realized then that if I was able to laugh, I was able to live. So I want to thank you for saving my life."

"No, I thank *you.*"

I shook his hand. He took his autographed book and disappeared into the crowd but not from my memory.

Because of a fluke combination of genes I inherited from my father, I am funny. I was given the gift of making people laugh. I am a very lucky man.

THE OTHER SIDE OF A LIMO

The security guards were escorting me hurriedly out of the back door of the concert hall, while the 6,000 fans were still applauding my performance. My manager was close behind me. The back door of the black stretch limo was open. We rushed inside it. The door slammed shut. The two motorcycle policemen turned on their sirens and the limo lurched forward in hot pursuit of our two-wheeled protectors who were leading the way back to our hotel.

I leaned my head on the soft, velvet seat back and spoke just loud enough to be heard above the wailing of the sirens. "I love my career and all that it has done for me and given me and my family and friends. I love how wonderful the public has been to me all these years, but no matter how good things are, no matter how great your life is, there comes that day when you need a change, when it's time to call it quits. It's going to happen to me someday. I know it. I know that some night, I'm going to walk out of the other side of a limo."

My manager didn't comment. He didn't have to. I knew he understood. I didn't say anything else, but my mind projected the images of what I meant on the inner screen of my mind.

I see myself being rushed out of a concert hall. The door of the awaiting stretch limo opens. I throw myself inside, but as the door is being slammed shut, I hurry to the other side, open that door, walk out, shutting it behind me. The limo pulls away with the police escort and I walk into the street, hail a cab, and go to the airport and fly somewhere, maybe back home to New York, maybe to St. Martin, where I take a sailboat across the seas, maybe to the south of France, or the Far East, or wherever I'm never going to have to perform on a stage again, where I can be whatever . . .

"We're at the hotel, David. Could I have your autograph for my kid. He loves you."

"Sure."

"I really enjoyed your show tonight. You were great. It was a pleasure driving for you."

"Thanks. Here you go."

"Thanks a lot. He'll be thrilled. You'll be back to see us again next year, won't you?"

"Of course. See you next year."

. . . whatever I want to be. Do whatever I want to do, whenever I want to do it. Free. Completely free. Just another person, just someone hoping to stay healthy and enjoy the precious gift of life . . . all of that is to be found for me someday on the other side of a limo.

IX

THOUGHTS AND FEELINGS

PICTURE TAKING

I don't own a camera. I hate to take pictures and I don't like to have my picture taken, in spite of what you may think after looking at all the pictures in this book. Sure, I take and pose for them but that doesn't mean that I like or understand picture taking. I especially feel this way while on vacation. Let's just look at the statistical logic of taking pictures during one's vacation.

Let's say you go away for two weeks. You load up with film and pack your camera. While on vacation, you take more pictures than you planned, right? So, now you have to buy a few rolls of film, which involves finding the location of and traveling to a camera store, waiting in line, selecting, paying. Let's allot 100 minutes for the whole procedure.

There's loading the camera. Figure it takes you one minute per loading, and, say, you shoot thirty rolls, so that's a total of 30 minutes. Another minute per roll for unloading adds up to another half hour.

You have to line up people for shots, get them to stand by the statue, near the waterfall, by the woman selling blankets, get them to push the hair out of their faces, look into the lens, keep their eyes open, hold it, smile. What would you say? A minute per pose? Okay, that would add up to 400 minutes.

We mustn't forget the procedures of taking a picture, opening the camera case, removing the lens cover, looking through the lens, wiping the lens, checking the speed and reading, focusing, snapping the picture, advancing the film, putting back the lens cover, closing the case, slinging it over one shoulder or hanging it from one's neck. Easily another 400 minutes.

Don't forget all the film has to be marked and packed. Say you're fast, so only a total of five minutes.

Now you have arrived home. Well, you've got to unpack the film, drive it over to your local camera store, pick it up when it is developed, look through the pictures to select the best ones and the ones you want to throw away.

Then it's time to sit with either the person or persons with whom you vacationed and/or your friends and neighbors and play still-picture show and tell.

Allowing 15 minutes to get to and from the camera store twice, one hour, and a preliminary and sharing screening of the pictures time of 120 minutes, the grand total comes to 1,145 minutes.

Divide this by 60 minutes and you find out that you have spent 19 hours and 5 minutes of your vacation and post-vacation time playing with a camera.

Personally, I'd rather just look at something or someone and remember it, and let's be honest, when was the last time you took out some old gone-by vacation pictures and looked at them?

I'm sure I'm going to hear from Kodak on this one. If they sue me and take me to court, I hope there isn't a court photographer there.

I must confess that occasionally I do take pictures, but of total strangers. It is a habit I picked up from my father.

My dad has a theory that people on vacation always come home with pictures that make it look like they weren't away together. There's always a shot of the husband standing with Mickey Mouse, then the wife standing with Mickey; then the husband sitting on the village cannon, then the wife mounted on it; then the husband making believe he's going to jump off the mountain, then the wife making believe she's going to leap. Whenever my father sees a couple preparing to go through double shots, he asks them if they'd like him to take their picture together. People always appreciate it. Almost always.

One time my father saw a man in his forties focusing to take a picture of his wife, a thirtyish blonde. She was posed cheesecake style against the boardwalk railing in Atlantic City. My father approached the husband. "Here, mister, give me the camera and go stand with your wife. I'll take both of you."

"That's okay."

"No problem. People always come home without any pictures together. Here, go next to your beautiful wife."

"Thanks, but this'll be fine."

"Look, I don't mind, really. Why should you be down here in Atlantic City and not have a picture of the two of you together. Go sit on the rail next to your wife."

"Sit on this, mister. That ain't my wife. Now get the hell away from me before I take a shot of you picking your teeth off the boardwalk."

"That wouldn't be difficult. Look."

My father pulled out his false teeth and put them down on the boardwalk.

"When you get it developed, send me two prints."

The man angrily walked away. My father picked up his teeth, cleaned them off with his handkerchief, put them back in his mouth, and smiled. It's a shame no one was there to take a picture of it.

So, if you're on a vacation and you see a man in his late eighties, with a full head of white hair and a good set of false teeth, come up to you and ask you if you want to have your picture taken together, say hello to my dad. He hasn't changed. Why should he?

COLLECTORS

It has been said that every human being collects something, from paperweights to weight lifters. I had always thought I was not a collector of anything, except maybe life's experiences, but I realized recently that I do sort of collect something—business cards. Let me explain how it came about.

When I was a teenager, I observed this American phenomenon—the handing out, exchange of and respect for business cards. By simply handing a doorman, a maître d', a nightclub owner, etc., a business card, which announces that you are a doctor, a detective, a lawyer, a rabbi, a bank president, etc., you get the go-ahead and get the royal treatment. From the moment the light bulb lit up in my head, I began asking everyone I could for their business card. Then I began to rehand them out. . . .

"Good evening, Dr. Goodman, we have a table for you in the loveliest corner in the restaurant. Please follow me."

"Thank you, pal."

"Good evening, Detective Ferguson. It is always a pleasure to have someone from the force in here. I'll lead you to your table right in front of the stage. Please follow me."

"Thank you, pal."

"I'm very glad to make your acquaintance, Mr. Brothmeyer. I have a cousin who used to be a district attorney. Let me show you our private fall collection. Please follow me."

"Thanks, pal."

I guess I used other people's business cards right up until I began doing stand-up comedy on TV and my face became my business card. However, I guess it is just out of habit that I still save them.

So, if you know anyone who has to or wants to make believe he or she is a coroner, taxidermist, astronaut, FBI agent, circus manager, nightclub owner, restauranteur, fashion designer, architect, interior decorator, trapeze-wire repairman, bomb-squad sergeant, window washer, cowboy, ranch owner, pilot, co-pilot, flight attendant, flight engineer, flight mechanic, car mechanic, car salesman, ticket seller, skycap, sanitation worker, telephone repairman, pimp, hooker—you name it—just have them give me a call. Here, I'll give you my card.

WET-MOP SYNDROME

I guess everyone has something that drives them crazy. Some little thing that seems to just pop up when they're around, picking on and punishing and torturing only them. Sort of a cinder in the shoe of life.

Well, mine is the restaurant mop. It seems that almost every time I go into a restaurant to eat, some guy comes whipping up to my table or booth with a mop soaked in penetratingly sickening disinfectant, which he proceeds to whip all around the floor by me and under me.

My first approach to the solution of the problem is to nicely ask the "gentleman" to postpone his chore until I have finished my food and left. This rarely works. Next, I make the request to either the hostess or manager. This, more often than not, also fails. It finally ends with me slipping one or all of these restaurant employees some bribe money.

My manager claims that this happens to me simply because I eat at odd hours of the day and night. He's probably right, but I have the distinct feeling that if I were on death row, about to begin eating my last meal, some idiot would come into my cell and start mopping. The solution then would be simple. I'd kill him. What would I have to lose?

RAIN

I think God invented rain to give dead people something to complain about.

PARANOIA

I've been paranoid all my life. I still don't believe it was the doctor who slapped me when I was born, and I've even made my parents show me ID on several occasions. I don't understand how anyone can help but be paranoid in this world. The place is overloaded with lunatics. Walk down any American street and you'll see some wacko talking to himself, some pervert whipping open his raincoat, someone dressed like a rabbit, a degenerate wacking off, a woman screaming obscenities to absolutely no one who has lived in the past century. How can you not be paranoid?

Whenever someone asks me why I wear a belt *and* suspenders, I always tell them it's because I am paranoid. If my suspenders break, the belt will hold up my pants, and if the belt breaks, my suspenders will do the job. This is actually my view of life itself: Put both a belt and suspenders on everything.

One time, someone who had become annoyed by one of my most extreme expressions of paranoia said to me, "David, why don't you put your paranoia up on a shelf for an hour?"

"I can't do that. I'm too afraid someone would steal it."

I'm so paranoid that right now I'm afraid that you think that you read this in another book and you are going to contact the author of that book and he will start a plagiarism suit against me, so I am not going to write one more word about paranoia. Who's there?

BEHIND BARS

I spent a good deal of time behind bars, almost a year. No, I wasn't sentenced to prison. I lived in and visited them during the many TV documentary films about prisons that I wrote, produced, and directed.

Jail is a horrible place, whether you're in one as a resident, an employee, or even an observer, but it is especially terrible when your category is prisoner. Worst of all, cruelest of all, is that penal institutions, as the so-called upstanding members of society call them, do not do their job, which is to rehabilitate while they incarcerate, remolding criminals into law-abiding and productive citizens, able to join the mainstream of society, able to become one of us. It is a bitter joke.

What prisons do, by and large, is make prisoners more bitter, angrier, more antisocial, and more knowledgeable of how to commit crimes once they are released. These walled worlds are primarily training schools for criminals, places in which you can exchange ideas and techniques so your craft can be better learned and executed. In other words, other than to take the criminal off the streets for a while, prisons accomplish the opposite results than those for which they are intended. Add to this the fact that this failure costs each of us lots of personal money, directly out of our pockets, and the whole idea of prisons becomes even more ludicrous. If anyone with any sort of business sense whatsoever were to be told what it cost to keep one man behind bars for one year and what we get for our investment, and were we to think of it not as the prison system but as a legitimate enterprise, then the citizens of this country would be demanding that something be done to change the system. However, it is not a legit business; it is dealing with criminals, persons who have violated our laws, who have hurt us in some way, humans about whom we want to just forget. Don't get the wrong idea. I am no bleeding heart, weeping liberal, head-in-the-clouds softy. I get sick to my stomach when I hear or read about some criminal animal getting a light sentence or no sentence at all for a heinous crime. All I am saying is that we are fooling ourselves when we think that when criminals are put away our problems with them are over. The reality is that our problems are just beginning. No, I don't have the answers, but I do know that answers are needed and should be sought, not for the criminals alone but for those of us who are violated by them.

It really bothers me, hurts me, actually, when I think that were any of my documentaries to be dusted off and put on TV today, you would think they were just produced (except for the hair and clothing styles), because almost every problem that existed in the correctional system way back then still exists today, along with a lot of new ones.

My purpose here is not to write a lengthy dissertation on the correctional system. All I guess I really want to do is get this off my chest, because it has been there for some time, and I do believe strongly that something should be done to make the system better, although I am as pessimistic as I always have been that whatever I do or say, be it in a documentary film or in a book, nothing will be done. This sort of thinking is one of the motivations for my abandoning my life as a social crusader and becoming a comedian, so that instead of pointing out the problems each of us is or will be facing in our lives, I now help persons superficially escape from the problems for the time I am on a stage or before the television cameras. I gave up the life of trying to change the world, but in spite of changing careers I have not allowed the world to change me. I still believe as I have always believed and feel about certain areas of life as I have always felt.

What I actually thought I was going to write about was some of the individual prisoners I met while doing my prison documentaries. So many of them were so interesting.

They called him Scratch. He called himself that, too. I don't know his real name. It doesn't matter. All I know is that he was a short, baldish Italian with a warm little boy's smile, a great sense of humor—and a fascinating character. Scratch was a second-story man, a house thief who had spent most of his forty-odd years behind bars. While he was working for me as a gofer, he told me about his not too glamorous and certainly not too successful life as a criminal.

"You know, Dave, one day while sitting in my cell I got to thinking that the reason I always got caught was because I never done really good, detailed planning before pulling off a job. I sorta just went into a rich-looking house and got what I could get. Real stupid-like. So I figured that the next time I got out, I was going to make one big score. I was going to do it like the real pros.

"When I got out, I rented me a small one-room apartment in South Philly. There was nothing in it but a small kitchen table, a few folding chairs, and a bare light bulb with a green shade over it. It was just like in the movies."

Scratch loved the expression "just like in the movies" and salted his whole conversation with it. He obviously thought of himself as Humphrey Bogart, Richard Conte, Edward G. Robinson, George Raft, and James Cagney.

"I used to get the paper every day and read it in my room, the society page. That's a great source of info for us guys. Anyway, one day I read that one of those posh, rich doctors from the Main Line is taking his old lady on a two-month cruise to Greece or one of those foreign kind of places. They're going to be gone for July and August.

"The next day I borrow some work clothes and a toolbox from my cousin Dom, who does all kinda odd jobs, and I go over to this doctor's house, making believe I'm an electrician who's there to check out the wiring. The maid falls for it, of course. She really believes I'm a city inspector and leads me through the whole house. Dave, I found out where all the good silver was and where the wall safes were hidden. It was just like in the movies. I mean, I worked out the best way to get into and out of the house and across the grounds, everything.

"I thanked the maid and told her I might have to come back for more survey. She said she'd be happy to take care of me. I wanted to take care of her, too, Dave, if you know what I'm talking about. Good-looking black chick with monster tits."

He laughed his contagious laugh, wiped invisible tears off his cheeks, and chain-lit another Camel cigarette. He blew the first puff of smoke toward the ceiling and winked at me with his boyish smile. I couldn't help but smile back. Scratch was a charmer.

"That day when I got back to my place, I drew the layout of the house, down to every detail, just like in the movies—doors, windows, stairs, safe. My drawings looked like some kind of architect's, I swear. The next week I got in my car and timed every possible route from the doc's house back to my hideout. I used a stopwatch. Just like in the movies. I even allowed for a possible, last-minute detour. I mean, you should've seen me, Dave. I allowed for lights changing and even for getting stuck behind a fire engine. I had it covered from A to Z. Just like in the movies. Man, I must've made fifty dry runs. This time I wasn't going to blow it. This time I was going to do it right. I was going to do it just like in the movies."

He lit another cigarette with the butt of the previous one, took off his Phillies' baseball cap, and wiped his brow with the sleeve of his prison shirt.

"I read the society page every day. Mostly boring shit. God, rich people really don't do nothin', do they? Anyway, one day, it's in there. The doc and his wife are taking off on the cruise. This is it. I call the maid and find out her day off by making an appointment to inspect the wiring. Smart, huh? Just like in the movies. Then on her day off, I go to the house that night. I park a few blocks away. I pick the front-door lock and go in. Man, it was just like in the movies. You know, with the long flashlight and climbing the dark stairs. The safe was in a bedroom closet, behind the doc's ties. Man, I opened it like a can of cocktail peanuts, nothing flat. Just like in the movies. You should've seen it, Dave. This guy had more cash. Piles of hundreds. You know how them doctors are. They collect all them bills in cash and never tell the government. Keep two sets of books, one for the IRS and one for themselves. Doctors are like the rest of us crooks except they don't get caught. Anyway, the safe was loaded, even got a few good diamond pieces that must've belonged to his old lady. Then I hit the first floor. The silverware. I loaded all of it in a couple of pillowcases. Just like in the movies. Dave, it went off like clockwork. Just like in the movies. Then I took all the loot, left the house, crossed the back lawn real low, in a crouch. There was a break in the high bushes, like a little door. I had seen it on my survey. I ducked into it and squirmed my way through the bushes to the pavement. When I got through, I got to my feet real fast and bumped into someone. We both fell down. As I was getting back up, I could see in the moonlight that there was two stripes up the sides of this guy's dark blue pants. A cop, Dave. I bumped into a fuckin' cop! Can you believe it, Dave?"

I didn't know whether I was supposed to laugh, but I did. The image was too much. The irony of it was too much. Finally, Scratch laughed, too. This time we both wiped real tears from our cheeks.

"I gotta tell you, Dave. You're looking at the worst thief in the world. I tell you something else, Dave. When I get out the next time, I'm going straight. I mean it. No more robbing houses. I'm never going back to prison. I learned something sitting here all these years. Robbing don't pay. I've kept my eyes open and you know what I've learned? You don't see no gamblers in here. Bookies and numbers writers never get caught. When I get out, I'm going legit. I'm going to be a bookie."

Scratch is what penologists call incorrigible. Scratch is what I label a character. One thing is for sure. If nothing else, Scratch learned that life is not a movie.

He was in his early thirties, tall and very good-looking. A strong, lean body and a soft voice that slipped out between a warm, friendly smile. He was exceptionally polite. He spoke intelligently. His vocabulary was extensive. He claimed to have a doctorate degree from a university in Switzerland, as well as one from a prominent university here in the States. I believed him.

This prisoner and I sat and spoke for over an hour while I waited for my film crew to set up the next location. I liked his calm, quiet manner and the way his conceptual mind and reasoning operated. His opinions were sound and astute. My crew announced that they were ready. The prisoner and I shook hands and said good-bye. He left the room and headed back to his cell. I turned to one of the guards assigned to us during the filming. "What did that guy do?"

"Oh, he's an interesting case, Mr. Brenner. He had a very successful career as a robber, mostly big estates or very wealthy people in their limos or on the street. One night, right after he pulled off a big haul at a small dinner party, he was sitting at a counter in a diner right out of Philly when he saw in the mirror a couple of state troopers enter the diner. They stood at the door looking around. They were actually looking for a couple of seats, but I guess he figured they were looking for him. Anyway, your friend spun around on his stool with his forty-five and blew those two cops away. He's in for life."

I was beginning to learn something about people, especially prison people. They are very much like icebergs. That is, only 10 percent of them shows above the surface; the remaining 90 percent is below.

He was old. He was black. He was wonderfully interesting. In his late sixties, always smiling, always a few kind words for everyone, a joke, a funny remark. Something to make people feel better. In the short time we had gotten to work together, a little more than a month, I and the entire film crew had gotten to love this old man.

One day, during a break in the filming, as he and I sat on empty equipment trunks, we had a casual one-to-one conversation. I asked him one of the first questions that always comes to mind when I spend a little time with an inmate.

"If you don't mind me asking, Pop, how long have you been in here?"

"Oh, I don't mind, David. Let's see now. I hope I can figure it out. Hmmmmm. Well, I remember Lincoln had already been assassinated."

I laughed. He smiled and then brushed an imaginary spot

from his prison pant leg, the smile leaving his face. "Come this June fifth, I'll be sixty-nine years old, and I came in a week after my seventeenth birthday, so what's that make it? A little over fifty-one years, right?"

I was dumbfounded. I couldn't believe it. This cheerful, sweet old man had spent the last fifty-one years of his life behind bars. Why?

"Why?"

"Why? Well, it was just one of those dumb things a young man does that he can be sorry for but can't change. No, he can't change it, no matter how much he wants to. It happened in a bar in North Philly, David. On Columbus Avenue. It was a Friday night. I was in there spending some of the money I made working in the wholesale meat market. I was having some scotch on the rocks. No water, no mix. I don't know who or what started it, but I got into an argument with some guy at the bar. A big dude. We both had too much to drink. I don't remember hardly too much about it, except he was yelling and cursing at me and I was yelling and cursing at him. What it was about I can't tell you. Next thing I knew we was in a fight. He broke a beer bottle and was trying to cut up my face with it. You may not believe it now, but I was good-looking when I was a kid. Anyway, I carried a knife in those days. I guess everybody did. Mine was one of those white, pearl-handled switchblades. The kind that is illegal nowadays. Well, he came at me with the bottle again. I guess I ducked and got him with my knife, right in the gut. That's what the witnesses said. I stabbed him and he died. I killed him. I don't remember. At my trial I had a public defender. Couldn't afford a lawyer. My father drove a coal wagon, made very little. Didn't seem like this young public defender was too interested in my case. Guess to him it was just another young nigger getting drunk and killing another young drunken nigger. Also, the judge seemed to be in a piss-poor mood that day. Maybe his wife didn't give him any the night before. Who knows. I didn't know what was happening. I was young and naïve. Next thing I heard was that I was sentenced to life in prison. Life for doing something I don't even remember doing. One night. One mistake. That's all it takes and your whole life is ruined, over."

We remained silent for a few moments. He just stared at his feet, sliding them back and forth on the cement floor.

"You don't have to answer this one, Pop, if you don't want, but how do you take spending your whole life behind bars? Doesn't it just rip you apart? I mean, can you ever really adjust, ever really get used to it?"

"Oh, I don't think nobody can ever get used to it. Man wasn't meant to spend his life locked away, but you got a misconception. I don't spend *all* my time behind bars. Sometimes, I get out of here. Beyond the big wall. On the outside."

I figured that Pop was suffering from illusions; understandably so, but illusions, nevertheless. Too much time in a cell. It wasn't for me to tell him the truth. To tell him that he never saw the "outside," that his whole world was within the tall, thick prison walls. Let him think he gets out. What's the harm?

About a week later, we had finished our filming and outside the prison walls we were loading up our station wagon with all our equipment. As I was tossing a sound cable up on the back of the vehicle I heard a soft whisper from directly behind me. "Told you I get out, David."

I turned around and looked into the soft brown eyes of Pop, who continued whispering, a sad sort of smile on his lips. "In the summertime, they lets me mow the grass, and, in the winter, they lets me shovel the snow. I get out."

Seven feet away from the mammoth walls was "getting out" to this old man. To him, not to me. It wouldn't be to you, either, would it? Seven feet isn't freedom, is it? No way.

Another man allowed outside the walls, of a different institution because he was a trustee, had been the leader of one of the most ferocious 1940s black street gangs in Philadelphia's history. He was sentenced to life imprisonment for killing one boy and cutting up another boy from a rival gang. When we met, he had already been behind bars for more than a quarter of a century. While my camera crew was taking general shots of the outside of the massive prison walls and guard posts, he was pruning the bushes and cutting away the weeds. The filming didn't really need a director, so I spent the time talking with the former gang leader and killer, a man grown old before his time.

"If you were able to say one thing to a young kid who's very much like you were, you know, kinda lost, mixed up in a street gang, living in a ghetto, what would you say?"

"You gonna put it on film? I mean, if you want me to say something, Dave, if you think I have something to say that might help someone, don't you wanna put it in your show?"

"Yeah, sure, you're right. Let me get my crew and set up the camera."

I called my crew over and they quickly set up. The former gang leader stopped pulling at the weeds. He put down his tools, wiped his hands on his prison pants, looked toward the sky for a moment, cleared his throat, and then spoke in a hoarse whisper.

"If I was to say anything to any young boy who is like I was as a boy, living and surviving in the streets of the ghetto, joinin' or leadin' a street gang like I did, I would say that what you are doin' is probably because you don't wanna be called a chicken. I know, because what I did—kill one boy and hurt another in a gang fight—was because somebody called me chicken. Now, let me tell you something. A chicken's only a bird. If you is going to be a bird, then be an eagle, all alone up there in the sky by yourself, flying higher than any other bird in the world. More beautiful and stronger. You don't wanna be coming down, playing on the ground with none of them crows and turkeys. That's right—if you is gonna be a bird, be an eagle. Otherwise you'll end up like me, a dumb crow trapped in a cage."

He went back to his weeds. We stopped the camera. I couldn't help but think that it was such a shame that he hadn't developed his philosophy and hadn't striven to become an eagle when he was a young man, when he could still learn to fly high, when he could still be free.

Women's prisons are so different from the stereotypes Hollywood produced on the silver screen. The women in the real prisons, unlike in those feature films, are not very attractive, very well built, misunderstood good hearts who only got into trouble because of their undying love for a bad man, forced now to live under the horror and torment of ugly, heavyset matrons, mean male guards, and satanic wardens. Most of the women I met in prison were, by and large, physically unattractive, extremely common, and tough as a piece of leather straight out of hell. Most of them made the matrons portrayed in the films look like angelic Cinderellas. Oh, they were female all right, but they were also criminals. Quasimodo's sister would have won a beauty contest in the prison in which I filmed.

One of them was beautiful, and not just compared to the general prison population. She would have been considered beautiful anywhere, anytime. In her early forties, long dark brown hair, soft expressive brown eyes, full lips, curvaceous body, long-legged and thin, full bust. In addition to her physical beauty, she had a special way about her. From the first time we spoke, we became friends, under the circumstances, of course. I believe she was flirtatious. Nothing ever happened between us other than good, challenging conversations. We spent a lot of time together discussing a thousand subjects, except crime and prison. The day I was leaving after saying good-bye to her, I asked the warden what the beautiful lady had done. The story was shocking.

"I thought you'd be asking me about that, David. She's a special case. Comes from a wealthy family. When she was seventeen years old, she had a steady boyfriend. Seems that her brother was jealous. It was believed that an incestuous relationship existed between them, but that was never proven at the trial. Anyway, one night, her brother stabbed the boyfriend to death. Then she and her brother dismembered his body, cutting it into little pieces, which they put into little plastic bags and distributed around the countryside from their car. Their trial was quite the thing. Lots of attention from the public and the press, as you can well imagine. Anyway, they were both found guilty. Her brother died in the electric chair, and she was given life. I had just started working here the day she arrived. I'll never forget it. She came up to the front gate in a chauffeur-driven limo. I watched her get out of the car, dressed in the latest fashion, and as she entered the front gate I thought to myself, What could this beautiful girl have done? I must tell you something else. She has always professed her innocence, claiming that her brother forced her to do what she did or he would have killed her, too, cut her up in little pieces, and spread her all over the state."

"What do you think, Warden?"

"I thought about it a lot. I've gotten to know her real well over all these years. I think she is telling the truth. I think she is innocent. I know I'd like to think she is."

"So would I."

Sometime after that, after the documentary aired and I was working on other projects, I thought about what the warden and I had said and I changed my mind. I hope she was guilty, because I would hate to think that someone so beautiful, so bright and alive, was spending her life behind prison walls, in a horrible place like that, for no reason.

In the 1920s he had made national headlines when he was caught and convicted for the kidnapping of the son of a prominently wealthy couple. He was sentenced to a long term and got out in the late 1950s on good behavior. After only a few days he was arrested for carrying a concealed weapon and given life. Rumor was that he purposely let himself get caught because after all those years behind bars he couldn't adjust to the outside world.

When I met him, he was a very old, withered man dying of cancer, who had spent the past seven years in a wheelchair. Although his body was constantly racked with pain, his mind was always alert and his spirit was always high. He was the oldest inmate and the most beloved by both his fellow prisoners and the guards. He was a very funny guy, a fabulous storyteller. I enjoyed the time I spent in his company and with the prisoner who wheeled him around and cared for him. We had some great laughs together.

A few years after my documentary experiences in the prisons, I got a phone call at my office. It was the man who wheeled the old man. He had gotten out of prison and had tracked me down.

"Hi, David. I hope this isn't a bother to you. I mean, if it is, just say so and I'll hang up."

"No bother at all. So, how are you? What can I do for you?"

"Nothing for me, thanks, I really just called to tell you that Pop passed away the other day. The cancer finally caught up to him."

"Oh, that's really a shame. He was a good old guy. I really liked him a lot."

"Yeah, I know you did. He liked you a lot, too. Often talked about you and all the laughs we had. That's really why I'm calling you. To invite you to the funeral tomorrow, if it's not a big inconvenience to you."

"I'd like to but I've got meetings and film editing tomorrow. I'm really jammed, but I guess there'll be a large turnout of all the guys who knew him over the years, and—"

"No there won't be, David. That's why I'm calling you. Only I'll be there. No one else is allowed."

"I don't understand."

"It's the law. When you're on parole, you're not allowed to be in the company of other parolees or it's a violation of parole and you get sent back to prison."

"Well, I'm sure an exception can be made for—"

"I tried. No dice. I spoke to a lot of the guys and they all felt I should represent them because I took care of Pop all those years, and, well, the reason I decided to ask you was because, well, I just hate to think that a man who was so loved by so many is going to be buried with only one person there to say good-bye."

It was raining like hell at the cemetery. As the coffin was lowered into the ground I looked at the man standing across the open grave from me. Even with the rain beating against his face, I could see the tears rolling down his cheeks. He mouthed the words "thank you" and walked away. I stood there a moment longer and then I, too, walked away, back to my freedom in a very strange world.

I sat on the bunk in the cell on death row, twenty-four hours after a man had been there prior to being killed in the electric chair. He had been convicted of murder. He was a murderer. He was also a husband and a father. Wife, children, murder, and electrocution all within forty-four years.

This is not an argument for or against capital punishment. The man had taken a life. The person whose life he took was also a husband and a father. Two men were dead. I was where one of them had lived, had been alive only hours before. Maybe it would have been easier if I had seen the man who was to die. Then he would have had a face, one particular face. Instead, he had no face, everyman's face. He was my father, my brother, my friend, even me.

I could see the impression his head had made as he lay on top of the covers of his bunk. Through the bars I could see the shiny brass crucifix that stood on the otherwise bare wooden table outside the cell. I stood and walked to the small sink. There was a hint of aftershave lotion. I thought how odd it was that a man about to die would care about shaving. Are we such creatures of habit or do habits bring hope that what is to be will not be? I looked down and floating in the toilet was a cigarette butt. It moved gently. His last cigarette. The last piece of evidence that a human being had been there, a man knowing that he was about to die, that he was going to leave this cubicle, walk down a short hall, enter a small room, look at the serious faces of witnesses peering silently through the glass windows, get strapped into a chair, feel electricity being shot through his body—death by electrocution.

I flushed the toilet, watching the cigarette disappear. I directed the film I had come to do, left the prison, got into my car, put the convertible top down, and drove through the crisp Pennsylvania night air at one hundred miles an hour. I was alive and wanted to feel it.

THE WAY IT IS

Nothing is as it seems to be and no one is as they appear. About all you can truly count on in this world are your fingers. Even then, you'd better look damn closely to make certain they are really yours.

GAS IS CHEAPER

The subject of a documentary on which I was working was the trauma of widowhood. We spent several months interviewing on camera women who had lost their husbands. One woman provided us with the most dramatic and touching story. She had lost her husband at a very early age. He had been her childhood sweetheart. Understandably, she was devastated. She sat at her kitchen table, where her young husband had sat only months before, and poured her heart out on camera. She was the most articulate subject we had and played a major role in our show.

We had a screening of the documentary for the TV executives and the sponsors, the Gas Company. The following day, a memo was sent to my executive producer and me that we were to delete this particular widow from the film, or it would not be allowed to air. The reason was that as she sat in her kitchen tearfully telling us how she contemplated suicide, we could see a gas stove in the background; the sponsor did not want this association of suicide with his product. The memo went on to state that had it been an electric stove, there would have been no problem, or if the widow had specified that she thought of blowing her brains out or taking poison or hanging herself, there would've been no problem, but the fact that she didn't specify the means of suicide she contemplated, the viewer might think she would take gas, to which the sponsor objected.

I was as disgusted by this memo as everyone else. We kept the widow in the show with no deletions. How? We sent a memo that I had placed their memo in a safe-deposit box and would release it to the press if they interfered with the film. The documentary aired as is and I hope it did some people some good. I know that it did me a lot of good, simply because I stood up for my principles. It's a damn shame that more idiots don't put their stupid ideas in memos, isn't it?

By the way, I still have that memo and it is still securely hidden, just in case some of you idiots are still around and would still like to cause some trouble.

SAVE THE SEALS

I had a dream one night that all those cute, little seals had baseball bats in their hands, and they were killing human hunters by bashing them over their heads, spilling their brains all over the ice. I was sorry it was only a dream.

PRICE TAGS

In order to earn college tuition and to get out of my sweltering city neighborhood, I spent my summer months as a camp counselor in Massachusetts. One of my twelve-year-old campers was casting his fishing line onto the roof of a bunkhouse. I had warned him several times that it was dangerous, but he was one of those know-it-all kind of kids. I noticed that the boy was suddenly standing as still as a statue. Something was wrong. Then I saw it. The hook had come flying off the roof and went through his eyelid.

I moved quickly but not so fast that I would alarm the boy and cause him to panic. I told him everything would be all right, not to move, and to keep his eye open. I picked him up in my arms, balancing the rod under one arm, and carried him the several hundred yards to the infirmary. The doctor told me that had the boy moved or had been jarred, he probably would have lost his eye.

At our next visiting day, the boy's wealthy parents drove up from their home in affluent Westchester County, New York. The father offered me twenty dollars for saving his son's eye. I refused to take it. To this day, I still don't understand how they determined the dollar value of an eye. What would they have offered if the hook had gone into their son's ear, or his chin, or his foot, or his lip? More perplexing than this is why they didn't offer me what I had expected, the most appropriate and priceless reward of all: a simple and sincere "thank you"?

GOOD DEEDS

My physician, Dr. Milton Reder, has a saying that, unfortunately, I believe is true most of the time: "No good deed goes unpunished."

MOGEN DAVID

I wear a tiny Mogen David (also called the Star of David and the Jewish Star) on a thin gold chain around my neck. People who have seen it on TV think it is a diamond. One fan asked me why I wear it.

"I wear it in memory of one of the more than one million Jewish children murdered by the Nazis in World War II."

"Oh, did you know any of the children who were killed?" she asked.

"I knew every one of them," I replied.

My little son wears an identical Mogen David and I hope that someday he'll "feel" why.

THE REAL DOPE

I was introduced to the world of drugs at age ten. Some older guys in the neighborhood, and by older I mean thirteen and fourteen, sometimes acted strangely, laughing too much and too loudly, staggering when they walked, slurring their words, acting real nervous, nodding out, talking to themselves, and getting into big trouble in school and with the law. Something was wrong. Oh, there were many reasons why kids living in that kind of environment engage in antisocial behavior, but theirs was really different, weird. Then I heard someone mention the word "dope," but not to mean someone was dumb. Then other words came into my young vocabulary, words like "heroin," "the big H," "horse," "speed," "marijuana," "grass," "joint," "weed," "stick," "powder," "dust," "reefer," "blow," "coke," "snow," "shoot," "drop."

When I was a kid, the drug culture had not yet reached the suburbs of middle-class America. It was only in the poor black and white ghettos of the big cities, and because it only attacked poor minority-group members, few other people cared. There were no social-service programs, no government action, no public concern. Only cops. Only arrests. Only jail. Only deaths.

At fourteen I started experimenting. I tried grass. I had been smoking cigarettes for five years, but for some reason marijuana and I never got along. It just gave me a headache, made me forget what I was talking about, made my throat sore, caused the giggles, and made me fall asleep. No thrill in any of that. Certainly not worth any of my precious hard-earned money. Cocaine was a different story. Dealers used to stand across the street from my high school and for twenty-five cents they would let you sniff a small spoon of the white powder up your nose.

213

They would always kid me: "Aw, man, here comes Brenner. With that nose of his, he's gonna snort away my profit." Funny, but not quite true. I liked coke. It made me feel energized, happy, confident to do all the things I otherwise might not think I could do. So, sometimes, instead of spending my money on a hoagie or a cheese-steak sandwich for lunch, I'd do some coke. I didn't do it too often, but whenever I did, I liked it. That's the danger signal.

By the time I was sixteen, drugs were running rampant in my neighborhood. The guys a couple of years older were really into it. We were on our way and probably would have caught up with them if tragedy hadn't struck.

Freddie was a star basketball player in spite of his shortness. He was also very handsome, very popular with the girls, bright and articulate, and one of the few from a family who had some money. On the day of his twentieth birthday, they buried him. He died of an overdose of heroin. Actually, the coroner determined that Freddie died from drowning. Two of his friends, attempting to revive him, put him in a shower and his lungs accidentally filled with water. They were sent to prison. The entire neighborhood was shocked. Society wasn't. News of Freddie's death took up three lines on a back page of a local paper.

The drug world started to close in on others in the neighborhood. The older crowd that hung out at the paint store diagonally across from our corner of Moe's Candy Shop at 60th and Osage streets in West Philly began paying the heavy price for their drug habits. Some of them started committing crimes to pay for their drugs, robbing friends, neighbors, and family. They were getting caught and being sent to jail. Some of them were brothers and cousins of guys in my gang. All of them were friends. In a short time, we witnessed the deterioration of an entire street-corner crowd that we had respected, looked up to, and emulated all our young lives. We started thinking twice. Their mistake was to our profit. We didn't make the move from grass to coke to heroin. None of us wanted to be like them anymore. We quit drugs—for a while anyway.

For me, it was a long while. A new drug, unknown to me, got me started again. I had discovered Quaaludes, or, as they're known by their street name, Ludes. Utopia and Valhalla in one little pill with the number 714 imprinted on it. A friend of mine was in the wholesale pharmaceutical business and got me as many jars of 1,000 Ludes as I wanted for free. I had about 3,000 sent to me.

I found out that if you broke the Ludes into quarters, you could pop them all day and night at intervals so you could have twenty-four hours of happy times. I used to hide the broken pieces in my socks. Whenever I wanted to feel good, I'd just slip my fingers into my socks, pinch my fingers around a quarter of a Lude, secretly slip it into my mouth, and wash it down. I couldn't keep something this good from my friends, so I shared the knowledge and the wealth. I was surprised how many of my friends were already popping Ludes. Some knew nothing about them, and their introduction to them was even more bizarre than mine.

His name has to remain anonymous. He is a fellow performer. In 1972 I was the opening act at the Sahara Hotel in Las Vegas for Sonny and Cher. My pal was working in a production show at one of the other hotels. At the end of the night, after we had finished our shows, we would meet to do some light gambling and share some heavy laughs. He was a big pothead. Matter of fact, his closets were filled with marijuana plants he was growing. Most of the time he was stoned, but in such an amiable and lovable way that no one ever minded. I never did Ludes prior to going on stage. I have never performed while the slightest bit stoned. I respected my fans and had too much pride in my profession to have done it, but after the shows was another matter.

One night we met after our shows and were playing twenty-one at one of the casinos. Both of us were laughing and having a great time. He turned to me. "What are you on, man? I mean, is there someone else who grows better pot than me?"

"No, man, everyone knows you're the best pot farmer in America."

"Then how come you seem to be having a big love affair with life tonight?"

"I popped half a Lude."

"Half a what?"

"Lude, man. Aren't you hip to Ludes?"

"No, man, you know I'm just a pothead. What's this Lude shit?"

"A muscle relaxer, sleeping pill, a downer. Makes you mellow and very happy."

"Is it like you take the best pot, press it into a pill, and pop it?"

"Not quite, but sorta."

"Lay one on me, man."

I told him what to expect and how to take them in quarters and halves, and reached into my sock and handed him a dozen unbroken Quaaludes.

The next night I had a night off, because Sonny and Cher had to go to L.A. to be on the Oscars. I sat in the show room to watch the replacement act. The maître d' tapped me on the shoulder and told me someone was outside to see me and said it was important, involving a friend. I left the show room. The fellow was a friend of my friend. He said that my friend came out on stage and during the opening number, in which the entire cast sings and dances in front of miniature models of the famous Paris buildings, my friend hit a high note, went up into the air, and crashed backward on top of the Paris skyline, destroying the Eiffel Tower, Notre Dame, and the Arch de Triomphe. They fired him, but he said he quit and was found on the expressway thumbing a ride back to L.A. in spite of the fact that he had his car with him in Vegas. He was presently being treated in the hospital and the doctors wanted to know what he had taken so they could treat him. I told him about the Ludes and to tell the doctors I gave them to him and they could contact me if they needed more information. They didn't have to talk to me. They pumped his stomach and released him. So he was rehired for the show and we met the next night. When I asked him what had happened, he told me that he had taken a Lude with his usual couple of preshow glasses of wine. I had forgotten to warn him not to drink alcohol with the Ludes. No wonder he had singlehandedly destroyed Paris!

I made the same mistake with another friend. He, too, had never heard of Ludes and he, too, washed them down with alcohol. We were at a discotheque when he did it. After about a half hour I noticed he was nowhere to be seen. No one had seen him since he left the table. I searched the dance floor, but he was not there. Not at the bar either. I went into the men's room. He wasn't at any of the urinals. I knocked on the stall doors, calling out his name. Finally, I heard a moan in response. I opened the door of the stall. There he was, this sophisticated, handsome man, on his hands and knees with his head in the toilet.

I pulled his head out of the bowl, wiped him dry with some paper towels, slung him over my shoulder, and carried him out of the disco. It was a freezing-cold night. I didn't know where to take him. There were no cabs and I couldn't carry him too far. There was a construction site across the street. I carried him over to it, got through the door, and laid him down on what would eventually be the main floor of a prominent bank. I sat with him until he awoke a few hours later. We both laughed our asses off talking about what happened.

Ludes and drugs sound like a lot of fun, don't they? Well, there's the flip side of the drug world and it's terrible. Take me, for example. I would wake up in the morning in New York and even before I got out of bed and brushed my teeth or had a sip of juice, I would light a cigarette and toot some coke, which I kept on my night table. By the time I had showered and left my apartment two hours later, I had already done ten toots and two half Ludes, and smoked a half pack of cigarettes. For the rest of the day and night, I would toot some coke to go up and then pop a quarter Lude to come down and then toot to get back up and pop to get back down, toot and pop, toot and pop all night long. Only when I was performing did I stay 100 percent clean. But, offstage I started having problems. I just couldn't seem to get through the day unless I was tooting and popping.

One afternoon in 1975, I was sitting at my desk in my apartment on East 69th Street in Manhattan, updating my records for TV appearances. I was tooting some coke a friend had given me. By the way, I never bought any drugs, ludes, or coke. All of it was always given to me by friends or fans. Anyway, I felt some moisture on my top lip. I wiped it off, making a mental note to take a Contac to stop the cold before it got started. A few moments later, I wiped off more moisture and then more. My nose kept running. Then I happened to glance down at my desk. There was a small puddle of blood on it, running off the end onto my pants. I was hemorrhaging from my nose. The coke was bad and the blood vessels in my nose had taken too much punishment over the years and had finally quit.

I rushed into the kitchen and made an ice pack, then I ran into the bathroom and lay on the floor with my legs up and the ice pack on my nose. The bleeding stopped. I threw out the coke.

That night I returned to my apartment. I had popped a Lude. Forgot I had popped it and popped another. A few minutes later I was staggering around my apartment, bouncing off the walls and falling over the furniture. I realized what I had done. I told the person with me to make a pot of strong coffee. I undressed, got into the stall shower, sat on the floor, and let the ice-cold water crash down on me while the hot coffee was poured down my throat. As I was lying on the floor of my shower, I started thinking.

Here I had done what few are able or lucky enough to do. I had climbed out of a slum and had become somebody. I was on the verge of realizing all my dreams. At the top of my life and near the top of the world and there I lay on the floor of a stall shower, wet and cold, like any other bum in the old neighborhood, throwing everything away, all my dreams, maybe my life itself, for a few pills and some powder. It was stupid, very stupid. Worse. It was a violation of all that is good in life. I decided to stop taking drugs. On the very rare and very stupid occasions after that when I ever did take anything, it was always in moderation. A few years ago I stopped altogether and forever.

In 1975 I spoke to one of my very best friends. We had done a lot of drugs together. I used to share my wealth of Ludes and coke with him when he was broke. Now he had made it and was financially well off. He was still on drugs, heavier than ever. I spoke and he listened. He always listened to me about his career and his life. I was like his big brother. We loved each other. This time he listened to me but he didn't heed my advice and warnings about drugs.

I recalled to him how when he and I were both in Las Vegas together, I was working a show room and had invited him to be my guest for a few days. Well, one night I did too many Ludes and passed out at a table in a disco. My friend lifted me onto his shoulders and carried me out, kiddingly telling everyone that he slipped me a mickey in my drink as a practical joke. He then rushed me back to my hotel suite and forced black coffee down my throat and walked me around until I revived. He probably saved my life.

He still wouldn't listen to my advice. He told me that he had his "shit together." I told him that a lot of people can get their shit together, that the real problem was whether you could lift it and carry it. He couldn't. He never did. We had a lot of heart-to-heart, soul-searching talks about drugs after that, but he couldn't quit.

One night, life and the drugs got to be too much for him. He washed down a few Ludes with a bottle of wine. Then he picked up a gun, put it next to his temple, and blew his brains out. He was twenty-two years old. This time it wasn't covered on the back pages of the local papers with three lines, like my childhood friend Freddie. This time it made headlines on the front page of every newspaper in the country, because this friend named Freddie had the last name of Prinze. The same Freddie Prinze who had carried me out of a Vegas disco on his shoulders and saved my life.

A short while ago I was cleaning out a bookcase in my house, sorting out the books to give to charity and those to keep, when a book fell to the floor and opened. It was a book Freddie Prinze had given to me as a joke, entitled *The Gourmet Cokebook*, filled with recipes for cooking with cocaine. I had read it when Freddie had given it to me, but I had never noticed the inscription he had written inside, which now lay open on the floor. The inscription reads:

MARCH 12, 1973
To David—
The nicest dude to be a funny man and not forget the street. Also, someone I love like my own brother. You'll always be everything you desire to be, because you deserve it, and just 'cause I'm giving you this funny book don't start taking this crap. You don't need it. (Sniff . . . sniff)

Always, Freddie Prinze

The next time I visit Freddie's grave, I'll tell him that I told you all this. I know he'll be happy I did.

One night a few years ago, for what reason I don't know, I went to the secret hiding place where I used to keep my old stash of drugs. I knew that I still had some supplies there. I think I kept them available just to prove to myself that I could resist all temptation even when it was so easily accessible. Anyway, there were over 300 pharmaceutical Ludes and a big rock of pure cocaine. I lifted the toilet seat and flushed it all down the john. The street value must have been over $10,000. The value to me wasn't even a dime.

I didn't write about my experiences with drugs in my first book because I guess I didn't want anyone to know about it. It's not something you want people to know about. I've written about it in this book because I do want people to know about it. I'm not preaching to anyone, trying to act holier than thou. I've been as weak and stupid as the next guy, but I've also been one of the lucky ones, real lucky. I have no right to tell you what to do with your life, maybe I'm not even smart enough to. It's your life, to do with it what you want. It's your body and your mind. I just thought that maybe if you were to know about my experiences, it might put a few thoughts in your head. Maybe some of you will want to continue drugging out as always. Well, that's for you to decide. Then again, maybe some of you will read what I have written and will stop using drugs, or maybe, if you have never experimented with them, you won't even try. I've done what I have always tried to do with you. I have laid my facts on the table for you to see. I've opened up. I have told you the truth. It is an ugly truth, but it's the truth and I wanted to tell you. You see, I know another irrefutable truth. When you use dope, the only real dope is you. Think about it and good luck.

LOOKING BACK

What is frightening about looking back on your life at all the stupid things you did is the revelation that you are doing stupid things today that you will someday examine in the future and

220

classify as stupid. For example, writing this is probably very stupid.

NICE

Jewish people have a favorite English word: "nice." We use it all the time. We use it with love and affection. It's only four letters, but it says so very much.

"Yes, we had a nice time. It was a very nice hotel. We took a nice drive through the country to get there. They have very nice service. We had a nice room overlooking this very nice valley. The waiter we had for the week was so nice. He had a nice face. I want to introduce him to my nice niece but he said he had a very nice Jewish girlfriend. We went for a nice walk after dinner. We saw a nice movie and then shared a nice dish of ice cream. It was very nice and worthwhile. Then we took a nice ride home, came into the house, had a nice surprise: Our daughter is going to get engaged to this nice Jewish boy. He has a nice job. He's an accountant with a nice Jewish law firm and they're going to have a nice wedding in June. Don't you think that's nice, Gertrude?"

"Yes, that's nice, Sarah, very nice."

And what about you, my nice reader? Do you think that's nice? Do you think this is a nice story? You do? That's nice. Have a nice day. Better yet, have a nice life.

PSYCHICS

I think that everyone should believe what they want to believe as long as it is not harmful to another human being. However, personally, I have trouble believing in psychics, people who can see into the future. Some personal experiences have reinforced my skepticism.

When I was working for Metromedia Television as a writer, producer, and film director, there was a psychic who had his own weekly show, on which he displayed his birth-given talent to see into the future. He made predictions about people and demonstrated various psychic phenomena. One afternoon, he came charging into my office.

"Brenner, you're never going to believe this. I just asked the boss for a lousy one-hundred-dollar-a-week raise or I'd quit and the dirty bastard fired me. What do you think about that?"

"If you really are a psychic, you would have known that before you went to see him. How come you're still in my office? Can't you tell I'm going to tell you I'm too busy for this bullshit?"

He left in a huff. I knew he would. I'm psychic.

I met a fellow who I was told was happily married to the same woman for eleven years and had three children. Now, I don't know about you, but I can count the number of people I know who are happily married on three fingers. I was curious to know the secret of his marital success, so I asked and he answered, "Well, David, my wife and I went to a psychic a few years ago. He told us that the reason my wife and I got along so well was because in five previous lives we had been married to each other."

"What did he charge you?"

"What do you mean?"

"I mean, how much money did he charge you for this information."

"The session was seventy-five dollars. Why?"

"Why didn't you tell him that in one of your previous lives with your wife, like back in the fifteenth century, you and he were in the army together and you loaned him one hundred dollars and that he was killed in battle and you didn't see him in any of your other lives until now and so you would appreciate the twenty-five-dollar difference, no interest?"

He didn't laugh. I knew he wouldn't. I told you, I'm psychic.

In case you're not psychic, let me tell you when I'll know a psychic is a true psychic and can actually see into the future. If, as I am walking into their office for a psychic consultation, they get on the phone right away and call the police because I am not going to pay them.

You think that was clever? I knew you would. That's right— I'm psychic. The next thing you're going to do is close this book or turn to the next page.

NEW WORLD

It is true that we are living in a new world, filled with push buttons, computers, atomic power, microchips, space vehicles, robots, electronic gadgetry, etc., but you still can't spit into the wind.

BROTHER, CAN YOU SPARE A DIME?

Panhandling must be as old as prostitution. Each of us has had our experiences with it. Some of mine are memorable.

He had a pirate's patch over one eye and worked on Broad Street, between Market and Arch streets in Center City in Philadelphia. His pitch was always the same. He talked to himself very loud.

"Damn Philadelphia. City of Brotherly Love, my ass. City of muggers is what it is. Stole all my money. Can't get back to Pittsburgh to visit my dying brother. Philly is shit. A cold-ass city with cold-ass people . . ." and so forth and so on, *ad infinitum*, until someone with civic pride would give him some change.

I had given him money a couple of times. One day, as he walked alongside me reciting his rift to himself, I joined him, reciting with him verbatim. He stopped and looked at me with his one good eye. "I've heard your act several times. Good luck."

I walked away and he headed in another direction, talking to himself and hoping for another Philadelphian with civic pride, which luckily for him, is a very easy person to find.

Then there was the young fella, my age, who walked up to me on Third Avenue in Manhattan and asked me to give him sixteen dollars so he and his three friends could see a movie. I delivered the only answer I felt was applicable: "Go fuck yourself."

I was standing on the corner of 48th Street and Eighth Avenue, at four A.M. with my good friends Steve Landesberg, Mike

Preminger, and Jimmy Walker, discussing each other's performance that night at a nearby local club, when a guy approached us.

"Could you guys help me out. I was on the train heading home to Brooklyn and fell asleep. When I woke up, my watch and wallet were gone and my pocket was cut open. Look at it. That's how they got my wallet, with a razor. Could you loan me some subway money so I can get home?"

I gave him the change I had. He thanked me and walked away. I called after him. "Yo, mister."

He turned.

"Buy yourself a new razor."

I smiled and waved. He smiled and waved. Did he actually think I would not wonder why he had gotten off the train once he was already on it heading home, got back on another train to come back to midtown to borrow money to get back on the same train again to go home? Did I really look like some sucker from out of town?

Why did I give him the money if I knew he was full of it? Because I had it and he didn't.

I've always liked the honest approach. I remember when I was a young teenager, a bum came up to me. "Listen, kid, I ain't gonna bullshit ya. I don't want no soup and no coffee. I hate that shit. I want to buy some wine and all I need is another fifty cents. What d'ya say?"

Of course I gave him the fifty cents. Honesty pays with me.

The most memorable panhandler I remember was a black kid about eight years old. As I was walking to my TV studio in Philly, he came up to me. He was crying. "Mister, can you help me? I was shopping with my mother and sister in Wanamaker's and got lost. I want to go home to North Philly but don't got enough money. Could you loan me a quarter?"

"Sure. Here you go. Now, you know how to get the train to North Philly?"

"Yeah, on Broad Street, northbound. Thanks a lot, mister."

"You're welcome, kid. Good luck."

I watched him as he ran off to Broad Street. I felt good.

About a month later, as I was walking down a different street on my way to work—I always took different walking routes to work so I wouldn't get bored—the same black kid, crying his eyes out as before, came up to me.

"Mister, can you help me? I was shopping—"

I cut him off. "With my mother and sister in Wanamaker's and got lost."

His eyes flew wide open. He turned to run, but I grabbed him by the front of his T-shirt and lifted him off the ground to my eye level.

"Let me go, man."

"No, man, I ain't going to let you go, but I'll tell you what you're going to do. You're going to reach in your pocket and give me back the quarter I loaned you a few weeks ago."

"Oh, come on, man."

"Come on, man, my ass. I'm teaching you something that's worth a helluva lot more than a quarter. As an old street hustler myself, what I'm teaching you, kid, is, if you're going to make this your gig, and it's a damn good rift, with the tears and all, then you've got to remember faces. You hit on me only a few weeks ago and already forgot me. You're dead if you continue to do this. Now, hand over my quarter."

He did. I put it in my pocket with my free hand and held him tightly with my other. "Thanks, kid. Now, I want you to look into my face. Study it. Pick out something about me that you'll always remember, like my big nose or crooked bottom teeth. Got it? Good."

I let him down on his feet and let go of his shirt. "Now, get the hell out of here."

He looked at me for a moment, smiled, and took off.

Why did I do what I did? Because we street kids got to stick together.

AFTER THE LAST BELL

I was a twenty-year-old going to the bathroom in one of Miami Beach's finest hotels when I heard voices behind me.

"Didn't I tell you to cover the broken urinals?"

"I put a string over them, and—"

"Damn it, a string won't stop people from using them. You could hog-tie them with rope and people'll ignore it. Do exactly what I told you. Put large cans inside and boards covering that. Now, do it."

"Yes, sir."

The all-too-familiar voice of a boss. I had heard it from my first job at age nine right through to the present time. People with authority pushing around and demeaning fellow human beings just so they can feel like some kind of big deals. Some people are so damn sick.

As I washed my hands, I glanced in the mirror at the black men's room custodian removing the strings from broken urinals. There was something so familiar about him, the way he moved his body and head, the sway of his shoulders, the shuffle from one side to another, the crouched posture, and his face, so familiar, something from out of the past, from TV. It couldn't be. My father had made me into a boxing fanatic. I am to this day. As a kid, my dad and I watched Wednesday and Friday night boxing on TV religiously. I read all I could about fighters and hung out at the gym to watch them spar.

I wiped my hands dry and walked over to him. "Excuse me, sir. My name is David Brenner. I'm down here from Philly and I was just wondering—you'll probably think I'm crazy—but, I was just wondering, are you—is your name Beau Jack?"

"Yes, it is."

"Wow! Oh, wow, wait'll I tell my dad I met you. Can I shake your hand? Thanks. Wow, Beau Jack. I used to watch you fight. You were sensational. You should've been the champ. Great punch, great defense. Man, you had it all. Wow, it's an honor to meet you."

"Thank you, son."

We talked for about fifteen minutes. All about boxing. I had a million questions to ask him about certain fighters and particular fights, but I couldn't get them all in. There was one big question in my mind, but I was afraid to ask. As we continued talking and I saw what a gentle, warm human being he was, even in that brief encounter I felt like we were friends, so I decided to ask it.

"Beau Jack, I have a personal kind of question to ask you. It's

226

not easy and you may get pissed off. I want you to know that I ask it with the greatest respect for you as a boxer and as a human being, so please don't take it the wrong way. Okay?"

"Okay, David. Shoot."

"Well, you were one of the greats in boxing. No, you really were. I'm not the only one who would say that. You fought a lot of fights and must've made a lot of money, maybe even over a million dollars. Well, with all that, with being somebody, making the big bucks, with all that, you . . . well, you end up in here, doing this, in a men's room. Don't you hate boxing for what it did to you, for making you end up like this?"

He didn't speak for a couple of moments, sort of just shuffling his feet and looking around here and there. I was very relieved when he looked into my eyes. He spoke softly. "You're right about the money, David. I made a lot of it in my time. Lots of people took advantage of me. And, yeah, I ended up in a men's room, but do I blame or hate boxing for it? No, absolutely not. You see, David, I look at it this way. With my background, where I was brought up, and the poor education I got, if it weren't for boxing, I would've spent my whole life doing this."

What a great attitude.

TOO OLD

I await the day when I can say, "I'm too old to die young."

EDGE OF THE LEAF

I always thought that if I were ever to write a book, I would entitle it *The Edge of the Leaf*. Well, my first literary endeavor was *Soft Pretzels With Mustard;* my second publication was *Revenge Is the Best Exercise;* and you know what this one you are reading is called. A few people felt that *The Edge of the Leaf* sounded too much like a soap opera, so it was vetoed. However, I thought I would at least explain why I wanted to use it. It has to do with my philosophy of life.

Most people in life cling to the most secure part, like the stem of the leaf. Then there are the adventurers, the take-a-chance souls, those willing to venture forth into the unknown and challenge life's mysteries. These persons walk on the edge of the leaf, where one can easily fall off into a dark abyss, possibly never to be able to climb back up, but they know that it is at the edge of the leaf where one finds all the excitement, the true adventures, all the glorious experiences life has to offer. It is here, at the edge of the leaf, that I have, do and always will walk.

There is always a chance that I may write another book and that I might entitle it *The Edge of the Leaf*, but meanwhile, I have expressed its meaning. And, what about you? Where on the leaf of life do you stand? Think hard about it because I truly believe that the shortest distance between life and death is a straight, safe line, so let's set 'em up, knock 'em down, and let the good times roll.

WHY NOT?

My brother first pointed it out to me. He calls it David's philosophy. I never even noticed that I did it. Whenever my brother, sister, parents, or I come up with a wild idea that will lead to fun or a new experience, and I'm asked my opinion of it, I always answer, "Why not?"

"David, what do you think about my going on a trip to Greece for a couple of weeks."

"Why not?"

"Hi, David. I wonder if maybe I could come to Vegas and spend a week with you."

"Why not?"

"Kingy, your mother and I would like to see an opening night of yours in Atlantic City. Do you think you could fly us up for it? We'll dress in a tuxedo and evening gown and have a great time and—"

"Why not?"

"Listen, Dad, Bib, Mom, Moby, I've quit my job as a writer, producer, film director, and I'm going to kick around and do stand-up comedy for a year or so until I find myself. I thought it over and I thought to myself, Hey, why not?"

So, my friends, if you are thinking of something crazy to do, I say to you, as long as you don't hurt the other guy, "Why not?"

SIMPLE TASTES

My tastes in life are simple, but thank God I have enough money to avoid them.

LONGEVITY

My maternal grandfather told me as a child that if I drank a glass of milk every day for one hundred years, I would live to be an old man. I drank my milk for years before I caught the joke. Then again, my grandpop was right, wasn't he?

LIVE FAST

People have sometimes asked me why I live my life so fast, always on the move, always doing, seeing, experiencing. The reason I've been this way as far back as my preteens is because I have always felt like I am in a footrace with Death, and as I get older, I can feel his cold breath on my heels, getting closer with every kick of my legs. I know that one day he is going to win, but until then, I am going to give him one helluva good race.

THE ANSWERS

When I was seventeen years old, I had all the answers to life. By the time I was twenty-five, and right up to today, I'm not even sure of the questions.

BEING RICH

All of us have heard a lot about the pitfalls and drawbacks to being rich. When I was a poor kid, I would hear other poor people ask, "Which would you rather be—poor and healthy or rich and unhealthy?"

I couldn't figure out why as soon as you became rich, you would also become unhealthy. Why couldn't the question be, "Which would you rather be—poor and healthy or rich and healthy, poor and unhealthy or rich and unhealthy?"

I guess you could say that I am rich today. I am also healthy. So, let me tell all of you something. Good health is definitely number one. If you have any chance to become rich, do it. Even if you are unhealthy, it is better to feel badly in a huge suite in Paris than in a row house in some broken-down neighborhood.

YOUR CAKE

All of us have heard the expression that you cannot have your cake and eat it, too. Well, I believe this is not valid. You can most certainly have your cake and eat it. The tough part is swallowing it and keeping it down.

THIRTY-ONE-INCH WAIST

When I was twenty years old, I weighed 175 pounds and had a thirty-one-inch waist. At age twenty-five, in order to keep the same waist measurement, I had to drop my weight to 170 pounds. At age thirty, I was down to 165; at forty, it had to be 155.

The body changes with age. We are at war with gravity constantly, and we cannot win. I have figured out, therefore, that if I live to be eighty, the only way I'll be able to maintain a thirty-one-inch waist will be if I weigh fifteen pounds.

TRADING PLACES

A friend and I were having a drink in a Manhattan West Side restaurant one night recently, when a group of ten or twelve young hopeful actors and actresses entered and were seated at a large table near us. They were chattering away exuberantly and enthusiastically about their near-careers, dreams, and aspirations, bursting with laughter and wonderful optimism.

I commented to my friend, "I envy them. I'd trade places with them tomorrow."

"Why do you say that, David. There's not one of them at that table who wouldn't give his or her right arm to be you. You are everything they dream of becoming. Why would you ever trade places?"

"Not because of their careers, but because they are so young. Because they have more to look forward to than back on."

EATING AND PLAYING

When you are a child, you eat and then you play. When you are a young adult, you play and then you eat. When you are old, eating is playing, and when you are very, very old, you play with your food.

DONE IT ALL

My good pal George Schultz, owner of Pips, the first comedy workshop in America, where I got my first professional money as a comedian, if you call thirty dollars for an eight-show-weekend money, was coughing his emphysema-riddled lungs out across from me at the dinner table in Joe's Clam Bar in Sheepshead Bay in Brooklyn, right next to Pips.

"George, I've been trying to get you to quit smoking for over seven years. You're going to die from them, you dumb bastard."

"I don't care. What have I got to live for? I've done it all— I've eaten Chinese food and I've come. What else is there?"

A very funny comment but not an answer, as George soon found out. George no longer smokes. He got a real scare. He had heart failure, his lungs collapsed, his liver is failing, his kidneys are shot, and he has diabetes, so I was right about the cigarettes. But let's face it, he was right about life.

TURNING EIGHTY

On my father's eightieth birthday, he and I were discussing the great event. He expressed his feelings about it in one sentence: "You know, Kingy, in my mind I am still twenty-one years old. Then I look into the mirror and I think, Who is that dried up old white monkey?"

It sounds funny at first, doesn't it, but, when you think about it, it isn't.

On July 18, 1985, my father turned eighty-nine. You don't have to think twice to know that this is wonderful.

LOOKING WAY BACK

Not only is Dr. Milton Reder the man who has saved me from crippling back pain for the past twelve years, he is also one of my favorite human beings, the grandfather I lost as a young boy. He is in his late eighties. His wisdom reflects his long life. His humor, on the other hand, is that of a young, hip man. One of the highlights in my life has been the time I have spent with this man. Not too many people would list sitting in their doctor's office as a highlight.

Usually, the doctor's office is packed with patients all day, from his starting hour of seven-thirty A.M. to his closing at six in the evening, seven days a week, 365 days a year. However, on this particular rainy April afternoon, there was a lull. For a short time, only he and I were there. The doctor slipped into a nostalgic mood and was telling me stories about his childhood in Dayton, Ohio, his parents, experiences as an intern, his becoming the first Jewish ear, nose, and throat doctor in New York, his experiences as a colonel surgeon during World War II, when he had become close friends with such greats as General George Patton and Winston Churchill, and his wartime correspondence with his longtime friend, and the dean of comedy writers, Goodman Ace.

After telling a particularly funny anecdote about Goody Ace, Dr. Reder commented that his pal was dead, adding that so was everyone else about whom he had spoken, as well as most of the people he had loved and known. He was silently reflective for a few moments, and then he spoke. "It's all a dream now, kid. It's all a dream."

A couple of months after that, I was holding my eighty-five-year-old mother's hand as she shuffled slowly along the boardwalk in Atlantic City. She turned her eyes, which see only light and shadow now, toward the beach and ocean.

"Are there people in the water today, darling?"

"Yes, Mom."

"I remember how much I used to swim way out when I was a young girl. I loved the ocean. There is so much you must learn to forget when you get old."

I hope I live long enough to remember all the things I should forget.

SIGNS OF AGE

You know you're getting old when
- You start to walk down stairs sideways.
- You go out with an older woman and it's not a thrill.
- You wave to a stranger.
- You wave to no one.
- You are horrified how wrinkled your long johns look in the full-length mirror and then realize you're naked.
- You're embarrassed to go topless on the beach and you're a man.
- The top part of your body runs.
- You start to dress in more than six colors.
- You no longer care what you look like at a pool or on a beach.
- The only thing you can get up at night is the hood of your car.
- You can no longer see out the window of your car when you're driving.
- You put on your glasses and then you look for your glasses.
- You notice a piece of broiled fish in your shoe.
- You consume more in your mouth for your bowels than for your taste buds.

- Your hand stops waving good-bye but the bottom of your arm doesn't.
- You notice the perfume you are wearing is the same as your teacher wore.
- You think carrying a radio on the shoulder is dumb but you'd love to be able to do it.
- Kids start to dress like you used to and movies are made about your teen life.
- You can't understand why someone in sports retires at only forty-two.
- You start a sentence with "When I was a kid ..."
- You say things like "What do you mean it's a dollar fifty?"
- Actors start to look old.
- Someone doesn't remember your favorite singer.
- You can't remember your favorite singer.
- You realize that your mother and father were right.
- You start to make up a list of the signs of age.

Who's that waving? Is someone waving? Where are my glasses?

THE LAST GOOD-BYE

I have been to more than one hundred funerals. I have been a pallbearer almost as many times. Death never gets easier to accept. If anything, it gets even harder. I've never been able to understand and accept death, and I doubt if I ever will.

The first living thing I ever saw die was a bird. I was four years old. I found the bird in the street. It had broken its wing. It was a sparrow. I carried it home and my mother and I nursed it back to health. We brought a little eyedropper and fed the bird every day. We made a splint for its wing. After a few weeks, it was able to walk, and soon after it was flying a little bit. It would hop-fly from the dining-room chair to the dining-room table, to another chair and to the windowsill. After a couple of months, it was flying around the house, completely recovered. Then for no reason at all, it died.

My mother helped me put it into an empty kitchen match-box, and we buried it in the backyard, marking the grave with a cross made of two popsicle sticks.

I had never seen anything die before. I felt a tremendous loss and a sense of total bewilderment. Why did anything have to die? Why did there have to be an ending from which there was no return? I couldn't understand.

A couple of months later I witnessed my second death. The neighborhood vegetable man was an old Italian who would ride through the streets on his horse-drawn wagon singing a song about the wonderful fresh vegetables he had for sale. One day, as I was standing on the street corner by my house, I saw the vegetable man climb off his wagon. He was in front of the church down the block and across the street. He took the reins of the horse, trying to coax it to move, but the horse just stood there with its head hanging low, not responding. I saw some kind of white stuff, like foam, coming out of the horse's mouth, and the head began drooping from side to side in a funny way. The horse would lift its head, then suddenly drop it, lift it again, and drop it again.

I crossed the street and walked up to the vegetable man. All of a sudden, the horse collapsed to the pavement, almost turn-ing the wagon over with it. The old man dropped to his knees and cradled the horse's head in his lap. A crowd gathered around. The old man was speaking in Italian. I could tell he was pleading with the horse to get up. The man began crying. The horse seemed to look at the old man and then it shook violently and died. The man pressed his face deep into the horse's neck and wept. I understood. I had lost a bird.

The first human death I experienced was my paternal grand-father's. He was the leading rabbi of Philadelphia. I remember that he was very tall. I later found out that he was exactly what I am—a shade under six foot two, a giant for his day. He had a long white beard and wore a black frock coat and a black yar-mulke. He had a very warm smile and a twinkle in his eye. I loved him.

When he was very ill, I used to visit him and stand by his bedside. He would talk to me in Yiddish and then he would reach under his pillow and give me a piece of chocolate, shaped like and with the imprint of a coin on its gold wrapper. I would thank him and he would smile. Then he would place his hand on my head and bless me in Hebrew. I would then leave his room and eat my delicious candy. One day, my mother told me that I would not be able to visit my grandfather anymore. I didn't understand.

That same year, my four-year-old cousin and playmate Sandy, a cute blonde who was a bit wild—I still bear a scar on my lip where she bit me—got brain cancer and died. This time I understood what had happened. This time I cried.

In those twelve months of my fourth year, I learned all about death.

Three years later, my maternal grandfather died. I loved him, too, very much. This time I did more than cry. This time I felt the agonizing pain of death. I felt the loss of a loved one. All that had been with Grandpop would never be again. All the games we played, all the laughs we shared, all the moments in his lap, all the walks hand in hand through the park, all of Grandpop would never be again. Only the memories would live on. And they do, even to this day. Grandpop, Grandpop . . .

He was a short man. Maybe five foot six. He wore his gray hair slicked back, parted on the left side, had silver-framed glasses and a walking cane. He dressed meticulously, in a three-piece suit and tie and shiny black shoes.

As a child I had a speech impediment. I couldn't pronounce my *l*'s. I turned them into a *y*. So, when we would be walking down the boardwalk in Atlantic City my grandpop would ask me to repeat the sentence, "Look at the ladies under the light." When I said, "Yook at the Yadies under the Yight," he would rock with laughter. It sounded correct to me, so I didn't understand why he was laughing, but I liked to see and hear him laugh, so it was fine with me. Actually, I got over my speech problem because of Grandpop.

We were sharing a guesthouse in Atlantic City when I was six years old. Grandpop's bedroom was next to mine. He snored horribly, keeping me awake and scaring the hell out of me every night. I asked him to please stop snoring. He said he would when I was able to correctly say, "Look at the ladies under the light." On my own time, when no one was around, I practiced it. I said it over and over thousands of times.

One morning I walked into the kitchen. Grandpop was reading the morning paper, sucking boiling-hot tea from a glass through a cube of sugar he held in his front teeth, something he learned to do as a little boy in Lithuania. I cleared my throat to get his attention. He put down the paper and looked at me with a slight smile on his face. He always had a slight smile.

"Look at the ladies . . . under the . . . light. Now, Grandpop, stop your snoring!"

He put back his head and roared with laughter. Maybe it was only my imagination, but I never heard Grandpop snore again that summer.

The next year, my family didn't let me go to the funeral to say good-bye to Grandpop. They made me sit in the car with my sister outside the funeral home and the cemetery.

I made believe I didn't know what was going on, because I knew that was what everyone wanted me to do, but I knew. I knew that Grandpop had died and that I would never see him again. That wonderful old man whom I loved so much was gone forever.

When we returned to Grandpop's house to sit shiva for him, a religious custom among Jews in which the immediate family sits shoeless and very low to the ground in mourning for a loved one for an entire week, while friends and relatives pay their last respects and comfort the family members, I ran around the house with my cousins playing as children are expected to do. When no one was looking, I went upstairs to my grandpop's bedroom, opened his closet, and took the cane I had seen him use all those years into my little hands, closed the door, turned out the light, and, then, with my face pressed against his tailored suits, I cried until tears no longer came.

One day, when I was about eight years old, I was walking down my street. A fire engine screeched to a stop, the firemen leaped off and ran up the steps of the house where I was standing. They smashed down the door and bashed out the front window with their axes and charged into the house. It was the widow's house, an elderly gray-haired woman who always smiled and said hello to me as I passed. Sometimes I would spend a few minutes talking to her. She was very nice. I liked her.

As soon as the odor hit my nostrils I recognized it—gas. A

moment later, the firemen carried out a stretcher on which was a body wrapped in a white bed sheet. I could see only some hair, long and gray. It was the widow. I had witnessed my first suicide. In the years to come, there were others, including a friend's father, who hanged himself.

My childhood suddenly became filled with deaths. The handsome Greek boy across the street got killed in the war. My friend's mother's cancer-ridden body was down to forty-eight pounds when she died in the makeshift bed she had been confined to in her living room for a few years. One of my best friend's father died of a heart attack at the age of thirty-eight. My other best friend's father passed away, then his mother, then another friend's mother and father.

I was attending funerals regularly, and as I grew taller and stronger, I was asked to be a pallbearer, to carry the coffin, toss the flimsy white gloves on top of it, and throw a handful of dirt on top of the coffin as it is lowered into the ground. I watched as loved ones disappeared, as relatives cried at gravesites. Death was on the attack. It was unrelenting.

My friend Jay Siegel died of leukemia at age seventeen; my pal Billy Meyers got killed in an airplane crash while in the air force, age nineteen; Freddie Gerber was the first drug-related death in the neighborhood, age twenty; my kid cousin Susan died on an operating table, age fourteen; then all my favorite aunts and uncles were struck down—Esther, Toby, Joe, Telli, Belle, Nisson, Lena, Jay; cousin Nessie in Chicago lost her fight with cancer; Freddie Prinze put a gun to his head and blew his brains out; Art Fisher lost control of a helicopter and was killed.

Why death? I think everyone should have the length of his life determined by how good or evil he or she is. We should all be given one thousand of one hundred thousand years of life, and every time we commit a bad deed, we lose a day, week, or years, according to the severity of the evil. That way, the good would live on and evil people would die young; Hitler would've died at age eighteen, Mussolini at twenty-one, Qadaffi at twenty-eight, and so on. The evil men of the world wouldn't live long enough to commit their worst deeds. If people knew that this is how life and death worked, they would strive to be good.

If there is some sort of existence after life, in a beyond some-where, and if I make it to the better one, I'm going to talk with God about my idea. If you suddenly notice the bad people dis-appearing rapidly, you'll know He bought my idea—and then you'd better straighten out your life. I wish you a long one.

ART FISHER

Art Fisher was a friend of mine. We met when I first became a TV writer/producer/film director. Art was a studio director, mostly of musical shows, and the best I had ever seen. When I got my job at Metromedia in New York, I talked the executives into hiring Art. We became a team on some projects, but it wasn't long before Art was making a name for himself. I quit TV and struggled as a stand-up comedian. I have a cassette of my first time ever on a stage, June 9, 1969. You can hear Art's mani-acal laugh on it. One of the reasons you can hear his laugh is because his was one of the only laughs I got that night.

Art went on to become one of the best studio directors in television. Many of your favorite musical series, variety shows, and specials were directed by Art Fisher. He was a wild man in and out of the studio, creative and mad, very strange, a loner, a man alone in crowds, recognized by many, yet truly known by and a friend of very few. I like to think that I was one of the few who was his friend. He was mine.

In March 1984, Art's helicopter crashed in Los Angeles and he was killed. In my eulogy, I said something that I feel was very true of the man: "Art Fisher was a very hard guy to get to know, but once you got to really know him, you realized that he was not a very hard guy." Suzanne Somers, who had worked on some specials with Art, sent me a poem he had written. The self-portrait of a loner, a lonely man, a friend.

I'D RATHER BE ALONE

> *I'd rather be alone*
> *If it's meant to be . . .*
> *Than play the game of caring for*
> *Anyone but me.*

I'm free to come and go
Alone if I must . . .
She doesn't live out there
The woman that I'll trust.

They want your love and life
On conditions they demand,
I'd rather be an island
Than a member of the band.

Loneliness is O.K. now
Before it was a lie
But we get along just fine today . . .
Me, myself and I.

No faceless names to remember
No errors for the score
Love . . . please leave, it's over now
You can find the door.

Valium sleep's upon me now
Hope the dream is real
Memories hold my hand tonight
But don't ask me to feel.

Yes I love you, no I don't
When will the sadness end?
I suppose it's up to him now
At least he is a friend.

I'd rather be alone, if it's meant to be
But God why now . . . why tonight . . . why me?

Art Fisher

THE FINAL DRAGON

I rubbed my forefinger over the dark spots on my left cheek and above my left eyebrow. "Dr. Reder, these marks I showed you a few weeks ago seem to be getting bigger and darker, especially this one above the eyebrow. It looks infected."

That's how it started. My week of hell in 1984. Upon a quick superficial examination, Dr. Reder's fear was that I might have melanoma, a fatal cancer. The closer to the brain, the faster you go. In my case, it couldn't get much closer. If it was melanoma, I probably wouldn't see the new year.

Dr. Reder made an appointment for me with one of America's foremost skin doctors for the following week. Normally, it takes six months to see him. I might not have had six months, so thank God I had Dr. Reder. Actually, the doctor was willing to squeeze me in the following day, but that would have meant cancelling the first of a series of seven one-night performances, and I had never missed a show or been late for one in fifteen years. I thought that if I did have the dreaded disease, the extra week of work wouldn't have mattered, and if, on the other hand, I did not have the disease, I would have disappointed a few thousand fans for no reason. So, either way, I decided to just go ahead with my life as planned—almost.

My immediate life's plan did not include the psychological effect brought on by thinking of imminent death. My first reaction was shock, and my second, disbelief. I just couldn't believe that in the prime of my life, after having accomplished what I had—after having risen from so low a station in life to so high, after having achieved the goals that seemed impossible when I first set out to reach them, after having fulfilled all the dreams I had dreamed as a poor kid living in a nowhere, nobody neighborhood, after bringing my family and loved ones up to the top with me, after all I had done—all of it was going to end because of a few innocuous marks on my cheek and forehead. I have never believed life is fair, but this was just too cruel a fate.

Then depression enveloped me like a summer rain cloud—suddenly and totally. I thought about how all that I see, feel, touch, taste, hear, all that I think and dream, all will be gone. The great gift of life was being taken from me, from someone who knew how to live every moment to the fullest, from someone who had so very much for which to live. The great adventure was coming to a close. Sorry, but all dreams, plans, expectations, and hopes are canceled. All that remains are the good-byes.

Then I stopped thinking about myself. I thought of others.

241

My parents, in their late eighties, losing their youngest child, their baby. My brother and sister suddenly without their crazy kid brother. All my childhood friends who had remained my friends throughout all these years losing their pal, their class comedian. Then I thought of my son, Cole Jay, only two years old. His being born a little late in my life stacked the odds against his ever knowing his father when he became a man. But now he would only know me through old video recordings of my television performances, books I had written, comedy albums I had recorded, newspaper clippings, and magazine articles—only through the superficiality of the mass media would he be able to find fragments of his father. My poor little boy.

I had to tell my manager, Steve Reidman, what was on my mind, just in case my performances that week were off. Funny how I would rather have him know that I'm worried about dying than have him think that I'm losing my touch. However, all the performances went great. It is truly strange how you forget all your problems onstage, the perfect world in which you're omnipotent, with no illnesses, no death, only joy.

After my tour, I went to see Dr. Reder for my daily back treatment. Even though I might have had only a few months to live, I didn't want to suffer the pain of a bad back. I had been going to Dr. Reder for more than ten years. It was more than a doctor-patient relationship; this eighty-four-year-old man and I were the best of friends.

"All right, David, your treatment is finished. Just let me get my hat and coat and we'll go."

"Go where?"

"To the skin doctor."

"Why are you going to the skin doctor? Besides, it is only eleven in the morning. You've got patients waiting out there."

"I've got an appointment with the skin doctor, if you must get nosy, and as far as my patients, I've been spoiling them all these years. The world won't come to an end because I'm closing the office a couple of hours early. Let's go."

Dr. Reder wanted to go with me. He was that worried. He is that wonderful.

We caught a cab and rode the ten blocks to the skin doctor's office. When we got out of the cab, we ran into students from a private elementary school, walking in regimented columns of two, holding hands. Dr. Reder suddenly grabbed hold of my hand and pulled me into the line with the children. Teachers and students cracked up at the ridiculous sight of this octogenarian with a hat half cocked on his head holding the hand of a tall, skinny man with a large nose. I also cracked up. There was a lot of laughter on that street that day. Wherever Dr. Reder is around there is a lot of laughter.

I lay on my back on the doctor's examining table. The doctor studied my face through a large, brightly lit magnifying glass. He scraped some skin off my face for a biopsy. I felt Dr. Reder's hand rest gently on my shoulder. He gave it a little squeeze. I looked up at him. His eyes were filled with tears. He spoke to the doctor. "Well, what do you think, Norman?"

"Well, Milton, I'm going to send this to the lab, but, from my preliminary examination, I'd rule out melanoma."

"Thank God."

Dr. Reder and I walked out of the office together. It was drizzling. Without looking at me, Dr. Reder spoke. "I was really afraid, David."

"So was I, Dr. Reder, and you know how I knew both of us were? Because we were so damn funny on the ride over here."

I'll never forget Dr. Reder. He's one of those rare human beings you can't forget. I will remember forever all he has done for me and my family as a doctor, all the laughter he has given me, all the fascinating stories he has told me. But the one moment I shall treasure forever is the feel of his gentle hand on my shoulder, the tears in his eyes and those whispered words "Thank God." I, too, say, "Thank God." Thank you for not taking my life and thank you for affording me the opportunity to know a really great man, Dr. Milton Reder.

My big brother, Moby, had a similar scare a couple of years before mine. A different medical problem but just as deadly and scary. I refused to believe the diagnosis he had been given and spoke about it to a doctor in New York, who recommended a specialist. He disagreed with the diagnosis. My brother was given a new lease on life. The doctor who recommended the specialist was Dr. Reder.

At that time, I sent my brother a framed calligraphy of an anonymous poem I had found in a magazine:

On an ancient wall in China
Where a brooding buddha blinks,
Deeply graven is the message—
It is later than you think.
The clock of life is wound but once,
And no man has the power to
Tell just when the hand will stop
At late or early hour.
Now is the time you own,
The past is a golden link,
Go cruising now, My Brother—
It is later than you think.

I also enclosed airline tickets for him and his lady, Sherry, for a trip through Europe.

When I had my big scare, my brother sent *me* a framed calligraphy, which today hangs on the wall of my office:

He who has encountered
in his own dark night
the final dragon
will find it difficult
forever afterwards
to take seriously
all lesser beasts

There is another quote. Neither my brother nor I have it framed and on a wall, because it has been with us all our lives. It is part of our heritage. The ancient Hebrew word spoken when toasting a drink with a friend or loved one: *"L'Chaim!"* It means "To Life!" Life—I love it. I live it.

FATHERS TELL SONS

Luckily, most of my life's dreams have come true, and for this I am thankful. However, one of my most precious dreams has turned into a nightmare of broken promises.

The epilogue of my first book, *Soft Pretzels with Mustard*, dealt with the birth of my son, Cole Jay Brenner, born in 1982. He was born without a marriage, but I had hoped he had come into this world loved and accepted by both parents. Since the publication of that book, many events have taken place that demand that untold truths from the past and new truths be told, not to get even with anyone or to be malicious against any person or persons, but solely because telling them might help other parents, especially fathers, who are going through the same experience, and, more importantly, because my son will deserve to know these truths when he is old enough to understand.

I am sharing with you this very private experience because I believe it is an important lesson for many of us. I hope that my frankness is helpful, and, if one child is spared unhappiness, or if one couple realize their mistakes from what I write, then regardless of the price I might have to pay in or out of the courts, I shall be happy I wrote this story.

Cole Jay's mother was never my girlfriend but someone I dated. When I learned she was pregnant I was immediately and totally supportive, both financially and spiritually, of my own free will. I had never intended to become a father, for many reasons, especially since I had never been in love with anyone enough to want to have a child with her. However, I had absolutely loved being a child myself and having the warmth of loving parents. Therefore I tried to establish some sort of quasi-family life for my son, something that became very difficult under the circumstances.

My relationship with my son's mother deteriorated, and I was barred from all visitations with my son, a special pain that all you parents will understand. My eighty-five-year-old mother and my eighty-eight-year-old father were also barred from seeing and talking with their grandson. It was always my intention and effort to settle all matters out of court, through reasonable and fair dealing. Unfortunately, this was not possible. A lawsuit in Connecticut was brought against me for paternity, even though I had always claimed Cole Jay as my son. I countersued. A New York City judge gave me immediate visitation rights, after I had not seen my son for over two months.

Eventually, the New York judge decided that jurisdiction was in Connecticut, so beyond the relationship infighting, I was now tangled up in legal wrangling across state lines. Again, my parents and I were denied visitation for over two months. As always, my three-year-old son was the big loser.

I went into the Connecticut court and won a temporary visitation schedule. I am presently trying to win total custody of my son.

These are the lessons I wish to share with others who have suffered the pain and frustration of similar situations: I have learned that there is no reason and no excuse for anyone ever to use a child as a tool or a weapon, and that what has happened to me is happening to a lot of fathers, which is why I have joined the Equal Rights for Fathers organization. And I feel obligated to plead with you, for God's sake—no, for your child's sake—I plead with you to fight it out adult to adult and leave the children to enjoy being children. Childhood is one of the few times in life we have any chance for happiness. Don't ruin it for your children—please.

Closing words: The other night I watched a movie starring Jason Robards, and a line he said stuck in my mind: "Fathers tell sons about fathers they loved." I always tell my son about my father. I can only hope that someday he will tell his son about me.

Cole Jay Brenner, my son, I am fighting for you very hard. I always will. I love you. I always will. Be a good boy and the best man. In every breath you ever take there will be a kiss from me.

In January 1986 Victoria and I took Cole Jay to Florida so my mother and father could see and say goodbye to their grandson prior to their leaving on their three-month cruise around the world. Only the long and insistent battling in custody court made this family visit possible. On March 5, while aboard the *Queen Elizabeth 2*, my mother passed away.

EPILOGUE

Thanks for reading this book. I hope you got something out of it. What you have read is the truth. Everything is the way it happened; everything is what I have seen, felt, and thought. I hope there is a lot more to come in my life—more adventures, more excitement, more accomplishments, more fulfillment of dreams, more expectations realized, more laughter, more joy, more life. You won't know about it, because this is the last book of this kind I am going to write. From now to the end of this wonderful gift we call life, I want to *live* a few books, not write them. I thank each of you for making my life so wondrous. I hope that you, too, have a rich and rewarding life and that you, too, are a breathing, living book. Now, let's all get out there and kick ass!

"*Like hell,* Mr. President!" Busick shouted. "We don't owe them *squat!* They started this whole thing—we just helped finish it. The general may have jumped the gun a little, but he did exactly what he thought was needed to be done to protect our guys out there."

"General, is that the way you see it?" Thorn asked.

Patrick looked at Thorn, then at Martindale, and finally back to Thomas Thorn. "No, sir—there was no misunderstanding," he replied. Both Martindale and Busick closed their eyes in frustration, and even Robert Goff shook his head sadly. "I was ordered by Secretary of Defense Goff directly to get my forces out of Turkmenistan after Deputy Secretary of State Hershel's flight was safe. My ground forces were only fifteen miles from the Uzbek border—they could have been picked up easily, before or after the attack on Charjew. Instead I kept my ground forces in place and planned an air attack on Engels."

"Because you *knew* that Gryzlov was going to launch more attacks on you."

"Yes, sir, but mostly because I wanted to hurt Gryzlov," Patrick admitted. "I wanted to defeat his bombers on the ground. I wanted to strike into the heart of Gryzlov's bomber force. I had the weapons and the opportunity, so I took it."

Thorn looked at each of his advisers in turn, then said angrily, "That's why we're paying reparations to the Russians, folks. America might be accused of being a bully every now and then, but when we screw up like that, we should at least have the guts to admit to it and pay for our mistake." He and everyone in the room fell silent. "That will be all, everyone."

Kevin Martindale stepped up to Thomas Thorn, looked him in the eye, shook his head, and said derisively, "You're going to be a pushover next fall, Mr. President." He turned to Patrick and said, so everyone including Thorn could hear him, "Don't let him get to you, Patrick. Gryzlov is right—but it doesn't mean it has to stay that way. Keep on fighting the way you know how to fight."

Finally it was just Thorn and McLanahan left in the Oval Office. Thorn looked at the two-star general. "You're dismissed, too, General," he said. Patrick looked as if he was about to say something, but Thorn held up a hand. "Don't say anything, General—I know you won't mean it anyway. Just get out. Go home and give your son a hug. Take him to the beach. I'll decide what to do with you later."

Patrick left the White House and made his way to the West Wing gate. As he waited to be let out, he heard a car horn beep behind him. Maureen Hershel rolled down her window in the backseat of her limousine. "Give you a lift somewhere, General?" she asked.

Patrick looked at her, then stood and looked back toward the Oval Office—and was surprised to see Thorn looking back at him through the window, the phone to his ear but still watching him intently. Patrick took a deep breath, confused and, yes, a little uncertain.

"C'mon, General," Maureen said. "I could use a drink right about now—and you look like you could use one too."

Patrick McLanahan stood at attention and saluted the Oval Office. The president saluted back, then returned his attention to his phone call. Patrick dropped his salute with a snap, smiled, and nodded. "I'd love to, Maureen," he said. "I'd love to. Let's go."